Jesus Firsthand

Daily Devotional Meditations For Knowing Jesus

DAVID FEDDES

Christian Leaders Press
Monee, Illinois
christianleadersinstitute.org

Jesus Firsthand: Daily Devotional Meditations For Knowing Jesus

Published by Christian Leaders Press
Monee, Illinois
www.christianleadersinstitute.org

Printed in the United States of America

Cover design: Jaclyn Feddes
Cover photo: R. Gino Santa Maria

Unless otherwise noted, Scripture readings are from the World English Bible, a public domain version. The author has edited some passages.

ISBN: 0615947093
ISBN-13: 978-0615947099

We want to see Jesus.
John 12:21

Christ is all.
Colossians 3:11

CONTENTS

Part One

JESUS FIRSTHAND

Jesus went about in all Galilee, teaching in their synagogues, preaching the Good News of the Kingdom, and healing every disease and every sickness. Matthew 4:23

Would you like to meet Jesus—hear him speaking, see him in action, know his personality? Don't just depend on a religious system or on what other people say. Come and see for yourself. Get to know Jesus firsthand. Go to a house where Jesus is having dinner. Hop into a boat with Jesus and his friends. Sit on a grassy hillside and listen to Jesus tell stories. Listen to him announce the nearness of God's kingdom. Watch him heal the sick. Walk with him down dusty roads and see how he relates to people. Notice who likes him, and why. Notice who hates him, and why. Come and see!

How can you do that? Do you need a magic machine to bring you to another time and place? No, you just need the New Testament gospels written by Matthew, Mark, Luke, and John. These inspired accounts of Jesus have miraculous power to carry you across time and space and into contact with Jesus. As you go to meet Jesus in that time and place, Jesus comes to meet you in this time and place. You enter his life, and he enters your life. Come and see!

Meet Jesus for yourself. Each day read the Bible passage on the left page. Let the reality of Jesus sink in as you read the meditation on the right page. Then talk to him in prayer.

PRAYER

Jesus, I want to know you firsthand, as you really are. Take away any junk that stands between you and me. Help me to connect with you and get better acquainted. Amen.

John 1:35-51

John was standing with two of his disciples, 36 and he looked at Jesus as he walked, and said, “Behold, the Lamb of God!” 37 The two disciples heard him speak, and they followed Jesus. 38 Jesus turned, and saw them following, and said to them, “What are you looking for?”

They said to him, “Rabbi” (which means Teacher), “where are you staying?”

39 He said to them, “Come, and see.”

They came and saw where he was staying, and they stayed with him that day. It was about the tenth hour. 40 One of the two who heard John, and followed Jesus, was Andrew, Simon Peter’s brother. 41 He first found his own brother, Simon, and said to him, “We have found the Messiah!” (which means Christ.) 42 He brought him to Jesus….

43 The next day, Jesus decided to go to Galilee, and he found Philip. Jesus said to him, “Follow me.” 44 Now Philip was from Bethsaida, the city of Andrew and Peter. 45 Philip found Nathanael, and said to him, “We have found him, of whom Moses in the law, and the prophets, wrote: Jesus of Nazareth, the son of Joseph.”

46 Nathanael said to him, “Can any good thing come out of Nazareth?”

Philip said to him, “Come and see.”

47 Jesus saw Nathanael coming to him, and said about him, “Behold, an Israelite indeed, in whom is no deceit!”

48 Nathanael said to him, “How do you know me?”

Jesus answered him, “Before Philip called you, when you were under the fig tree, I saw you.”

49 Nathanael answered him, “Rabbi, you are the Son of God! You are King of Israel!”

50 Jesus answered him, “Because I told you, ‘I saw you underneath the fig tree,’ do you believe? You will see greater things than these!” 51 He said to him, “Most certainly, I tell you, you will see heaven opened, and the angels of God ascending and descending on the Son of Man.”

COME AND SEE

"Come and see." John 1:46

As you watch Jesus in action, you see that he has a remarkable effect on people. Just a few hours with him—sometimes just a few minutes—is enough to make people realize that Jesus is like nobody they've ever met before. Some conclude that he is the key to everything they have been looking for. That may be your experience too.

Andrew, Peter, Philip, and Nathaniel meet Jesus at the start of his ministry, before Jesus has begun to do mighty miracles or preach to enormous crowds. Even before he works wonders, they marvel at Jesus himself. They are amazed and gripped by his personality. Jesus is so magnetic, so magnificent, that they sense he must be the Messiah, the one promised by the prophets, the Son of God, their King. They still have a lot to learn, but one thing they know: in meeting Jesus, they have met more than just another man. In meeting Jesus, they are getting to know God in a fresh, wonderful way and are having their deepest longings satisfied.

When they want to share their discovery with family and friends and others, they don't give a long speech. They just say, "Come and see. Check him out for yourself." The invitation still stands: Come and see. As the biblical gospels bring you into contact with Jesus, you find that Jesus is pleased that you want to know him. You also find that he already knows you. Like Nathaniel, you might ask Jesus, "How do you know me?" You will discover that Jesus is the all-knowing Son of God. He saw you and sought you before you knew anything of him. When you believe in him based on what you've seen thus far, Jesus promises, "You shall see greater things than these." So come and see!

PRAYER

Thank you, Jesus, for knowing me and calling me into a relationship with you. Help me to walk with you and to see greater things of your glory every day. Amen.

John 2:1-11

1 The third day, there was a marriage in Cana of Galilee. Jesus' mother was there. 2 Jesus also was invited, with his disciples, to the marriage. 3 When the wine ran out, Jesus' mother said to him, "They have no wine."

4 Jesus said to her, "Woman, what does that have to do with you and me? My hour has not yet come."

5 His mother said to the servants, "Whatever he says to you, do it." 6 Now there were six stone water pots standing there, the kind the Jews used for ceremonial washing. Each held about twenty to thirty gallons. 7 Jesus said to them, "Fill the water pots with water." They filled them up to the brim. 8 He said to them, "Now draw some out, and take it to the ruler of the feast." So they took it. 9 When the ruler of the feast tasted the water, which had become wine, he didn't know where it came from (but the servants who had drawn the water knew). The ruler of the feast called the bridegroom, 10 and said to him, "Everyone serves the good wine first, and when the guests have drunk freely, then that which is worse. You have kept the good wine until now!" 11 This, the first of his signs, Jesus did in Cana of Galilee, and revealed his glory; and his disciples believed in him.

John 8:10-13

10 Jesus said, "Have the people sit down." Now there was much grass in that place. So the men sat down, about five thousand of them. 11 Jesus took the [five] loaves; and having given thanks, he distributed to the disciples, and the disciples to those who were sitting down; likewise also of the [two] fish as much as they desired. 12 When they were filled, he said to his disciples, "Gather up the broken pieces which are left over, that nothing be lost." 13 So they gathered them up, and filled twelve baskets with broken pieces from the five barley loaves, which were left over by those who had eaten.

WINE AND BREAD

This, the first of his signs, Jesus did in Cana of Galilee, and revealed his glory. John 2:11

Jesus' first miracle was to change water into wine at a wedding banquet. Jesus did this not only to keep the party going but also to show his divine glory.

It was an amazing miracle, but notice that the Creator is continually changing vast amounts of water into wine. It's just that most of the time he uses vines and grapes and natural processes rather than an instant miracle.

Later, Jesus took a little bread and fed over five thousand people with it. A miracle indeed! But don't miss the fact that right now the Creator is taking a little grain, transforming it gradually with soil, sun, and water, and making enough bread for billions of people. We call it a miracle when the Lord fed five thousand, but when he feeds billions, we yawn and take it for granted.

Scripture says that God "makes grass grow for the cattle, and plants for man to cultivate—bringing forth food from the earth: *wine* that gladdens the heart of man ... and *bread* that sustains his heart" (Psalm 104:14-15). When Jesus changed water to wine and fed thousands with bread, he showed that he is the Creator who has always done these things for us and continues to do them. Your food today is from the hand of Jesus as surely as if you were among the five thousand eating miracle bread. Your drink today is from the hand of Jesus as surely as if you were drinking miraculous wine at the Cana wedding feast.

PRAYER

Dear God, thank you for all you do behind the scenes as our hidden Creator and Sustainer. And thank you for showing yourself and revealing your glory in Jesus. Amen.

Mark 10:13-16, 46-52 NIV

13 People were bringing little children to Jesus for him to
place his hands on them, but the disciples rebuked them.
14 When Jesus saw this, he was indignant. He said to them,
"Let the little children come to me, and do not hinder them,
for the kingdom of God belongs to such as these. 15 Truly I
tell you, anyone who will not receive the kingdom of God
like a little child will never enter it." 16 And he took the children in his arms, placed his hands on them and blessed
them…

46 Then they came to Jericho. As Jesus and his disciples,
together with a large crowd, were leaving the city, a blind
man, Bartimaeus (which means "son of Timaeus"), was sitting by the roadside begging. 47 When he heard that it was
Jesus of Nazareth, he began to shout, "Jesus, Son of David,
have mercy on me!"

48 Many rebuked him and told him to be quiet, but he
shouted all the more, "Son of David, have mercy on me!"

49 Jesus stopped and said, "Call him."

So they called to the blind man, "Cheer up! On your feet!
He's calling you." 50 Throwing his cloak aside, he jumped to
his feet and came to Jesus.

51 "What do you want me to do for you?" Jesus asked
him.

The blind man said, "Rabbi, I want to see."

52 "Go," said Jesus, "your faith has healed you." Immediately he received his sight and followed Jesus along the road.

ANYBODY WELCOME

"Whoever comes to me I will never drive away." John 6:37

Jesus welcomes anybody. It doesn't matter who you are—man or woman, grandparent or child, fisherman or farmer, priest or prostitute, soldier or rebel, cop or criminal, ruler or slave, rich or poor, educated or uneducated, healthy or disabled, religious or rotten, sensible or demon-possessed—Jesus warmly welcomes anyone who wants to meet him and get to know him better. He never tells anyone that he's too important or too busy or too good for them.

As you hang around with Jesus, you see young mothers with little ones, wanting Jesus to touch their children. Some people around Jesus say that Jesus can't be bothered with babies and housewives. But when Jesus sees women and children treated as though they don't count, it makes him mad. "Let the little children come to me," he says. "Don't hinder them. God's kingdom is for kids like these."

Then you hear a guy yelling, "Son of David, have mercy on me." It's a blind beggar who sits beside the road every day asking for handouts. The crowd tells him to shut up. Jesus has important things to do. Why should a disabled loudmouth make a scene and interfere with Jesus' schedule? But the blind man yells all the louder, and Jesus doesn't mind. In fact, he's pleased. Jesus touches the man's eyes. Suddenly he can see, and he joins Jesus' other followers.

Jesus not only makes time for women and children and disabled people but also for people who are downright bad. He eats with crooks and prostitutes and riffraff of every kind. He accepts invitations from almost anybody, and he even invites himself to their place if they feel unworthy to invite him. Jesus never turns away anyone who comes to him.

PRAYER

Thank you, Jesus, for welcoming me, just as I am, and not driving me away. Touch me with your love, heal me by your power, and take away all my sins by your mercy. Amen.

Matthew 10:24-42

24 "A disciple is not above his teacher, nor a servant
above his lord. 25 It is enough for the disciple to be like his
teacher, and the servant like his lord. If they have called the
master of the house Beelzebul, how much more those of his
household! 26 Therefore don't be afraid of them, for there is
nothing covered that will not be revealed; and hidden that
will not be known. 27 What I tell you in the darkness, speak
in the light; and what you hear whispered in the ear, proclaim on the housetops. 28 Don't be afraid of those who kill
the body, but are not able to kill the soul. Rather, fear him
who is able to destroy both soul and body in hell.

29 "Aren't two sparrows sold for a penny? But not one of
them falls to the ground apart from your Father's will. 30 And
the very hairs of your head are all numbered. 31 Therefore
don't be afraid. You are of more value than many sparrows.
32 Everyone therefore who confesses me before men, him I
will also confess before my Father who is in heaven. 33 But
whoever denies me before men, him I will also deny before
my Father who is in heaven.

34 "Don't think that I came to bring peace on the earth. I
did not come to bring peace, but a sword. 35 For I came to set
a man at odds against his father, and a daughter against her
mother, and a daughter-in-law against her mother-in-law.
36 A man's foes will be those of his own household. 37 He
who loves father or mother more than me is not worthy of
me; and he who loves son or daughter more than me isn't
worthy of me. 38 He who doesn't take his cross and follow
after me, isn't worthy of me. 39 He who seeks his life will
lose it; and he who loses his life for my sake will find it.
40 He who receives you receives me, and he who receives me
receives him who sent me. 41 He who receives a prophet because he is a prophet will receive a prophet's reward. He
who receives a righteous man because he is a righteous man
will receive a righteous man's reward. 42 Whoever gives one
of these little ones just a cup of cold water to drink because
he is a disciple, I tell you truly, he will not lose his reward."

FIGHTING FOR FREEDOM

"I did not come to bring peace but a sword." Matthew 10:34

Jesus does not make peace with Satan or this wicked world. Jesus brings a sword "to destroy him who holds the power of death—that is, the devil—and free those who all their lives were held in slavery by their fear of death" (Hebrews 2:14-15). "The Lord is a warrior" (Exodus 15:3). As Jesus fights, he calls you to join him in the fight for freedom from sin and Satan.

When you join the military, you must be loyal to your commander and obey orders. If he orders you into combat, you must go. You must be willing to give up family and friends and even your own life. This is true of a nation's military; it's also true of Jesus' army. If you put family and friends above Christ, you can't join his army. If you value your own life more than freedom in Christ, you can't join Jesus' army.

It would be crazy to follow Jesus if he were just a religious nut who causes conflict, disrupts families, and demands complete loyalty. But Jesus isn't just a crazy guy who thinks he's God; Jesus *is* God. Only God has the right to call for the absolute loyalty Jesus demands.

When we enlist in the Lord's army, we become friends of freedom. If political freedom is worth celebrating and fighting for, spiritual freedom is worth far more. The cost of following Jesus may sound extreme, but the commander who calls us to give up everything for him is the same Jesus who gave up everything for us.

PRAYER

Lord Jesus, if you set us free, we are free indeed. Strengthen our hearts with complete loyalty to you, and protect us with the armor of God. Amen.

Luke 4:31-44

[31] Jesus came down to Capernaum, a city of Galilee. He
was teaching them on the Sabbath day, [32] and they were
astonished at his teaching, for his word was with authority.
[33] In the synagogue there was a man who had a spirit of an
unclean demon, and he cried out with a loud voice, [34] saying,
"Ah! what have we to do with you, Jesus of Nazareth? Have
you come to destroy us? I know you who you are: the Holy
One of God!"

[35] Jesus rebuked him, saying, "Be silent, and come out of
him!" When the demon had thrown him down in the middle
of them, he came out of him, leaving him unharmed.

[36] Amazement came on all, and they said to one another,
"What is this word? For with authority and power he commands the unclean spirits, and they come out!" [37] News
about him went out into every place of the surrounding region.

[38] He rose up from the synagogue, and entered into Simon's house. Simon's mother-in-law was afflicted with a
great fever, and they begged him to help her. [39] He stood
over her, and rebuked the fever; and it left her. Immediately
she rose up and served them. [40] When the sun was setting, all
those who had any sick with various diseases brought them
to him; and he laid his hands on every one of them, and
healed them. [41] Demons also came out of many, crying out,
and saying, "You are the Christ, the Son of God!" Rebuking
them, he didn't allow them to speak, because they knew that
he was the Christ.

[42] When it was day, he departed and went into an unin-
habited place. The crowds looked for him, and came to him,
and held on to him, so that he wouldn't go away from them.
[43] But he said to them, "I must preach the good news of
God's Kingdom to the other cities also. For this reason I
have been sent." [44] He kept preaching in the synagogues of
Galilee.

DEFEATING DEMONS

"What is this word? For with authority and power he commands the unclean spirits, and they come out!" Luke 4:36

Demons are not wimps. They are rebel angels who have lost all goodness but still have terrible strength. When evil spirits take possession of someone, it's not easy to drive them out. No mere human can do it. People aren't strong enough to defeat demons.

It's astounding, then, when someone comes along who makes demons tremble and run. Evil spirits that nobody could drive away are suddenly in full retreat. When a demon-possessed man makes an awful scene in a worship service, Jesus merely speaks, and the demon flees.

Another man is possessed by a whole army of demons and lives in a graveyard. He is naked, uncontrollable, foaming at the mouth, screaming in a demonic voice. He is a danger to himself and others. Then Jesus gives an order. The next moment the man is well-dressed, in his right mind, talking with Jesus, beaming with joy (see Mark 5:1-20).

What sort of person can order demons around? Some of Jesus' enemies think that the reason demons listen to Jesus is that Jesus himself is possessed by the chief demon of them all. But Jesus does so much damage to the cause of the demons that he can't possibly be a tool of the chief demon. If Jesus' power isn't demonic or merely human, there's one possibility left: his power is divine. He must be God the Son. "The reason the Son of God appeared was to destroy the devil's work" (1 John 3:8).

PRAYER

All glory to you, Jesus, for defeating demons. How awesome are your deeds! So great is your power that your enemies cringe before you. Amen. (Psalm 66:3)

Mark 2:13-22

13 He went out again by the seaside. All the multitude
came to him, and he taught them. 14 As he passed by, he saw
Levi, the son of Alphaeus, sitting at the tax office, and he
said to him, "Follow me." And he arose and followed him.

15 He was reclining at the table in his house, and many
tax collectors and sinners sat down with Jesus and his disciples, for there were many, and they followed him. 16 The
scribes and the Pharisees, when they saw that he was eating
with the sinners and tax collectors, said to his disciples,
"Why is it that he eats and drinks with tax collectors and sinners?"

17 When Jesus heard it, he said to them, "Those who are
healthy have no need for a physician, but those who are sick.
I came not to call the righteous, but sinners to repentance."

18 John's disciples and the Pharisees were fasting, and
they came and asked him, "Why do John's disciples and the
disciples of the Pharisees fast, but your disciples don't fast?"

19 Jesus said to them, "Can the groomsmen fast while the
bridegroom is with them? As long as they have the bridegroom with them, they can't fast. 20 But the days will come
when the bridegroom will be taken away from them, and
then will they fast in that day. 21 No one sews a piece of un-
shrunk cloth on an old garment, or else the patch shrinks and
the new tears away from the old, and a worse hole is made.
22 No one puts new wine into old wineskins, or else the new
wine will burst the skins, and the wine pours out, and the
skins will be destroyed; but they put new wine into fresh
wineskins."

Luke 7:34

34 "The Son of Man has come eating and drinking, and you
say, 'Behold, a gluttonous man, and a drunkard; a friend of
tax collectors and sinners!'"

LIFE OF THE PARTY

"Why is it that he eats and drinks with tax collectors and sinners?" Mark 2:16

When you meet Jesus, you find that he practices what he preaches. There's nothing greedy about him. He can't be flattered or bribed or seduced. He treats women with utmost respect, with no hint of lust. He lives one day at a time, trusting his heavenly Father, without using his fame to pile up money. Even his enemies have nothing to say when Jesus asks, "Can any of you prove me guilty of sin?" (John 8:46). Never has anyone been so pure and perfect.

But Jesus' perfect purity isn't a sour strictness. He often speaks of God's reign in terms of a huge party, and almost everywhere he goes, people are throwing parties. In fact, he's involved in so many parties that some folks criticize him for not being stern and strict enough. He has the wrong kind of friends, and they enjoy themselves far too much to suit the grim guardians of decency. But despite the complaints, Jesus keeps making friends who keep throwing parties for him.

Jesus himself is the life of the party. The sinners he befriends can't help celebrating (Mark 2:19). "I have come," explains Jesus, "that they may have life, and have it to the full" (John 10:10). That's why there are parties wherever he goes. People have never been so happy as when they are with Jesus, and they keep inviting others to come and see.

Have you joined the party of sinners who celebrate with their Savior? Are you inviting others to meet Jesus too?

PRAYER

Lord, you are holy and we are sinful. Thank you for bridging the gap that divides us, so that your joy may be in us and our joy may be complete. Amen.

Luke 7:36-50

36 One of the Pharisees invited him to eat with him. He entered into the Pharisee's house, and sat at the table. 37 Behold, a woman in the city who was a sinner, when she knew that he was reclining in the Pharisee's house, she brought an alabaster jar of ointment. 38 Standing behind at his feet weeping, she began to wet his feet with her tears, and she wiped them with the hair of her head, kissed his feet, and anointed them with the ointment. 39 Now when the Pharisee who had invited him saw it, he said to himself, "This man, if he were a prophet, would have perceived who and what kind of woman this is who touches him, that she is a sinner."

40 Jesus answered him, "Simon, I have something to tell you."

He said, "Tell me, Teacher."

41 "A certain lender had two debtors. The one owed five hundred denarii, and the other fifty. 42 When they couldn't pay, he forgave them both. Which of them therefore will love him most?"

43 Simon answered, "I suppose the one whom he forgave the most."

He said to him, "You have judged correctly." 44 Turning to the woman, he said to Simon, "Do you see this woman? I entered into your house, and you gave me no water for my feet, but she has wet my feet with her tears, and wiped them with the hair of her head. 45 You gave me no kiss, but she, since the time I came in, has not ceased to kiss my feet. 46 You didn't anoint my head with oil, but she has anointed my feet with ointment. 47 Therefore I tell you, her sins, which are many, are forgiven, for she loved much. But the one who is forgiven little, loves little." 48 He said to her, "Your sins are forgiven."

49 Those who sat at the table with him began to say to themselves, "Who is this who even forgives sins?"

50 He said to the woman, "Your faith has saved you. Go in peace."

WHO IS THIS?

"Who is this who even forgives sins?" Luke 7:49

The woman had lived a bad life, and everybody knew it. How could Jesus let such a woman touch him and kiss his feet? That was shocking—but even more shocking was what Jesus said to the woman: "Your sins are forgiven." That statement stunned the others in the room. They exclaimed, "Who is this who even forgives sins?" Good question!

No mere human can forgive sins committed against other people. If someone wronged you, and then I came along and told that person, "I forgive you," I would be out of line. You are the one who was hurt, not I; so I have no right to forgive wrongs done to you. The only sins I may forgive are those that have been committed against me personally.

So how could Jesus forgive this woman? Her immorality harmed other people's marriages and may have spread diseases. If she had children, her lifestyle would have harmed them. Her parents and extended family were probably wounded and embarrassed. She had sinned against lots of people, but how had she ever wronged Jesus?

If Jesus wasn't the one she had wronged, how could he say, "Your sins are forgiven"? He couldn't—unless he was the main one offended, the God whose law is broken and whose love is wounded in every sin. Jesus' words of forgiveness were words that only God could speak.

Who is this who even forgives sins? He is God with us.

PRAYER

Lord, who is a God like you, who pardons sin and forgives? You will tread our sins underfoot and hurl them into the depths of the sea (Micah 7:18-19). Thank you, Jesus. Amen.

Mark 2:1-12

1 When he entered again into Capernaum after some
days, people heard that he was in the house. 2 Immediately
many were gathered together, so that there was no more
room, not even around the door; and he spoke the word to
them. 3 Four people came, carrying a paralytic to him.
4 When they could not come near to him because of the
crowd, they removed the roof where he was. When they had
broken it up, they let down the mat that the paralytic was lying on. 5 Jesus, seeing their faith, said to the paralytic, "Son,
your sins are forgiven you."

6 But there were some of the scribes sitting there, and
thinking in their hearts, 7 "Why does this man speak blas-
phemies like that? Who can forgive sins but God alone?"

8 Immediately Jesus, perceiving in his spirit what they
were thinking within themselves, said to them, "Why do you
think these things in your hearts? 9 Which is easier, to tell
the paralytic, 'Your sins are forgiven;' or to say, 'Arise, and
take up your bed, and walk'? 10 But that you may know that
the Son of Man has authority on earth to forgive sins"—he
said to the paralytic— 11 "I tell you, arise, take up your mat,
and go to your house."

12 He arose, and immediately took up the mat, and went
out in front of them all; so that they were all amazed, and
glorified God, saying, "We never saw anything like this!"

GOD ALONE

"Who can forgive sins but God alone?" Mark 2:7

Some religious groups claim to believe the Bible but deny that Jesus is God. They knock on doors and tell people there's no Bible verse which proves Jesus is God. They somehow sidestep John 1:1, which says of Jesus, "The Word was God." They dodge John 20:28, where Thomas calls Jesus, "My Lord and my God!" But even if the Bible did not state directly that Jesus is God, his divine glory would still shine in the way the Lord Jesus of the New Testament matches Old Testament descriptions of the Lord Yahweh.

Old Testament Scripture says, "Praise Yahweh... who forgives all your sins and heals all your diseases" (Psalm 103:2-3). God alone can forgive all our sins. God alone can heal all our diseases. Jesus' opponents were right in saying, "Who can forgive sins but God alone?" But they were wrong not to see Jesus as God.

When Jesus said, "Son, your sins are forgiven," he was saying what only God could say. When opponents objected, Jesus responded by doing what only God could do: he healed a paralyzed man. His healing work confirmed his forgiving word, and both confirmed his identity as God.

Jesus' divine glory shines not only in Bible verses that directly call him God but in all Jesus says and does. If Jesus forgives sins and makes a paralyzed person dance, who can he be but "Yahweh, who forgives all your sins and heals all your diseases"?

PRAYER

Praise to you, Lord, almighty forgiver and healer. Give me faith to recognize your divine glory and love, and help many more people to see you for who you are. Amen.

Mark 4:24-41

24 Jesus said to them, "Pay attention to what you hear.
With whatever measure you measure, it will be measured to
you, and more will be given to you who hear. 25 For whoever
has, to him will more be given, and he who doesn't have,
even what he has will be taken away from him."

26 He said, "God's Kingdom is like this: A man scatters
seed on the earth. 27 Night and day, whether he sleeps or rises, the seed springs up and grows, he doesn't know how.
28 For the earth bears fruit: first the blade, then the ear, then
the full grain in the ear. 29 But when the fruit is ripe, immediately he puts in the sickle, because the harvest has come."

30 He said, "To what will we compare God's Kingdom?
Or with what parable will we illustrate it? 31 It's like a grain
of mustard seed, which is the smallest seed planted in the
earth. 32 Yet when it is sown, it grows up, and becomes
greater than all the herbs, and puts out great branches, so that
the birds of the sky can lodge under its shadow."

33 With many such parables he spoke the word to them,
as they were able to hear it. 34 Without a parable he didn't
speak to them; but privately to his own disciples he explained everything.

35 On that day, when evening had come, he said to them,
"Let's go over to the other side." 36 Leaving the multitude,
they took him with them, just as he was, in the boat. Other
small boats were also with him. 37 A big wind storm arose,
and the waves beat into the boat, so much that the boat was
already filling. 38 Jesus was in the stern, asleep on the cush-
ion. They woke him up, and told him, "Teacher, don't you
care that we are dying?"

39 He awoke, and rebuked the wind, and said to the sea,
"Peace! Be still!" The wind ceased, and there was a great
calm. 40 He said to them, "Why are you so afraid? How is it
that you have no faith?"

41 They were greatly afraid, and said to one another,
"Who is this, that even the wind and the sea obey him?"

RULER OF WIND AND SEA

"Who is this, that even the wind and the sea obey him?" Mark 4:41

Jesus is human, with a body like ours. During his time on Earth, Jesus could get as tired as we do. If you ever doubt whether Jesus is really human, just look at him sprawled in the stern of a boat, catching up on his sleep.

But he isn't only human. If you ever doubt whether Jesus is divine, just look at him giving orders to waves and weather. The Psalms declare: "O Lord God Almighty, who is like you? You are mighty, O Lord, and your faithfulness surrounds you. You rule over the surging sea; when its waves mount up, you still them" (Psalm 89:8-9). "Mightier than the thunder of the great waters, mightier than the breakers of the sea—the Lord on high is mighty" (Psalm 93:4). Only God Almighty can rule the sea and put a storm to sleep.

Jesus has two natures, a human nature and a divine nature. Though these two natures are joined in him, they are not mixed together into some third thing that is 50 percent human and 50 percent divine. Jesus is 100 percent human and 100 percent divine. His humanity and deity are unmixed. His divine nature didn't keep his human nature from getting tired like any other man, and his human nature didn't keep his divine nature from directing the weather like the God he is. As a man Jesus knows our weakness firsthand. As Lord of all things, he has almighty power to rescue us from any storm.

PRAYER

Dear Jesus, human brother and divine Master, forgive us when our faith is too small. Help us to trust you at all times and to live in your peace. Amen.

Luke 5:1-11

[1] Jesus was standing by the lake of Gennesaret, while the multitude crowded around him and heard the word of God. [2] He saw two boats standing by the lake, but the fishermen had gone out of them, and were washing their nets. [3] He got into one of the boats, which was Simon's, and asked him to put out a little from the land. Jesus sat down and taught the multitudes from the boat. [4] When he had finished speaking, he said to Simon, "Put out into the deep, and let down your nets for a catch."

[5] Simon answered him, "Master, we worked all night, and caught nothing; but at your word I will let down the net." [6] When they had done this, they caught so many fish that their net was breaking. [7] They signaled to their partners in the other boat, that they should come and help them. They came, and filled both boats, so that they began to sink. [8] But Simon Peter, when he saw it, fell down at Jesus' knees, saying, "Depart from me, for I am a sinful man, Lord." [9] For he and all who were with him were amazed at the catch of fish which they had caught; [10] and so were James and John, sons of Zebedee, who were partners with Simon.

Jesus said to Simon, "Don't be afraid. From now on you will be catching people."

[11] When they had brought their boats to land, they left everything, and followed him.

SCARY GLORY

"Depart from me, for I am a sinful man, Lord." Luke 5:8

Miracles can be scary. Jesus' disciples were scared during a wild storm, but when Jesus calmed the storm, they were downright terrified (Mark 4:41). Something about Jesus was scarier than any storm.

Catching fish doesn't sound so scary. After fishing all night and catching nothing, Peter suddenly caught two boatloads of fish with Jesus' help. Why was that so scary? Peter suddenly sensed that he was a mere man in the presence of the divine, a sinner in the presence of the blinding holiness that angels dare not look upon.

Peter feared that he was too small and sinful to hang around with someone so great and holy. He said, "Depart from me, for I am a sinful man, Lord." Peter thought it would be simpler and safer if Jesus would just go away and leave him to his fishing and his sinning. But Jesus told Peter not to be afraid, and Peter ended up following Jesus into something far greater than fishing or sinning.

If you've never felt afraid of Jesus, you probably don't know him well and don't know yourself well. "The fear of the Lord is the beginning of wisdom" (Proverbs 9:10). As you sense the Lord's majesty and your own sin, humble fear is healthy. But don't let fear scare you away from Jesus. "Don't be afraid," he says. "From now on you will be catching people." Jesus calls you to share his glory and to become a partner in his mission. Will you follow him?

PRAYER

Father in heaven, thank you for showing us your glory through Jesus. Forgive my sins and calm my fears. Make me a follower of Jesus and a fisher of men. Amen.

Mark 10:17-31

17 As Jesus was going on his way, a man ran to him, knelt before him, and asked him, "Good Teacher, what shall I do that I may inherit eternal life?"

18 Jesus said to him, "Why do you call me good? No one is good except one—God. 19 You know the commandments: 'Do not murder,' 'Do not commit adultery,' 'Do not steal,' 'Do not give false testimony,' 'Do not defraud,' 'Honor your father and mother.'"

20 He said to him, "Teacher, I have observed all these things from my youth."

21 Jesus looked at him and loved him. He said to him, "One thing you lack. Go, sell whatever you have, and give to the poor, and you will have treasure in heaven; and come, follow me."

22 But his face fell at that saying, and he went away sorrowful, for he had great possessions. 23 Jesus looked around, and said to his disciples, "How difficult it is for those who have riches to enter into God's Kingdom!"

24 The disciples were amazed at his words. But Jesus answered again, "Children, how hard is it for those who trust in riches to enter into God's Kingdom! 25 It is easier for a camel to go through a needle's eye than for a rich man to enter into God's Kingdom."

26 They were exceedingly astonished, saying to him, "Then who can be saved?"

27 Jesus, looking at them, said, "With men it is impossible, but not with God, for all things are possible with God."

28 Peter began to tell him, "Behold, we have left all, and have followed you."

29 Jesus said, "I tell you truly, there is no one who has left house, or brothers, or sisters, or father, or mother, or wife, or children, or land, for my sake, and for the sake of the Good News, 30 who will not receive one hundred times more now in this time, houses, brothers, sisters, mothers, children, and land, with persecutions; and in the age to come eternal life. 31 But many who are first will be last; and the last first."

WHO IS GOOD?

"Why do you call me good? No one is good except one—God." Mark 10:18

A rich young man thinks he's good; he thinks Jesus is good too. The man is half right.

When the man addresses Jesus as "good teacher," Jesus challenges him to think harder. Only God is truly good; all mere humans have sinned and fall short of God's glory. So if Jesus is not God, he is not good. But if Jesus *is* good, then he must be God. This forces a decision: either stop calling Jesus a good teacher, or start honoring him as God.

The young man needs to accept the truth about Jesus: if Jesus is good, he's God. The young man also needs to accept the truth about himself: he's not as good as he thinks he is. He claims that throughout his life he has kept all God's commands. But when he actually meets God in the person of Jesus and hears the Lord's command to choose Christ over money, the young man's face falls, and he walks away. He loves money more than he loves God, thus breaking God's greatest commandment to love the Lord with all his heart.

If God alone is good and if none of us is good enough to measure up to God's standard, what hope is there? If prosperous, well-behaved, religious people who call Jesus a good teacher can't earn eternal life, we might ask with Jesus' disciples, "Who then can be saved?" Our only comfort is Jesus' reply: "With men it is impossible, but not with God, for all things are possible with God."

PRAYER

Lord, you are more precious than silver, more costly than gold, more beautiful than diamonds. Nothing I desire compares with you. Do the impossible and save me. Amen.

Luke 7:11-23

11 Soon afterwards, he went to a city called Nain. Many
of his disciples, along with a great multitude, went with him.
12 Now when he came near to the gate of the city, a dead man
was carried out, the only son of his mother, and she was a
widow. Many people of the city were with her. 13 When the
Lord saw her, he had compassion on her, and said to her,
“Don’t cry.” 14 He came near and touched the coffin, and the
bearers stood still. He said, “Young man, I tell you, arise!”
15 The dead man sat up, and began to speak. And he gave
him to his mother.

16 Fear took hold of all, and they glorified God, saying,
“A great prophet has arisen among us!” and, “God has visited his people!” 17 This report about him went out in the
whole of Judea, and in all the surrounding region.

18 The disciples of John told him about all these things.
19 John, calling to himself two of his disciples, sent them to
Jesus, saying, “Are you the one who is coming, or should we
look for another?” 20 When the men had come to him, they
said, “John the Baptizer has sent us to you, saying, ‘Are you
he who comes, or should we look for another?’”

21 In that hour he cured many of diseases and plagues and
evil spirits; and to many who were blind he gave sight.
22 Jesus answered them, “Go and tell John the things which
you have seen and heard: that the blind receive their sight,
the lame walk, the lepers are cleansed, the deaf hear, the
dead are raised up, and the poor have good news preached to
them. 23 Blessed is he who is not offended at me.”

ARE YOU THE ONE?

"Are you he who comes, or should we look for another?" Luke 7:20

Before Jesus came, there had never been a greater man of God than John the Baptist (Luke 7:28). But even John had his times of doubt and confusion. John prepared the way for Jesus and directed other people to Jesus, but after several months in prison, John couldn't help wondering if he had been right about Jesus. He wanted to make sure.

John sent a message to Jesus: "Are you he who comes, or should we look for another?" John knew the Old Testament Scripture: "Your God will come… he will come to save you… Then will the eyes of the blind be opened and the ears of the deaf unstopped. Then will the lame leap like a deer and the mute tongue shout for joy" (Isaiah 35:4-6).

John believed that God would come and that Jesus was the one, but he wavered. Jesus sent back a message showing that Isaiah's words were coming true: "The blind receive their sight, the lame walk, the lepers are cleansed, the deaf hear, the dead are raised up, and the poor have good news preached to them" (Luke 7:22). Everything Isaiah had predicted was coming true, and more besides.

Should we look for another? No, God has come. We might not know why the miracle-working Christ left John to die in prison, nor do we know why we sometimes suffer the blows of a cruel world. But we do know that our God has come, accompanied by the promised signs.

PRAYER

Father in heaven, when fears and doubts attack us, help us to hear your Word afresh and to know Jesus anew as the fulfillment of all your promises. Amen.

John 5:1-18

1 After these things, there was a feast of the Jews, and Jesus went up to Jerusalem. 2 Now in Jerusalem by the sheep
gate, there is a pool, which is called in Hebrew, “Bethesda”,
having five porches. 3 In these lay a great multitude of those
who were sick, blind, lame, or paralyzed, waiting for the
moving of the water; 4 … Whoever stepped in first after the
stirring of the water was healed of whatever disease he had.
5 A certain man was there, who had been sick for thirty-eight
years. 6 When Jesus saw him lying there, and knew that he
had been sick for a long time, he asked him, “Do you want to
be made well?”

7 The sick man answered him, “Sir, I have no one to put
me into the pool when the water is stirred up, but while I’m
coming, another steps down before me.”

8 Jesus said to him, “Arise, take up your mat, and walk.”

9 Immediately, the man was made well, and took up his
mat and walked. Now it was the Sabbath on that day. 10 So
the Jews said to him who was cured, “It is the Sabbath. It is
not lawful for you to carry the mat.”

11 He answered them, “The man who made me well said
to me, ‘Take up your mat, and walk.’”

12 Then they asked him, “Who is the man who said to
you, ‘Take up your mat, and walk’?” 13 But he who was
healed didn’t know who it was, for Jesus had withdrawn, as
there was a crowd in the place.

14 Afterward Jesus found him in the temple, and said to
him, “Behold, you are made well. Sin no more, so that nothing worse happens to you.”

15 The man went away, and told the Jews that it was Jesus
who had made him well. 16 For this reason the Jews persecuted Jesus, and sought to kill him, because he did these things
on the Sabbath. 17 But Jesus answered them, “My Father is
still working, so I am working, too.” 18 For this reason therefore the Jews sought all the more to kill him, because he not
only broke the Sabbath, but also called God his own Father,
making himself equal with God.

EQUAL WITH GOD

He called God his own Father, making himself equal with God. John 5:18

For thirty-eight years a man is unable to walk or take care of himself. Then along comes someone who tells him to pick up his mat and walk. The man is instantly cured, picks up his mat and walks. What a horrible sin! The rule-makers have decreed that it's wrong to carry a mat on the Sabbath. They seem to think it's more holy to lie on the ground paralyzed than to walk in the strength of the Lord.

When religion is nothing but rules and has no power to transform, all it can do is paralyze and criticize: it keeps people down and criticizes any life and vigor that doesn't fit the rules. Such religion angers Jesus (Mark 3:5).

Jesus is "Lord of the Sabbath" (Luke 6:5). Together with his Father, Jesus is the Lawgiver who commanded, "Remember the Sabbath day by keeping it holy" (Exodus 20:8). By claiming authority over the Sabbath and calling God his Father, Jesus declares himself equal with God.

That makes Jesus' enemies want to kill him. They love dead religion and hate the living God. Jesus' enemies eventually do kill him—but they can't make him stay dead.

Because Jesus is equal with God, he defeats death as well as paralysis. The Lord of the Sabbath rises from the dead, and he makes the day of his resurrection, Sunday, into the new Lord's Day. Every Sunday is a day to celebrate the life-giving power of Jesus and to worship him as equal with God.

PRAYER

Lord, you give movement to the paralyzed and life to the dead. Free us from dead rules to serve the living God. Fill us with your life and love. Amen.

John 7:31-52

31 Many of the multitude believed in Jesus. They said,
"When the Christ comes, he won't do more signs than those
which this man has done, will he?" 32 The Pharisees heard
the multitude murmuring these things concerning him, and
the chief priests and the Pharisees sent officers to arrest him.

33 Then Jesus said, "I will be with you a little while longer, then I go to him who sent me. 34 You will seek me, and
won't find me; and where I am, you can't come." …

37 Now on the last and greatest day of the feast, Jesus
stood and cried out, "If anyone is thirsty, let him come to me
and drink! 38 He who believes in me, as the Scripture has
said, from within him will flow rivers of living water." 39 But
he said this about the Spirit, which those believing in him
were to receive. For the Holy Spirit was not yet given, because Jesus wasn't yet glorified.

40 Many of the multitude therefore, when they heard these
words, said, "This is truly the prophet." 41 Others said, "This
is the Christ." But some said, "What, does the Christ come
out of Galilee? 42 Hasn't the Scripture said that the Christ
comes of the offspring of David, and from Bethlehem, the
village where David was?" 43 So there arose a division in the
multitude because of him. 44 Some of them would have arrested him, but no one laid hands on him. 45 The officers
therefore came to the chief priests and Pharisees, and they
said to them, "Why didn't you bring him?"

46 The officers answered, "No man ever spoke like this
man!"

47 The Pharisees therefore answered them, "You aren't
also led astray, are you? 48 Have any of the rulers believed in
him, or of the Pharisees? 49 But this multitude that doesn't
know the law is accursed."

50 Nicodemus (he who came to him by night, being one
of them) said to them, 51 "Does our law judge a man, unless
it first hears from him personally and knows what he does?"

52 They answered him, "Are you also from Galilee?
Search, and see that no prophet has arisen out of Galilee."

ARRESTING WORDS

The officers answered, "No man ever spoke like this man!" John 7:46

Jesus spoke with unmatched power. Even when Jesus was a boy, "everyone who heard him was amazed at his understanding" (Luke 2:47). As an adult, Jesus' words amazed almost everybody, whether they loved or hated him.

Jesus had astonishing insight into deep truths, yet he spoke in simple words and gripping stories. Expert scholars tried to stump him or trick him into saying something foolish, but Jesus always had the perfect answer. The smartest people couldn't outwit him, yet the simplest people could benefit from his teaching. Jesus' simple brilliance made people wonder, "How did this man get such learning without having studied?" (John 7:15).

People were amazed not only at Jesus' brilliance but by the sheer authority of how he spoke. He wasn't like other teachers who debated the fine points of religion and piled up quotes from other experts. Jesus often challenged expert opinion and declared the truth, based on divine authority. "The crowds were amazed at his teaching, because he taught as one who had authority, and not as their teachers of the law" (Matthew 7:28-29).

Jesus' enemies sent guards to arrest him, but those tough, no-nonsense officers found themselves arrested by Jesus' words. They drank in his words and then went away without seizing him. Asked why they didn't arrest Jesus, they declared, "No man ever spoke like this man!" That's because no one but Jesus ever spoke as God with us.

PRAYER

Father in heaven, thank you for sending your Son, your eternal Word, to speak your truth. Arrest our hearts by your Spirit, and captivate us by your wisdom. Amen.

Matthew 7:13-29

[13] "Enter in by the narrow gate; for wide is the gate and
broad is the way that leads to destruction, and many are
those who enter in by it. [14] How narrow is the gate, and re-
stricted is the way that leads to life! Few are those who find
it.

[15] "Beware of false prophets, who come to you in sheep's
clothing, but inwardly are ravening wolves. [16] By their fruits
you will know them. Do you gather grapes from thorns, or
figs from thistles? [17] Even so, every good tree produces good
fruit; but the corrupt tree produces evil fruit. [18] A good tree
can't produce evil fruit, neither can a corrupt tree produce
good fruit. [19] Every tree that doesn't grow good fruit is cut
down, and thrown into the fire. [20] Therefore by their fruits
you will know them. [21] Not everyone who says to me, 'Lord,
Lord,' will enter into the Kingdom of Heaven; but he who
does the will of my Father who is in heaven. [22] Many will tell
me in that day, 'Lord, Lord, didn't we prophesy in your
name, in your name cast out demons, and in your name do
many mighty works?' [23] Then I will tell them, 'I never knew
you. Depart from me, you who work iniquity.'

[24] "Everyone therefore who hears these words of mine,
and does them, I will liken him to a wise man, who built his
house on a rock. [25] The rain came down, the floods came,
and the winds blew, and beat on that house; and it didn't fall,
for it was founded on the rock. [26] Everyone who hears these
words of mine, and doesn't do them will be like a foolish
man, who built his house on the sand. [27] The rain came
down, the floods came, and the winds blew, and beat on that
house; and it fell—and great was its fall."

[28] When Jesus had finished saying these things, the multitudes were astonished at his teaching, [29] for he taught them
with authority, and not like the scribes.

THE ROCK

"Everyone therefore who hears these words of mine, and does them, I will liken him to a wise man, who built his house on a rock." Matthew 7:24

Old Testament Scripture often speaks of God as the Rock. "Oh, praise the greatness of our God. He is the Rock" (Deuteronomy 32:3-4). "Come, let us sing for joy to Yahweh; let us shout aloud to the Rock of our salvation" (Psalm 95:1). "Trust in Yahweh forever, for Yahweh, Yahweh, is the Rock eternal" (Isaiah 26:4).

Old Testament Scripture warns against building our lives on anything but God the Rock. "Is there any God besides me? No, there is no other Rock" (Isaiah 44:8). When people don't build on the Rock, they might still try to look good and impress others, but they are just putting whitewash on a weak wall with no foundation. "Rain will come in torrents… and violent winds will burst forth," says God. "I will tear down the wall you have covered with whitewash and will level it to the ground so that its foundations will be laid bare" (Ezekiel 13:11,14).

When Jesus speaks of himself and his words as the Rock, he speaks with divine authority. Jesus is not just one more teacher of Old Testament law; he is the Lawgiver, the Lord Yahweh. He is the only foundation to build upon. "For no one can lay any foundation other than the one already laid, which is Jesus Christ" (1 Corinthians 3:11). Without Jesus as your foundation, you collapse. But built on Christ the Rock, you stand strong through every storm.

PRAYER

When all around my soul gives way,
you then are all my hope and stay.
On Christ the solid rock I stand;
all other ground is sinking sand. Amen.

John 8:12-27

12 Jesus again spoke to the people: “I am the light of the world. He who follows me will not walk in the darkness, but will have the light of life.”

13 The Pharisees therefore said to him, “You testify about yourself. Your testimony is not valid.”

14 Jesus answered them, “Even if I testify about myself, my testimony is true, for I know where I came from, and where I am going; but you don’t know where I came from, or where I am going. 15 You judge according to the flesh. I judge no one. 16 Even if I do judge, my judgment is true, for I am not alone, but I am with the Father who sent me. 17 It’s also written in your law that the testimony of two people is valid. 18 I am one who testifies about myself, and the Father who sent me testifies about me.”

19 They said therefore to him, “Where is your Father?”

Jesus answered, “You know neither me, nor my Father. If you knew me, you would know my Father also.” 20 Jesus spoke these words in the treasury, as he taught in the temple. Yet no one arrested him, because his hour had not yet come. 21 Jesus said therefore again to them, “I am going away, and you will seek me, and you will die in your sins. Where I go, you can’t come.”

22 The Jews therefore said, “Will he kill himself, that he says, ‘Where I am going, you can’t come’?”

23 He said to them, “You are from beneath. I am from above. You are of this world. I am not of this world. 24 I said therefore to you that you will die in your sins; for unless you believe that I AM, you will die in your sins.”

25 They said therefore to him, “Who are you?”

Jesus said to them, “Just what I have been saying to you from the beginning. 26 I have many things to speak and to judge concerning you. However he who sent me is true; and the things which I heard from him, these I say to the world.”

27 They didn’t understand that he spoke to them about the Father.

LIGHT OF THE WORLD

"I am the light of the world." John 8:12

When Jesus says, "I am the light of the world," he makes an astonishing claim. He doesn't just claim to teach how to be enlightened. He declares himself to *be* the light. In doing so, Jesus declares himself to be Yahweh, the living God.

In Old Testament Scripture, who is the light? Psalm 27:1 says, "Yahweh is my light and my salvation." So when Jesus says, "I am the light," he is saying, "I am Yahweh, your light and salvation." Psalm 18:28 says, "For you will light my lamp, Yahweh. My God will light up my darkness." So when Jesus says, "Whoever follows me will never walk in darkness but will have the light of life," he is saying, "I am Yahweh God, who lights up your darkness."

The light of the world is the great I AM, who told Moses, "I am who I am." When the Pharisees heard Jesus claim to be the light, they immediately challenged him. And still today there are people who challenge Jesus' divine claims. Satan "has blinded the minds of unbelievers, so that they cannot see the light of the gospel of the glory of Christ, who is the image of God" (2 Corinthians 4:4).

But some do see the light of the world and recognize Jesus as God with us. "For God, who said, 'Let light shine out of darkness,' made his light shine in our hearts to give us the light of the knowledge of the glory of God in the face of Christ" (2 Corinthians 4:6).

PRAYER

Lord, with you is the fountain of life; in your light we see light. Let your face shine on us, that we may be saved. Amen. (Psalm 36:9; 80:19).

Luke 8:4-15

4 When a great multitude came together, and people from
every city were coming to him, he spoke by a parable. 5 "A
farmer went out to sow his seed. As he sowed, some fell
along the road, and it was trampled under foot, and the birds
of the sky devoured it. 6 Other seed fell on the rock, and as
soon as it grew, it withered away, because it had no mois-
ture. 7 Other seed fell amid the thorns, and the thorns grew
with it, and choked it. 8 Other seed fell into the good ground,
and grew, and produced one hundred times as much fruit."
As he said these things, he called out, "He who has ears to
hear, let him hear!"

9 Then his disciples asked him, "What does this parable
mean?"

10 He said, "To you it is given to know the mysteries of
God's Kingdom, but to the rest in parables; that 'seeing they
may not see, and hearing they may not understand.' 11 Now
the parable is this: The seed is the word of God. 12 Those
along the road are those who hear, then the devil comes, and
takes away the word from their heart, that they may not believe and be saved. 13 Those on the rock are they who, when
they hear, receive the word with joy; but these have no root,
who believe for a while, then fall away in time of temptation.
14 The seed which fell among the thorns, these are those who
have heard, and as they go on their way they are choked with
cares, riches, and pleasures of life, and bring no fruit to maturity. 15 The seed in the good ground, these are such as in an
honest and good heart, having heard the word, hold it tightly,
and produce fruit with patience."

GOOD SOIL

"The seed in the good ground, these are such as in an honest and good heart, having heard the word, hold it tightly, and produce fruit with patience." Luke 8:15

If you hear God's Word but it goes in one ear and out the other, you're like hard soil. If you get excited about the Lord but later lose interest, you're like shallow soil. If you believe some things about God but your heart is crowded with worries or pleasures, you're like thorny soil. The only soil that produces a crop is good soil, "an honest and good heart."

What if you don't have an honest and good heart? You can still get one, but only by having your heart plowed through repentance. In Old Testament Scripture, God says, "Break up your unplowed ground and do not sow among thorns" (Jeremiah 4:3). "Sow for yourselves righteousness, reap the fruit of unfailing love, and break up your unplowed ground; for it is time to seek the Lord, until he showers righteousness upon you" (Hosea 10:12).

Jesus, as Lord of Old Testament and New, brings this message afresh through his parable of the four soils. To bear a crop for the Lord, you must become good soil. The plowing of repentance loosens and softens your hard heart so that God's Word can sink in. Repentance cuts deep so that your response to Christ is not shallow but lasting. Repentance roots out weeds of worldliness so that God's Word has space to grow and bear fruit in you. Has your heart been plowed by repentance? Is Jesus' Word producing fruit in you?

PRAYER

Lord, produce the fruit of your Spirit in me. Break up my unplowed ground, and give me a good and noble heart that lives by your Word. For Jesus' sake, Amen.

Luke 15:11-32

11 Jesus said, “A certain man had two sons. 12 The younger of them said to his father, ‘Father, give me my share of
your property.’ He divided his livelihood between them.
13 Not many days after, the younger son gathered all of this
together and traveled into a far country. There he wasted his
property with riotous living. 14 When he had spent all of it,
there arose a severe famine in that country, and he began to
be in need… 17 But when he came to himself he said, ‘How
many hired servants of my father’s have bread enough to
spare, and I’m dying with hunger! 18 I will get up and go to
my father, and will tell him, “Father, I have sinned against
heaven, and in your sight. 19 I am no more worthy to be
called your son. Make me as one of your hired servants.”’

20 “He arose, and came to his father. But while he was
still far off, his father saw him, and was moved with compassion, and ran, and fell on his neck, and kissed him. 21 The son
said to him, ‘Father, I have sinned against heaven, and in
your sight. I am no longer worthy to be called your son.’

22 “But the father said to his servants, ‘Bring out the best
robe, and put it on him. Put a ring on his hand, and shoes on
his feet. 23 Bring the fattened calf, kill it, and let us eat, and
celebrate; 24 for this, my son, was dead, and is alive again. He
was lost, and is found.’ So they began to celebrate.

25 “Now his elder son was in the field. As he came near to
the house, he heard music and dancing… 28 But he was angry, and would not go in. Therefore his father came out, and
begged him. 29 But he answered his father, ‘Behold, these
many years I have served you, and I never disobeyed a
commandment of yours, but you never gave me a goat, that I
might celebrate with my friends. 30 But when this, your son,
came, who has devoured your living with prostitutes, you
killed the fattened calf for him.’

31 “He said to him, ‘Son, you are always with me, and all
that is mine is yours. 32 But it was appropriate to celebrate
and be glad, for this, your brother, was dead, and is alive
again. He was lost, and is found.’”

THE SINGING GOD

"Let us eat, and celebrate; for this, my son, was dead, and is alive again. He was lost, and is found." Luke 15:23-24

Old Testament Scripture says, "The Lord your God is with you, he is mighty to save. He will take great delight in you, he will quiet you with his love, he will rejoice over you with singing" (Zephaniah 3:17). Jesus' parable of the prodigal son drives that message home. As the father in Jesus' story saved his son from starvation, so God saves us from damnation. As the father delighted to see his son back, so God delights over all who seek his help. As the father hugged his son and quieted him before the boy could make his offer to become a slave, so God quiets us with his love and welcomes us not as slaves but as sons and daughters. As the father celebrated with music and dancing, so God rejoices over his people with singing.

Can you picture God throwing a party? Can you imagine the Lord standing up in the middle of the party, singing a happy song, and dancing for joy? Maybe you think of God as solemn and somber and silent. In your mind, God isn't the type to sing and dance—or at least he shouldn't be, not when the people he sings over have been so rotten. God should be more dignified. If he celebrates at all, he should sing only over those who deserve it.

But God's glory in Christ overflows with delight and music. In Christ we meet a glad God, a Father who sings for joy whenever a wandering child returns home. God's glorious gladness is what every sinful, prodigal son needs—and what every sour older brother needs.

PRAYER

Father, I have sinned and am not worthy to be called your son. Thank you for saving me, loving me, delighting in me, and singing over me. I love you, Lord. Amen.

Luke 11:1-13

1 When Jesus finished praying in a certain place, one of
his disciples said to him, “Lord, teach us to pray, just as John
also taught his disciples.”
2 He said to them, “When you pray, say,
‘Our Father in heaven,
may your name be kept holy.
May your Kingdom come.
May your will be done on earth, as it is in heaven.
3 Give us each day our daily bread
4 Forgive us our sins,
for we ourselves also forgive
everyone who is indebted to us.
Bring us not into temptation,
but deliver us from the evil one.’”
5 He said to them, “Which of you, if you go to a friend at
midnight, and tell him, ‘Friend, lend me three loaves of
bread, 6 for a friend of mine has come to me from a journey,
and I have nothing to set before him,’ 7 and he from within
will answer and say, ‘Don’t bother me. The door is now shut,
and my children are with me in bed. I can’t get up and give it
to you’? 8 I tell you, although he will not rise and give it to
him because he is his friend, yet because of his persistence,
he will get up and give him as many as he needs.
9 “I tell you, keep asking, and it will be given you. Keep
seeking, and you will find. Keep knocking, and it will be
opened to you. 10 For everyone who asks receives. He who
seeks finds. To him who knocks the door will be opened.
11 “Which of you fathers, if your son asks for bread, will
give him a stone? Or if he asks for a fish, he won’t give him
a snake instead of a fish, will he? 12 Or if he asks for an egg,
he won’t give him a scorpion, will he? 13 If you then, being
evil, know how to give good gifts to your children, how
much more will your heavenly Father give the Holy Spirit to
those who ask him?”

POUNDING ON HEAVEN'S DOOR

"To him who knocks the door will be opened." Luke 11:10

Who would dare say that praying to God is like pounding on a door and yelling to wake someone up in the middle of the night? That sounds rash and rude, but God himself urges us to pray this way.

God inspired Old Testament writers to pray, "Awake, my God; decree justice" (Psalm 7:6). "Awake, and rise to my defense!" (Psalm 35:23) "Awake, Yahweh! Why do you sleep? Rouse yourself! Do not reject us forever" (Psalm 44:23). "Awaken your might; come and save us" (Psalm 80:2). God told his people, "You who call on Yahweh, give yourselves no rest and give him no rest" (Isaiah 62:7).

The Son of God, the fulfillment of Old Testament Scripture, compares prayer to waking up a sleepy friend at midnight. Later Jesus goes even further and compares prayer to hassling a crooked judge into upholding justice even when he doesn't feel like it (Luke 18:1-8). Jesus' point is not that our Father in heaven is sleepy or crooked. His point is that we should be as aggressive and persistent in prayer as we would be if we were trying get food from a drowsy friend, or struggling to get justice from an unjust judge who won't pay attention unless we keep bothering him.

The fact that God is perfectly just and never slumbers should increase our confidence but should not decrease our urgency or boldness. Pray aggressively for the honor of God's name, the coming of his kingdom, and the doing of his will. Give yourself no rest, and give God no rest. Keep pounding on heaven's door until the Lord answers with a greater outpouring of his Holy Spirit.

PRAYER

O Thou by whom we come to God,
the life, the truth, the way,
the path of prayer thyself hast trod:
Lord, teach us how to pray. Amen.

John 8:3-11

3 The scribes and the Pharisees brought a woman taken in
adultery. Having set her in the middle, 4 they told Jesus,
"Teacher, we found this woman in adultery, in the very act.
5 Now in our law, Moses commanded us to stone such wom-
en. What then do you say about her?" 6 They said this testing
him, that they might have something to accuse him of.

But Jesus stooped down, and wrote on the ground with
his finger. 7 But when they continued asking him, he looked
up and said to them, "He who is without sin among you, let
him throw the first stone at her." 8 Again he stooped down,
and with his finger wrote on the ground.

9 They, when they heard it, being convicted by their conscience, went out one by one, beginning from the oldest,
even to the last. Jesus was left alone with the woman where
she was, in the middle. 10 Jesus, standing up, saw her and
said, "Woman, where are your accusers? Did no one condemn you?"

11 She said, "No one, Lord."

Jesus said, "Neither do I condemn you. Go your way. From now on, sin no more."

FULL OF GRACE AND TRUTH

"Neither do I condemn you. Go your way. From now on, sin no more." John 8:11

Jesus is "full of grace and truth" (John 1:14). When a sinful woman was in danger of being killed, Jesus told her accusers, "Let him who is without sin cast the first stone." They left one by one until only Jesus remained.

Jesus truly was without sin, so he had the right to throw the first stone. He had the right to judge and destroy the woman. But Jesus told her, "Neither do I condemn you." That's grace. Then he added, "Sin no more." That's truth. Jesus showed her God's loving grace *and* told her the truth about her sin and her need to change.

Jesus' grace and truth shone even in his dealings with Pharisees, super-strict religious leaders who didn't really know God. Jesus was painfully truthful, calling them hypocrites, snakes, and blind guides. He warned of hell for those who didn't change. But in telling the truth, Jesus remained gracious. When the Pharisee Nicodemus wanted to talk with him, Jesus explained the way of salvation. Later, when the Pharisee Saul of Tarsus was killing Jesus' followers, the Lord showed Saul the truth about his evil conduct and the truth of Jesus' divine lordship. Jesus also showed grace by forgiving Saul and making him into Paul, the great missionary. Grace and truth, even for stubborn, cruel Pharisees!

This beautiful blend of grace and truth is nothing less than divine glory. "We have seen his glory, the glory of the One and Only, who came from the Father, full of grace and truth" (John 1:14).

PRAYER

Lord God, fountain of grace and truth, in your grace forgive our sleazy sins and our proud self-righteousness, and guide us by your truth in Christ. Amen.

John 1:1-18

1 In the beginning was the Word, and the Word was with
God, and the Word was God. 2 He was in the beginning with
God. 3 All things were made through him. Without him nothing was made that has been made. 4 In him was life, and the
life was the light of men. 5 The light shines in the darkness,
and the darkness has not overcome it. 6 There came a man,
sent from God, whose name was John. 7 He came as a witness, that he might testify about the light, that all might believe through him. 8 He was not the light, but was sent that he
might testify about the light. 9 The true light that enlightens
everyone was coming into the world.

10 He was in the world, and the world was made through
him, and the world didn't recognize him. 11 He came to his
own, and those who were his own did not receive him. 12 But
as many as received him, to them he gave the right to become God's children, to those who believe in his name:
13 who were born not of blood, nor of the will of the flesh,
nor of the will of man, but of God. 14 The Word became
flesh, and lived among us. We saw his glory, such glory as of
the only begotten Son of the Father, full of grace and truth.
15 John testified about him. He cried out, saying, "This was
he of whom I said, 'He who comes after me has surpassed
me, for he was before me.'" 16 From his fullness we all received grace upon grace. 17 For the law was given through
Moses. Grace and truth came through Jesus Christ. 18 No one
has seen God at any time. The only begotten God, who is in
the bosom of the Father, he has declared him.

GRACE AND TRUTH UNITED

The Word became flesh, and lived among us. We saw his glory, such glory as of the only begotten Son of the Father, full of grace and truth. John 1:14

Grace and truth belong together but are often separated. Churches eager to be gracious can lose biblical truth. If two people with no Christian commitment request a church wedding, the church does the ceremony. If people who don't follow Jesus want their baby baptized out of tradition or superstition, the church gladly gets the child wet. The sermons are all positive thinking, no Bible. All love, no judgment. All grace, no truth.

Other churches go to the opposite extreme. Anxious about truth, they neglect grace. They emphasize Bible knowledge and theology, they have detailed rules for every situation, but grace is in short supply. The sermons are all judgment, no love. There's not much room for people who don't have perfect behavior and perfect beliefs. Every few years there's another nasty quarrel and another church split over some detail of doctrine. All truth, no grace.

Grace and truth belong together. Grace without truth isn't grace at all; it's permissiveness. And truth without grace isn't God's truth; it's legalism. What churches need, what families need, what we all need, isn't a little more grace or a little more truth. What we need is a lot more of Jesus. "Grace and truth came through Jesus Christ" (John 1:17). It is the glory of Christ to be full of grace *and* truth. If we are full of Christ, we will be full of grace and truth, and divine glory will overflow from us.

PRAYER

Father, fill us with the Spirit of Christ. Warm our hearts with the grace of Jesus, guide our minds by the truth of Jesus, and reveal your glory in us. Amen.

Luke 1:30-37

30 The angel said to Mary, “Don’t be afraid, Mary, for
you have found favor with God. 31 Behold, you will conceive
in your womb, and give birth to a son, and will call his name
‘Jesus.’ 32 He will be great, and will be called the Son of the
Most High. The Lord God will give him the throne of his
father, David, 33 and he will reign over the house of Jacob
forever. There will be no end to his Kingdom.”
34 Mary said to the angel, “How can this be, seeing I am a
virgin?” 35 The angel answered her, “The Holy Spirit will
come on you, and the power of the Most High will over-
shadow you. Therefore the holy one who is born from you
will be called the Son of God… 37 For with God nothing is
impossible.”

Matthew 1:18-25

18 Now the birth of Jesus Christ was like this; for after his
mother, Mary, was engaged to Joseph, before they came together, she was found pregnant by the Holy Spirit. 19 Joseph,
her husband, being a righteous man, and not willing to make
her a public example, intended to end the relationship secretly. 20 But when he thought about these things, behold, an angel of the Lord appeared to him in a dream, saying, “Joseph,
son of David, don’t be afraid to take to yourself Mary, your
wife, for that which is conceived in her is of the Holy Spirit.
21 She shall give birth to a son. You shall call his name Jesus,
for it is he who shall save his people from their sins.”
22 Now all this has happened, that it might be fulfilled
which was spoken by the Lord through the prophet, saying,
23 “Behold, the virgin shall be with child, and shall give
birth to a son. They shall call his name Immanuel” which is,
being interpreted, “God with us.”
24 Joseph arose from his sleep, and did as the angel of the
Lord commanded him, and took his wife to himself; 25 and
didn’t know her sexually until she had given birth to her
firstborn son. He named him Jesus.

HARD TO BELIEVE

Joseph intended to end the relationship secretly. Matthew 1:19

Skeptics claim that people in the past believed in Jesus' miracles only because they were less scientific than we are. But that's nonsense. Miracles were just as hard to believe then as they are now.

When Mary got pregnant, Joseph didn't need a biology degree to know where babies come from. He didn't yawn and say, "Another virgin birth—happens all the time." Joseph figured Mary must have been with another man. It took an angel visit to make Joseph believe the miracle.

When Jesus' disciples were in a boat and saw Jesus walking toward them on the water, they didn't say, "What else is new? Some people were wave-walking just yesterday." The disciples didn't need advanced physics to know that people don't walk on water.

On the first Easter, when Jesus' friends found that his tomb was empty, they didn't smile and say, "Must be another resurrection—knew it all along." They didn't need modern science to know that dead people tend to stay dead. The disciples believed only after Jesus came to them and ate with them and convinced them he really was alive.

Modern science doesn't make miracles harder to believe. Miracles have always been impossible in terms of ordinary patterns of nature. But what if the God who designed those patterns decides to do something different? If you deny Jesus' miracles, it's not because you're too scientific. "You are in error because you do not know the Scriptures or the power of God" (Matthew 22:29). "For with God nothing is impossible." (Luke 1:37)

PRAYER

Lord, I believe. Help me overcome my unbelief. Expand my mind to accept biblical realities, and touch my heart by the power of God in Christ. Amen.

John 9:1-38

[1] As he passed by, he saw a man blind from birth. [2] His
disciples asked him, "Rabbi, who sinned, this man or his
parents, that he was born blind?"

[3] Jesus answered, "It's not that this man sinned, nor his
parents; but, that the works of God might be revealed in him.
[4] I must work the works of him who sent me, while it is day.
The night is coming, when no one can work. [5] While I am in
the world, I am the light of the world." [6] When he had said
this, he spat on the ground, made mud with the saliva,
anointed the blind man's eyes with the mud, [7] and said to
him, "Go, wash in the pool of Siloam" (which means
"Sent"). So he went away, washed, and came back seeing…

[13] They brought him who had been blind to the Pharisees… [17] Therefore they asked the blind man again, "What
do you say about him, because he opened your eyes?"

He said, "He is a prophet." …

[24] They called the man who was blind a second time, and
said to him, "Give glory to God. We know that this man is a
sinner."

[25] He therefore answered, "I don't know if he is a sinner.
One thing I do know: that though I was blind, now I see…
[31] We know that God doesn't listen to sinners, but if anyone
is a worshiper of God, and does his will, he listens to him.
[32] Since the world began it has never been heard of that anyone opened the eyes of someone born blind. [33] If this man
were not from God, he could do nothing."

[34] They answered him, "You were altogether born in sins,
and do you teach us?" They threw him out.

[35] Jesus heard that they had thrown him out, and finding
him, he said, "Do you believe in the Son of God?"

[36] He answered, "Who is he, Lord, that I may believe in
him?"

[37] Jesus said to him, "You have seen him, and it is he
who speaks with you."

[38] He said, "Lord, I believe!" and he worshiped him.

SIGHT FOR THE BLIND

"Since the world began it has never been heard of that anyone opened the eyes of someone born blind. If this man were not from God, he could do nothing." John 9:32-33

God has a special purpose for people with physical challenges. It is not just random chance that makes a person blind or deaf. God does. "Who makes a man deaf or mute? Who gives him sight or makes him blind? Is it not I, the Lord?" (Exodus 4:11) At some point the Lord will give full physical abilities to all his people. Meanwhile, hearing and sight are God's to withhold or to give. That raises the question why God would make someone blind. Some might think God singled out such a person for special punishment, but in fact, God singled him out for a special purpose: to display God's work in his life.

God's work is Jesus' work. When Jesus gave sight to the blind, he showed his divine glory. Jesus' enemies called him a sinner, and even some of his friends saw him only as a prophet. But Old Testament Scripture had said, "*Yahweh* gives sight to the blind" (Psalm 146:8), so Jesus was doing work that only Yahweh God could do. The man whom Jesus healed came to understand this. He said, "'Lord, I believe!' and he worshiped him" (John 9:38).

Do you believe and worship the Lord Jesus? Blind eyes might be troublesome, but a blind soul is far worse. The Lord Jesus is the only one who can remove either kind of blindness. As the Creator of light and eyes, Jesus alone can give physical sight. As the spiritual light of the world, Jesus alone can open the eyes of our hearts.

PRAYER

Lord, save us from blind souls and deaf hearts. Help us to hear your voice, to see your glory, and to love you as our light and salvation. Amen.

John 10:1-18

1 “Most certainly, I tell you, one who doesn’t enter by the
door into the sheep fold, but climbs up some other way, is a
thief and a robber. 2 But one who enters in by the door is the
shepherd of the sheep. 3 The gatekeeper opens the gate for
him, and the sheep listen to his voice. He calls his own sheep
by name, and leads them out. 4 Whenever he brings out his
own sheep, he goes before them, and the sheep follow him,
for they know his voice. 5 They will by no means follow a
stranger, but will flee from him; for they don’t know the
voice of strangers.” 6 Jesus spoke this parable to them, but
they didn’t understand what he was telling them.

7 Jesus therefore said to them again, “Most certainly, I
tell you, I am the sheep’s door. 8 All who came before me are
thieves and robbers, but the sheep didn’t listen to them. 9 I
am the door. If anyone enters in by me, he will be saved, and
will go in and go out, and will find pasture.

10 The thief only comes to steal, kill, and destroy. I came
that they may have life, and may have it abundantly. 11 I am
the good shepherd. The good shepherd lays down his life for
the sheep. 12 He who is a hired hand, and not a shepherd, who
doesn’t own the sheep, sees the wolf coming, leaves the
sheep, and flees. The wolf snatches the sheep, and scatters
them. 13 The hired hand flees because he is a hired hand, and
doesn’t care for the sheep. 14 I am the good shepherd. I know
my own, and I’m known by my own; 15 even as the Father
knows me, and I know the Father. I lay down my life for the
sheep. 16 I have other sheep, which are not of this fold. I must
bring them also, and they will hear my voice. They will become one flock with one shepherd. 17 Therefore the Father
loves me, because I lay down my life, that I may take it
again. 18 No one takes it away from me, but I lay it down by
myself. I have power to lay it down, and I have power to take
it again. I received this commandment from my Father.”

THE GOOD SHEPHERD

"I am the good shepherd. The good shepherd lays down his life for the sheep." John 10:11

Perhaps the best-loved statement in the Old Testament is Psalm 23:1: "The Lord is my shepherd." Other Old Testament scriptures also speak of God as a shepherd: "He gathers the lambs in his arms and carries them close to his heart" (Isaiah 40:11). "This is what the Sovereign Lord says: I myself will search for my sheep and look after them… I myself will tend my sheep and have them lie down, declares the Sovereign Lord… I will shepherd the flock with justice" (Ezekiel 34:11-16).

When Jesus says, "I am the good shepherd," he speaks as God. Jesus isn't just another religious leader. He is the Lord of glory who has come to Earth to be our shepherd.

Some religious leaders are thieves or hired hands, says Jesus, but the good shepherd is different. A thief rips off and ruins the sheep, but the good shepherd gives them abundant life. A hired hand is in the religion business only for the money and abandons his flock if danger threatens, but the good shepherd stays with his sheep no matter what. He is even willing to die for them.

Is the Lord Jesus your shepherd? Don't fall for phony religion. Only Jesus can bring you to green pastures and still waters. Only Jesus can restore your soul and guide you in paths of righteousness. Only Jesus can bring you through the valley of the shadow of death, defeat Satan and all enemies, and give you a place in God's house forever. So trust the good shepherd, God with us.

PRAYER

Good shepherd, forgive me for all the times I wander away from you. Thank you for laying down your life to save me. Lead me and keep me in your care forever. Amen.

John 10:22-39

22 It was the Feast of the Dedication at Jerusalem. 23 It
was winter, and Jesus was walking in the temple, in Solo-
mon's porch. 24 The Jews therefore came around him and
said to him, "How long will you hold us in suspense? If you
are the Christ, tell us plainly."

25 Jesus answered them, "I told you, and you don't believe. The works that I do in my Father's name, these testify
about me. 26 But you don't believe, because you are not of
my sheep, as I told you. 27 My sheep hear my voice, and I
know them, and they follow me. 28 I give eternal life to them.
They will never perish, and no one will snatch them out of
my hand. 29 My Father, who has given them to me, is greater
than all. No one is able to snatch them out of my Father's
hand. 30 I and the Father are one."

31 Therefore Jews took up stones again to stone him.
32 Jesus answered them, "I have shown you many good
works from my Father. For which of those works do you
stone me?"

33 The Jews answered him, "We don't stone you for a
good work, but for blasphemy: because you, being a man,
make yourself God."

34 Jesus answered them, "Isn't it written in your law, 'I
said, you are gods?' 35 If he called them gods, to whom the
word of God came (and the Scripture can't be broken), 36 do
you say of him whom the Father sanctified and sent into the
world, 'You blaspheme,' because I said, 'I am the Son of
God?' 37 If I don't do the works of my Father, don't believe
me. 38 But if I do them, though you don't believe me, believe
the works; that you may know and believe that the Father is
in me, and I in the Father."

39 They sought again to seize him, and he went out of
their hand.

IS FAITH FOOLISH?

"The works that I do in my Father's name, these testify about me. But you don't believe." John 10:25-26

A man phoned me to complain about one of my radio messages. He complained that I was foolish to preach Jesus' resurrection. He thought I was terribly irrational. But as the conversation continued, the caller went on to tell me that magician David Copperfield made the Statue of Liberty go away completely and then made it come back. I urged him to get serious, but he was dead serious. He knew for sure that this happened because he saw it on television! For him, seeing was believing. If seeing is believing, then television is the standard of truth.

Many people know enough not to believe everything they see on TV—but they still take their own ideas more seriously than God. Francis Crick won a Nobel Prize for his discoveries in the structure of DNA. After studying complex genetic codes, this brilliant scientist doubted that random evolution could ever produce DNA from scratch. So did he conclude that God was involved? No, he said that perhaps aliens from outer space put genetic material on Earth. In Dr. Crick's opinion, belief in the Creator God is unscientific—but belief in space aliens makes good sense!

Is faith foolish? Not nearly as foolish as unbelief. If you shut your eyes to God's glory in Christ, other things become darker too. But if you believe Jesus and his mighty works, you start seeing the whole world more clearly.

PRAYER

Dear Lord, forgive us when we feel foolish for believing you. Help us to believe your Word, to marvel at your miracles, and to prize you above all else. Amen.

Matthew 17:1-13

1 After six days, Jesus took with him Peter, James, and John his brother, and brought them up into a high mountain by themselves. 2 He was transfigured before them. His face shone like the sun, and his garments became as white as the light. 3 Behold, Moses and Elijah appeared to them talking with him.

4 Peter answered, and said to Jesus, “Lord, it is good for us to be here. If you want, let’s make three tents here: one for you, one for Moses, and one for Elijah.”

5 While he was still speaking, behold, a bright cloud overshadowed them. Behold, a voice came out of the cloud, saying, “This is my beloved Son, in whom I am well pleased. Listen to him.”

6 When the disciples heard it, they fell on their faces, and were very afraid. 7 Jesus came and touched them and said, “Get up, and don’t be afraid.” 8 Lifting up their eyes, they saw no one, except Jesus alone. 9 As they were coming down from the mountain, Jesus commanded them, saying, “Don’t tell anyone what you saw, until the Son of Man has risen from the dead.”

10 His disciples asked him, saying, “Then why do the scribes say that Elijah must come first?”

11 Jesus answered them, “Elijah indeed comes first, and will restore all things, 12 but I tell you that Elijah has come already, and they didn’t recognize him, but did to him whatever they wanted to. Even so the Son of Man will also suffer by them.” 13 Then the disciples understood that he spoke to them of John the Baptizer.

THE SHINING SAVIOR

His face shone like the sun, and his clothes became as white as the light. Matthew 17:2

Paintings of Jesus make him look handsome, but Jesus probably looked ordinary, perhaps even homely. "He had no beauty or majesty to attract us to him, nothing in his appearance that we should desire him" (Isaiah 53:2). Jesus didn't look like a movie star; and, living among the poor, he didn't have costly clothes to look fashionable or important. Even Jesus' best friends didn't always sense his divine majesty.

Jesus' looks and his clothes were not awe-inspiring, but one day, that plain face suddenly shone like the sun. Those worn, dirty clothes became white as the light. It lasted only a short time, but the Transfiguration gave a glimpse of who Jesus was all along: the Son of the living God. It also previewed the glory that would shine after Jesus defeated death and ascended to heaven.

Peter never forgot what he saw and heard that day, and he wanted everyone else to know. "We were eyewitnesses of his majesty," wrote Peter. "For he received honor and glory from God the Father when the voice came to him from the Majestic Glory, saying, 'This is my Son, whom I love; with him I am well pleased.' We ourselves heard this voice that came from heaven when we were with him on the sacred mountain." The Bible reveals Jesus' glory, so "you will do well to pay attention to it, as to a light shining in a dark place, until the day dawns and the morning star rises in your hearts" (2 Peter 1:16-19).

PRAYER

Father in heaven, shine the light of Jesus' face into our hearts. By your Spirit speak to us of your beloved Son, that we may know your glory in him. Amen.

Matthew 25:31-46

31 “When the Son of Man comes in his glory, and all the
holy angels with him, then he will sit on the throne of his
glory. 32 Before him all the nations will be gathered, and he
will separate them one from another, as a shepherd separates
the sheep from the goats. 33 He will set the sheep on his right
hand, but the goats on the left. 34 Then the King will tell
those on his right hand, ‘Come, blessed of my Father, inherit
the Kingdom prepared for you from the foundation of the
world; 35 for I was hungry, and you gave me food to eat. I
was thirsty, and you gave me drink. I was a stranger, and you
took me in. 36 I was naked, and you clothed me. I was sick,
and you visited me. I was in prison, and you came to me.’

37 “Then the righteous will answer him, saying, ‘Lord,
when did we see you hungry, and feed you; or thirsty, and
give you a drink? 38 When did we see you as a stranger, and
take you in; or naked, and clothe you? 39 When did we see
you sick, or in prison, and come to you?’”

40 “The King will answer them, ‘Most certainly I tell you,
because you did it to one of the least of these my brothers,
you did it to me.’ 41 Then he will say also to those on the left
hand, ‘Depart from me, you cursed, into the eternal fire
which is prepared for the devil and his angels; 42 for I was
hungry, and you didn’t give me food to eat; I was thirsty, and
you gave me no drink; 43 I was a stranger, and you didn’t
take me in; naked, and you didn’t clothe me; sick, and in
prison, and you didn’t visit me.’

44 “Then they will also answer, saying, ‘Lord, when did
we see you hungry, or thirsty, or a stranger, or naked, or sick,
or in prison, and didn’t help you?’

45 “Then he will answer them, saying, ‘Most certainly I
tell you, because you didn’t do it to one of the least of these,
you didn’t do it to me.’ 46 These will go away into eternal
punishment, but the righteous into eternal life.”

THE PLATINUM RULE

"Whatever you did for one of the least of these brothers of mine, you did for me." Matthew 25:40

One important way God displays his glory is by standing with poor people. Old Testament Scripture says, "Yahweh will maintain the cause of the afflicted, and justice for the needy" (Psalm 140:12). Indeed, God cares so much about poor people that he actually identifies with them. Any action toward the poor is an action toward God himself. "He who has pity on the poor lends to Yahweh; he will reward him" (Proverbs 19:17).

When Jesus says that he will judge the world on the final day, he speaks as the Lord Yahweh, who brings "justice for the poor." When Jesus says, "Whatever you did for one of the least of these brothers of mine, you did for me" (Matthew 25:40), he speaks as the Lord Yahweh, who identifies with the needy. Kindness to needy people is kindness to the Lord Jesus. Neglecting others is neglecting the Lord Jesus.

Jesus said, "Do to others as you would have them do to you" (Luke 6:31). That became known as the Golden Rule. If that's the golden rule, here's the Platinum Rule: "Do to others as you would do to Christ." As Creator and brother of the poor, Jesus takes personally everything done to his people. Whether you treat others well or badly, Jesus takes it personally. So do to others as you would do to Christ.

To meet Jesus firsthand and see God's glory in Christ, don't just look for a mystical experience. Look for people who need help and can't get justice. Hidden in those suffering faces is the glory of God in the face of Christ.

PRAYER

Father in heaven, help us to see you as Father of the poor and to see Christ in the faces of the needy. Move us to show love for them and you. Amen.

John 11:1-44

[1] Now a certain man was sick, Lazarus from Bethany, of
the village of Mary and her sister, Martha. [2] This was the
same Mary who had anointed the Lord with ointment, and
wiped his feet with her hair, whose brother, Lazarus, was
sick. [3] The sisters therefore sent to Jesus, saying, "Lord, behold, he whom you love is sick." [4] But when Jesus heard it,
he said, "This sickness is not to death, but for the glory of
God, that God's Son may be glorified by it." [5] Now Jesus
loved Martha, and her sister, and Lazarus. [6] When therefore
he heard that he was sick, he stayed two days in the place
where he was…

Jesus said to them plainly then, "Lazarus is dead. [15] I am
glad for your sakes that I was not there, so that you may believe. Nevertheless, let's go to him."

[21] … Martha said to Jesus, "Lord, if you would have been
here, my brother wouldn't have died. [22] Even now I know
that, whatever you ask of God, God will give you." [23] Jesus
said to her, "Your brother will rise again."

[24] Martha said to him, "I know that he will rise again in
the resurrection at the last day."

[25] Jesus said to her, "I am the resurrection and the life. He
who believes in me will still live, even if he dies. [26] Whoever
lives and believes in me will never die. Do you believe this?"

[27] She said to him, "Yes, Lord. I have come to believe
that you are the Christ, God's Son, he who comes into the
world." …

[41] So they took away the stone from the place where the
dead man was lying. Jesus lifted up his eyes, and said, "Father, I thank you that you listen to me. [42] I know that you always listen to me, but because of the multitude that stands
around I said this, that they may believe that you sent me."
[43] When he had said this, he cried with a loud voice, "Lazarus, come out!"

[44] He who was dead came out, bound hand and foot with
wrappings, and his face was wrapped around with a cloth.

Jesus said to them, "Free him, and let him go."

THE LAZARUS PRINCIPLE

"This sickness is not to death, but for the glory of God, that God's Son may be glorified by it." John 11:4

When Jesus was asked to come and help Lazarus, why did he stay away? Why did Jesus let his friend suffer and die? Why did Jesus let Mary and Martha go through the horror of burying their brother? Why does Jesus still allow dreadful things to happen to his friends? Why doesn't he answer all prayers right away and prevent all pain?

I don't know easy answers to such questions, but I do know the one who says, "I am the resurrection and the life." For a friend of Jesus, death is never the end. The end, the final destination, is resurrection. This was true for Lazarus, and it is true for *all* of Jesus' friends.

When we go through terrible times, we might wonder whether Jesus cares and whether he is in charge. But Jesus never stops loving his friends, and he never loses control. The Lord doesn't always keep death away, but when he allows death to come, it is only so that he may conquer death.

A deadly illness can be "for the glory of God, that God's Son may be glorified" (11:4). It can also be "for your sake" (11:14) to increase faith and resurrection joy. Do you prize God's glory in Christ enough to say, "I eagerly expect and hope that … Christ will be exalted in my body, whether by life or by death" (Philippians 1:20)? Count on the Lazarus principle: *For a friend of Jesus, death is never the end.* The Lord of resurrection directs all things for our good and his glory.

PRAYER

Lord of life, conqueror of death, we give all glory to you. Glorify yourself in us, whether by our life or death. Come soon and resurrect all your people. Amen.

John 13:1-17

1 Now before the feast of the Passover, Jesus, knowing that his time had come that he would depart from this world to the Father, having loved his own who were in the world, he loved them to the end. 2 During supper, the devil having already put into the heart of Judas Iscariot, Simon's son, to betray him, 3 Jesus, knowing that the Father had given all things into his hands, and that he came from God, and was going to God, 4 arose from supper, and laid aside his outer garments. He took a towel, and wrapped it around his waist. 5 Then he poured water into the basin, and began to wash the disciples' feet, and to wipe them with the towel that was wrapped around him. 6 Then he came to Simon Peter. He said to him, "Lord, do you wash my feet?"

7 Jesus answered him, "You don't know what I am doing now, but you will understand later."

8 Peter said to him, "You will never wash my feet!"

Jesus answered him, "If I don't wash you, you have no part with me."

9 Simon Peter said to him, "Lord, not my feet only, but also my hands and my head!"

10 Jesus said to him, "Someone who has bathed only needs to have his feet washed, but is completely clean. You are clean, but not all of you." 11 For he knew him who would betray him, therefore he said, "You are not all clean." 12 So when he had washed their feet, put his outer garment back on, and sat down again, he said to them, "Do you know what I have done to you? 13 You call me, 'Teacher' and 'Lord.' You say so correctly, for so I am. 14 If I then, the Lord and the Teacher, have washed your feet, you also ought to wash one another's feet. 15 For I have given you an example, that you also should do as I have done to you. 16 Most certainly I tell you, a servant is not greater than his lord, neither one who is sent greater than he who sent him. 17 If you know these things, blessed are you if you do them."

HUMILITY AND AUTHORITY

"You call me, 'Teacher' and 'Lord.' You say so correctly, for so I am. If I then, the Lord and the Teacher, have washed your feet, you also ought to wash one another's feet." John 13:13-14

In meeting Jesus, you meet a combination of humility and authority you won't meet anywhere else, an astonishing union of tenderness and toughness. One moment, he's cuddling babies; the next he's confronting rulers. One moment, he's lying exhausted and asleep in a boat that's being tossed by a storm; the next, he's giving orders to the storm. One moment, he's weeping at the grave of his dead friend, Lazarus; the next, he's ordering death itself to release his friend. One moment, he's on his knees like a slave, washing his disciples' dirty feet; the next, he says he's their Lord.

Jesus feels the weakness, pain and poverty of humanity, and at the same time he unleashes the power, healing, and abundance of God. He doesn't have even a small hut for a home, yet he strides through God's temple as though he owns the place. He doesn't have a penny to his name, yet he talks like the whole world is his. Could even the least human be humbler and more vulnerable? Could even almighty God be greater and more powerful? What else can we think except that Jesus must be completely human and at the same time fully divine?

The Son of God makes us sons of God and daughters of God. He gives believers authority to reign with him, and he calls us to serve with him. If you have the Spirit of Christ, you become more and more like Jesus in his authority and in his humility. Divine glory shines in humble acts of love.

PRAYER

Lord Jesus, bold as a lion, gentle as a lamb, make us bold with your authority and gentle with your humility. By your Spirit, display your glory in us. Amen.

Part Two

WERE YOU THERE?

If you want to know Jesus, it is not enough to hear him speaking or to watch him working wonders. You must know Jesus in his suffering, death, and resurrection.

The Scriptures and meditations in Part Two look at the suffering Savior through the eyes of those who were there when he died. Many had a part in killing him. In fact, we all did. Jesus died, not just because of someone else's sins, but because of yours and mine. Were you there?

No, it was not the Jews who crucified,
Nor who betrayed You in the judgment place,
Nor who, Lord Jesus, spat into Your face,
Nor who with buffets struck You as You died.

No, it was not the soldiers fisted bold
Who lifted up the hammer and the nail,
Or raised the cursed cross on Calvary's hill,
Or, gambling, tossed the dice to win Your robe.

I am the one, O Lord, who brought You there,
I am the heavy cross You had to bear,
I am the rope that bound You to the tree,
The whip, the nail, the hammer, and the spear,
The blood-stained crown of thorns You had to wear:
It was my sin, alas, it was for me.

(Jacob Revius, trans. Henrietta Ten Harmsel)

Isaiah 53 NIV

1 Who has believed our message and to whom has the arm of
the LORD been revealed? 2 He grew up before him like a
tender shoot, and like a root out of dry ground. He had no
beauty or majesty to attract us to him, nothing in his appearance that we should desire him. 3 He was despised and rejected by men, a man of sorrows, and familiar with suffering.
Like one from whom men hide their faces he was despised,
and we esteemed him not. 4 Surely he took up our infirmities
and carried our sorrows, yet we considered him stricken by
God, smitten by him, and afflicted. 5 But he was pierced for
our transgressions, he was crushed for our iniquities; the
punishment that brought us peace was upon him, and by his
wounds we are healed. 6 We all, like sheep, have gone astray,
each of us has turned to his own way; and the LORD has laid
on him the iniquity of us all. 7 He was oppressed and afflicted, yet he did not open his mouth; he was led like a lamb to
the slaughter, and as a sheep before her shearers is silent, so
he did not open his mouth. 8 By oppression and judgment he
was taken away. And who can speak of his descendants? For
he was cut off from the land of the living; for the transgres-
sion of my people he was stricken. 9 He was assigned a grave
with the wicked, and with the rich in his death, though he
had done no violence, nor was any deceit in his mouth. 10 Yet
it was the LORD's will to crush him and cause him to suffer,
and though the LORD makes his life a guilt offering, he will
see his offspring and prolong his days, and the will of the
LORD will prosper in his hand. 11 After the suffering of his
soul, he will see the light [of life] and be satisfied; by his
knowledge my righteous servant will justify many, and he
will bear their iniquities. 12 Therefore I will give him a portion among the great, and he will divide the spoils with the
strong, because he poured out his life unto death, and was
numbered with the transgressors. For he bore the sin of
many, and made intercession for the transgressors.

ISAIAH

He was despised and rejected by men, a man of sorrows and familiar with suffering. Isaiah 53:3

Isaiah the prophet has seen the Lord, high and lifted up, so dazzling that angels hide their eyes. He's been told of someone who will be God's light in a dark world, who will himself be called "Mighty God." He has seen visions of the Lord's mighty judgments on the nations of the earth. And now, at last, the moment has come. Isaiah's next vision will provide his closest look yet at the person who embodies the mighty and magnificent God.

What? Can this be the one? Is this pathetic figure the person who embodies God? Who can believe this message? Who can see the strong arm of God revealed in this haggard weakling? Even if his face weren't such a mess, it probably wouldn't be much to look at. Even if he didn't have stripes of blood caked on his torso, he wouldn't be much of a physical specimen. Everybody hates him, it seems. He's being tortured, yet he doesn't say a word. They beat him, they pierce his flesh, they kill him, and then they bury him in a sinner's grave. Is this the one who embodies you, Almighty Lord?

Yes. He looks like a reject. From his condition, you'd think God hated him. But he is God's own Son, and he is doing all this for us. We have all sinned, but the Lord has laid our sins on him. He is suffering what we deserve. It is the Lord's will to cause him to suffer and make him a guilt offering. By going through all this, he will justify many. And in the end, he will live again in triumph.

Isaiah's vision is horrifying and thrilling.

PRAYER

Lord, with Isaiah we marvel at your suffering servant. Grant us pardon through his condemnation, healing through his wounds, life through his death, joy through his sorrow. For Jesus' sake, Amen.

Mark 10:32-45

32 They were on the way, going up to Jerusalem; and Jesus was going in front of them, and they were amazed; and those who followed were afraid. He again took the twelve, and began to tell them the things that were going to happen to him. 33 "Behold, we are going up to Jerusalem. The Son of Man will be delivered to the chief priests and the scribes. They will condemn him to death, and will deliver him to the Gentiles. 34 They will mock him, spit on him, scourge him, and kill him. On the third day he will rise again."

35 James and John, the sons of Zebedee, came near to him, saying, "Teacher, we want you to do for us whatever we will ask."

36 He said to them, "What do you want me to do for you?"

37 They said to him, "Grant to us that we may sit, one at your right hand, and one at your left hand, in your glory."

38 But Jesus said to them, "You don't know what you are asking. Are you able to drink the cup that I drink, and to be baptized with the baptism that I am baptized with?"

39 They said to him, "We are able."

Jesus said to them, "You shall indeed drink the cup that I drink, and you shall be baptized with the baptism that I am baptized with; 40 but to sit at my right hand and at my left hand is not mine to give, but for whom it has been prepared."

41 When the ten heard it, they began to be indignant towards James and John.

42 Jesus summoned them, and said to them, "You know that they who are recognized as rulers over the nations lord it over them, and their great ones exercise authority over them. 43 But it shall not be so among you, but whoever wants to become great among you shall be your servant. 44 Whoever of you wants to become first among you, shall be bondservant of all. 45 For the Son of Man also came not to be served, but to serve, and to give his life as a ransom for many."

JAMES

"Teacher," they said, "we want you to do for us whatever we will ask." Mark 10:35

James and his brother John are quite a pair. Born the sons of Zebedee, they are nicknamed "Sons of Thunder" by Jesus (Mark 3:17). The tag fits. When Jesus sets out on his final journey to Jerusalem, he sends messengers ahead to make arrangements. However, at a Samaritan village, their plans hit a snag. The villagers know he's heading for Jerusalem. They hate Jerusalem, and so they tell Jesus and his group to get lost. Well, the Sons of Thunder aren't about to take that lying down. They ask, "Lord, do you want us to call fire down from heaven to destroy them?" But Jesus rebukes them, and they go on to another village (Luke 9:51-56).

As Jesus continues toward Jerusalem, his disciples are astonished, and many tagging along are afraid. He has dangerous and powerful enemies in Jerusalem. Why go there? Jesus then tells the Twelve about his impending death.

When James hears this, it goes in one ear and out the other. He's thinking about power and glory. He wants to be first in line, along with his brother, to share his Lord's destiny. Jesus replies that they will indeed share his destiny—like him, they will serve and suffer. James is perplexed. Why doesn't the Master wipe out his enemies in a blaze of fire? What's so great about being a slave? And what's this about serving and giving his life as a ransom for many?

Eventually, James does get to be first among the Twelve—the first apostle to die for his faith (Acts 12:2).

PRAYER

Lord, you came not to destroy your enemies but to die for them, not to be served but to serve. Free us from our lust for power, and help us serve each other humbly for Jesus' sake. Amen.

John 11:41-53, 12:9-11

41 They took away the stone from the place where the
dead man was lying. Jesus lifted up his eyes, and said, "Father, I thank you that you listen to me. 42 I know that you always listen to me, but because of the multitude that stands
around I said this, that they may believe that you sent me."
43 When he had said this, he cried with a loud voice, "Lazarus, come out!"

44 He who was dead came out, bound hand and foot with
wrappings, and his face was wrapped around with a cloth.

Jesus said to them, "Free him, and let him go."

45 Therefore many of the Jews, who came to Mary and
saw what Jesus did, believed in him. 46 But some of them
went away to the Pharisees, and told them the things which
Jesus had done. 47 The chief priests therefore and the Pharisees gathered a council, and said, "What are we doing? For
this man does many signs. 48 If we leave him alone like this,
everyone will believe in him, and the Romans will come and
take away both our place and our nation."

49 But a certain one of them, Caiaphas, being high priest
that year, said to them, "You know nothing at all, 50 nor do
you consider that it is advantageous for us that one man
should die for the people, and that the whole nation not perish." 51 Now he didn't say this of himself, but being high
priest that year, he prophesied that Jesus would die for the
nation, 52 and not for the nation only, but that he might also
gather together into one the children of God who are scattered abroad. 53 So from that day forward they took counsel
that they might put him to death…

12:9 A large crowd therefore of the Jews learned that he
was there, and they came, not for Jesus' sake only, but that
they might see Lazarus also, whom he had raised from the
dead. 10 But the chief priests conspired to put Lazarus to
death also, 11 because on account of him many of the Jews
went away and believed in Jesus.

CAIAPHAS

"You know nothing at all, nor do you consider that it is better for us that one man should die for the people, and that the whole nation not perish." John 11:49-50

How can the members of the ruling council be so stupid? Can't they see the obvious? Here they are, dithering over what to do about this guy Jesus. Rumors have been flying about his miracles in the backwater areas of Galilee. Now, in the Jerusalem suburb of Bethany, he supposedly raised a dead man named Lazarus to life. All sorts of rabble are tagging along with him. If his following gets too big, the Romans might get nervous. They might send in the legions and destroy Jerusalem, the temple, and the nation.

But why panic? The solution is simple. There won't be a Jesus movement to provoke the Romans if there isn't any Jesus. Nobody follows a dead man. Can't these fools see that? It's a matter of national security. Anybody can see it's better to terminate one individual than to jeopardize the whole country. Just kill Jesus, and everything will be fine.

"You know nothing at all!" Caiaphas snorts. "You do not realize that it is better for you that one man die for the people than that the whole nation perish." One man dies, everybody else lives. Simple logic. The logic of hell.

But the logic of heaven shines through. Caiaphas becomes God's mouthpiece in spite of himself. "He did not say this on his own, but as the high priest that year he prophesied that Jesus would die for the Jewish nation, and not only for that nation but also for the scattered children of God, to bring them together and make them one" (John 11:51-52 NIV).

PRAYER

Father, we marvel that even in wicked scheming, your perfect plan can be fulfilled. Lord Jesus, we praise and thank you for giving yourself as a ransom for many. Amen.

John 12:1-8

[1] Then six days before the Passover, Jesus came to Bethany, where Lazarus was, who had been dead, whom he
raised from the dead. [2] So they made him a supper there.
Martha served, but Lazarus was one of those who sat at the
table with him. [3] Mary, therefore, took a pound of ointment
of pure nard, very precious, and anointed the feet of Jesus,
and wiped his feet with her hair. The house was filled with
the fragrance of the ointment. [4] Then Judas Iscariot, Simon's
son, one of his disciples, who would betray him, said,
[5] "Why wasn't this ointment sold for three hundred denarii,
and given to the poor?" [6] Now he said this, not because he
cared for the poor, but because he was a thief, and having the
money box, used to steal what was put into it. [7] But Jesus
said, "Leave her alone. She has kept this for the day of my
burial. [8] For you always have the poor with you, but you
don't always have me."

MARY OF BETHANY

Mary took a pound of ointment of pure nard, very precious, and anointed the feet of Jesus, and wiped his feet with her hair. The house was filled with the fragrance of the ointment. John 12:3

Mary isn't efficient, and she's not proper. She squanders a bundle of money on a bottle of perfume and pours the whole thing over Jesus' feet. Then she lets her hair down like a woman of the street and uses it to wipe Jesus' feet. The men in the room are upset, especially Judas. How could Mary be so careless with her money? Why waste money on a sweet smell, when it could be used to fund a soup kitchen for the poor? Judas talks like an efficiency expert, and the others agree. Judas makes more sense than Mary.

Only one person approves of Mary's extravagance—Jesus. He likes this wonderful waste. True, the soup kitchen will have to get funding elsewhere for today—but doesn't the room smell wonderful? While everyone else is calculating costs and thinking about proper behavior, Jesus is enjoying the fragrance of Mary's extravagant love. He's thinking that her perfume is preparing him in advance for burial.

A while back, Mary's sister Martha criticized her for sitting and listening to Jesus instead of working like a good hostess. Now Judas is criticizing Mary for her wastefulness. But Jesus sides with Mary. Some things are more important than hard work, careful spending, and good manners. Loving Jesus lavishly is better than all these.

Jesus blesses extravagant Mary. Meanwhile, Mr. Efficiency, the embezzling bookkeeper, begins calculating how much silver Jesus is worth.

PRAYER

Lord, you told us that we can't serve both God and money, that we will hate one and love the other. Free us from the grip of money, and teach us to love you with our whole heart. For Jesus' sake, Amen.

Luke 22:37-54 ESV

37 Jesus said, “I tell you that this Scripture must be fulfilled in me: ‘And he was numbered with the transgressors.’
For what is written about me has its fulfillment.” 38 And they
said, “Look, Lord, here are two swords.” And he said to
them, “It is enough.”

39 And he came out and went, as was his custom, to the
Mount of Olives, and the disciples followed him. 40 And
when he came to the place, he said to them, “Pray that you
may not enter into temptation.” 41 And he withdrew from
them about a stone’s throw, and knelt down and prayed,
42 saying, “Father, if you are willing, remove this cup from
me. Nevertheless, not my will, but yours, be done.” 43 And
there appeared to him an angel from heaven, strengthening
him. 44 And being in an agony he prayed more earnestly; and
his sweat became like great drops of blood falling down to
the ground. 45 And when he rose from prayer, he came to the
disciples and found them sleeping for sorrow, 46 and he said
to them, “Why are you sleeping? Rise and pray that you may
not enter into temptation.”

47 While he was still speaking, there came a crowd, and
the man called Judas, one of the twelve, was leading them.
He drew near to Jesus to kiss him, 48 but Jesus said to him,
“Judas, would you betray the Son of Man with a kiss?”
49 And when those who were around him saw what would
follow, they said, “Lord, shall we strike with the sword?”
50 And one of them struck the servant of the high priest and
cut off his right ear. 51 But Jesus said, “No more of this!”
And he touched his ear and healed him. 52 Then Jesus said to
the chief priests and officers of the temple and elders, who
had come out against him, “Have you come out as against a
robber, with swords and clubs? 53 When I was with you day
after day in the temple, you did not lay hands on me. But this
is your hour, and the power of darkness.” 54 Then they seized
him and led him away.

ANGELS

And there appeared to him an angel from heaven, strengthening him. And being in an agony he prayed more earnestly; and his sweat became like great drops of blood falling down to the ground. Luke 22:43-44

The angels can only watch and wonder. When their divine King became human, they heralded the news. After he was tempted by Satan, they came and strengthened him. During his anguished prayers in Gethsemane, an angel came and ministered to him. But now they can only watch. Jesus must face the worst alone, without them.

As armed thugs grab the King, the angels reach for their weapons. It would be so easy to destroy the puny humans. But the heavenly hosts hold their place, as Jesus says, "Do you think I cannot call on my Father, and he will at once put at my disposal twelve legions of angels? But how then would the Scriptures be fulfilled that say it must happen this way" (Matthew 26:53-54). The King has a plan, and he always fulfills his plans.

When the Lord of the universe, whose splendor dazzled even the noblest of angels, became a helpless baby in a feed box, the angels were astonished. But this! Allowing a filthy gang of human roughnecks to seize him, spit on him, taunt him, punch him, flog him, and then crucify him—that staggers even the angelic imagination. How their King must love the human creatures!

What must it be like, the angels wonder, to be so favored by the Holy One that he becomes one of you—and even dies for you? He never did that for angels. Angels can't figure out what it's like. You have to be human to know.

Even angels long to look into these things (1 Peter 1:12).

PRAYER

Lord Jesus, you have favored us even above the angels. We can only marvel that you became one of us, suffered for us, and are not ashamed to be our brother. Amen.

John 18:1-11

1 When Jesus had spoken these words, he went out with
his disciples over the brook Kidron, where there was a garden, into which he and his disciples entered. 2 Now Judas,
who betrayed him, also knew the place, for Jesus often met
there with his disciples. 3 Judas then, having taken a detachment of soldiers and officers from the chief priests and the
Pharisees, came there with lanterns, torches, and weapons.
4 Jesus therefore, knowing all the things that were happening
to him, went out, and said to them, "Who are you looking
for?"

5 They answered him, "Jesus of Nazareth."

Jesus said to them, "I am he."

Judas also, who betrayed him, was standing with them.
6 When therefore he said to them, "I am he," they went
backward, and fell to the ground.

7 Again he asked them, "Who are you looking for?"

They said, "Jesus of Nazareth."

8 Jesus answered, "I told you that I am he. If therefore
you seek me, let these go their way," 9 that the word might be
fulfilled which he spoke, "Of those whom you have given
me, I have lost none."

10 Simon Peter therefore, having a sword, drew it, and
struck the high priest's servant, and cut off his right ear. The
servant's name was Malchus. 11 Jesus therefore said to Peter,
"Put the sword into its sheath. The cup which the Father has
given me, shall I not surely drink it?"

Luke 22:51-53 NIV

And he touched the man's ear and healed him. 52 Then
Jesus said to the chief priests, the officers of the temple
guard, and the elders, who had come for him, "Am I leading
a rebellion, that you have come with swords and clubs?
53 Every day I was with you in the temple courts, and you did
not lay a hand on me. But this is your hour—when darkness
reigns."

MALCHUS

But Jesus answered, "No more of this!" And he touched the man's ear and healed him. Luke 22:51 NIV

Malchus wakes up with a start. He raises his right hand to his head. Sure enough, the ear is still there. Was everything last night just a dream? Malchus yawns and rubs his eyes. Then he looks down at the tunic lying on the floor. He blinks and looks again. Unbelievable! The tunic is spattered with red, like a butcher's apron. Again he gingerly fingers his ear. His eyes dart again to the bloodstained tunic.

So it really happened, after all. Malchus remembers seeing a flash in the corner of his eye and ducking instinctively. Too late. His ear was hanging by a shred of skin, and his tunic was sprayed with blood. The burly fellow with the sword was about to finish him off when Jesus stepped in.

Malchus remembers doubling over in pain. Then he felt someone touch his ear. He lifted his head and found himself looking into the Nazarene's face. Suddenly the throbbing ceased. The bleeding stopped. At that moment, the squad arrested Jesus, and all his followers fled into the night.

Now here Malchus is, back in his room, with one bloody tunic, two healthy ears, and a lot of questions. What was it about the man from Nazareth that had made the whole squad back off and fall to the ground? How did he restore a severed ear? And why would he want to, when Malchus was there to harm him? If he had the power to do such things, why would he let himself be arrested?

By his wounds we are healed (Isaiah 53:5).

PRAYER

Lord Jesus, thank you for loving us while we were still your enemies, and for enduring such terrible agony to bring us healing. Now help us to love our enemies. Amen.

John 18:12-14, 19-24

12 So the detachment, the commanding officer, and the
officers of the Jews, seized Jesus and bound him, 13 and led
him to Annas first, for he was father-in-law to Caiaphas, who
was high priest that year. 14 Now it was Caiaphas who ad-
vised the Jews that it was expedient that one man should perish for the people…

19 The high priest therefore asked Jesus about his disciples, and about his teaching. 20 Jesus answered him, "I spoke
openly to the world. I always taught in synagogues, and in
the temple, where the Jews always meet. I said nothing in
secret. 21 Why do you ask me? Ask those who have heard me
what I said to them. Behold, these know the things which I
said."

22 When he had said this, one of the officers standing by
slapped Jesus with his hand, saying, "Do you answer the
high priest like that?"

23 Jesus answered him, "If I have spoken evil, testify of
the evil; but if well, why do you beat me?"

24 Annas sent him bound to Caiaphas, the high priest.

ANNAS

They bound him and brought him first to Annas, who was the father-in-law of Caiaphas. John 18:12-13

Don't do anything without first seeing Annas. He's the power broker, the one who calls the shots. It's been nearly twenty years since the old man was officially high priest, but most people still refer to him as the high priest anyway. He might as well be. You can bet that whoever is high priest is really a front man for Annas. Five sons, one grandson, and currently, his son-in-law Caiaphas, have held the office.

As a card-carrying Sadducee, Annas turns up his nose at silly superstitions like resurrection. He believes in getting his fair share in *this* life. And religion is a lucrative business. Annas has transformed God's temple into a mall, with shops selling various animals for sacrifices. He also runs a currency exchange in the temple that makes a handsome profit from pilgrims wanting to turn foreign money into shekels. Annas is not going to sit idly by after some peasant from Nazareth assaults the merchants, drives them out of the temple, and disrupts Annas's cash flow.

So after the old godfather's goons arrest Jesus, the first order of business is a visit to Annas. When they get there, the prisoner pipes up and asks why a secret interrogation is necessary, when his ministry has been open and public.

Just who does this pauper think he's talking to? Is he implying that Annas—make that "Mister Annas, Sir"—is sneaky and underhanded? Nobody talks to Annas that way! One of his lieutenants hammers the prisoner in the face.

Old Annas has seen enough. He sends Jesus, still bound, off to Caiaphas. His son-in-law will know what to do.

PRAYER

Lord, when manipulators like Annas exploit your people, turn us again to the perfect high priest. Thank you, Jesus, for seeking our good rather than your own. Amen.

Mark 14:53-65

53 They led Jesus away to the high priest. All the chief
priests, the elders, and the scribes came together with him.
54 Peter had followed him from a distance, until he came
into the court of the high priest. He was sitting with the officers, and warming himself in the light of the fire. 55 Now
the chief priests and the whole council sought witnesses
against Jesus to put him to death, and found none. 56 For
many gave false testimony against him, and their testimony
didn't agree with each other. 57 Some stood up, and gave
false testimony against him, saying, 58 "We heard him say, 'I
will destroy this temple that is made with hands, and in three
days I will build another made without hands.'" 59 Even so,
their testimony did not agree.

60 The high priest stood up in the middle, and asked Jesus, "Have you no answer? What is it which these testify
against you?" 61 But he stayed quiet, and answered nothing.
Again the high priest asked him, "Are you the Christ, the
Son of the Blessed?"

62 Jesus said, "I am. You will see the Son of Man sitting
at the right hand of Power, and coming with the clouds of the
sky."

63 The high priest tore his clothes, and said, "What further
need have we of witnesses? 64 You have heard the blasphemy! What do you think?" They all condemned him to be
worthy of death. 65 Some began to spit on him, and to cover
his face, and to beat him with fists, and to tell him, "Prophesy!" The officers struck him with the palms of their hands.

CROOKED COURT

Now the chief priests and the whole council sought witnesses against Jesus to put him to death, and found none. Mark 14:55

Already before the trial, the sentence is determined: death. Therefore, the verdict is also determined: guilty as charged. Now, all that's needed is an offense to charge him with, and some evidence to back it up. Should be easy enough. The prosecution has been keeping paid witnesses on standby, so that if the paid traitor would come through in leading the midnight arrest, everything would be ready for a quick, pre-dawn trial. (Never mind that night trials and instant verdicts are illegal—that's just a technicality.)

Here goes. Oh, for crying out loud! Can't these witnesses even keep their stories straight? It certainly is hard to buy good witnesses these days. Well, if the prosecution can't do its job, at least the judge knows what to do. Time to stop presiding and start prosecuting. Caiaphas badgers the prisoner: "What about all these charges?" Silence. Then Caiaphas gets an idea: "Are you the Christ, the Son of the Blessed One?"

Finally, the prisoner speaks: "I am. And you will see the Son of Man sitting at the right hand of the Mighty One and coming on the clouds of heaven." That's it. Caiaphas shrieks and tears his clothes for dramatic effect. Surely this is blasphemy. Almost everybody agrees.

Is Joseph of Arimathea challenging the Council's consensus (Luke 23:51)? Sit down and shut up, Joseph. No punishment is too cruel for this guy Jesus. How about a spitting contest? Or how about blind man's buff, with the blindfolded one guessing who hit him? Sounds fun. Then off to Pilate.

PRAYER

We're amazed, dear Jesus, when we think of the injustice and mockery you endured. You not only told us to turn the other cheek, but you showed us how. Thank you. Amen.

Luke 22:54-62

54 They seized him, and led him away, and brought him
into the high priest's house. But Peter followed from a distance. 55 When they had kindled a fire in the middle of the
courtyard, and had sat down together, Peter sat among them.
56 A certain servant girl saw him as he sat in the light, and
looking intently at him, said, "This man also was with him."

57 He denied Jesus, saying, "Woman, I don't know him."

58 After a little while someone else saw him, and said,
"You also are one of them!"

But Peter answered, "Man, I am not!"

59 After about one hour passed, another confidently af-
firmed, saying, "Truly this man also was with him, for he is a
Galilean!"

60 But Peter said, "Man, I don't know what you are talking about!" Immediately, while he was still speaking, a
rooster crowed. 61 The Lord turned, and looked at Peter.
Then Peter remembered the Lord's word, how he said to
him, "Before the rooster crows you will deny me three
times." 62 He went out, and wept bitterly.

PETER

The Lord turned, and looked at Peter. Then Peter remembered the Lord's word, how he said to him, "Before the rooster crows you will deny me three times." He went out, and wept bitterly. Luke 22:61-62

When Jesus tells Peter what will happen, Peter doesn't believe it. Deny Jesus? Never! Peter thinks he knows himself better than Jesus knows him. He's Peter the Rock, the spokesman, the boldest of the disciples. Can't Jesus see that?

Later that evening, however, when Jesus is agonizing and praying in an olive grove, Peter can't even stay awake. He sleeps when he's supposed to be praying. When the mob comes to arrest Jesus, Peter finally awakens. He slashes at one of them with his sword. But when Jesus stops him, Peter turns tail and runs. He'd rather kill for Jesus than die for him.

All brave and blustery in a room full of Jesus' friends, Peter the Rock turns to jelly in a courtyard full of potential enemies. Even a servant girl scares him to death. Before long, Peter is swearing up and down for the third time that he's got nothing to do with Jesus. Cockadoodledoo! At the sound of the rooster, Peter suddenly finds his Lord looking directly into his eyes. Peter remembers. And the tears begin.

Jesus knows. He's always known. What was it he said? "Simon, Simon, Satan has asked to sift you as wheat. But I have prayed for you, Simon, that your faith may not fail. And when you have turned back, strengthen your brothers" (Luke 22:31-32). Simon Peter overestimated himself and he underestimated Satan; but Jesus has always known both Peter and the enemy. Peter failed to pray; but Jesus has prayed for him. On his own, Peter is finished; but Jesus won't leave Peter on his own.

PRAYER

Lord Jesus, you know us better than we know ourselves. You know how we sleep instead of praying. You know our sin and cowardice. Forgive us; pray for us; transform us. Amen.

Matthew 27:1-10

1 Now when morning had come, all the chief priests and
the elders of the people took counsel against Jesus to put him
to death: 2 and they bound him, and led him away, and delivered him up to Pontius Pilate, the governor. 3 Then Judas,
who betrayed him, when he saw that Jesus was condemned,
felt remorse, and brought back the thirty pieces of silver to
the chief priests and elders, 4 saying, "I have sinned in that I
betrayed innocent blood."

But they said, "What is that to us? You see to it."

5 He threw down the pieces of silver in the sanctuary, and
departed. He went away and hanged himself. 6 The chief
priests took the pieces of silver, and said, "It's not lawful to
put them into the treasury, since it is the price of blood."
7 They took counsel, and bought the potter's field with them,
to bury strangers in. 8 Therefore that field was called "The
Field of Blood" to this day. 9 Then that which was spoken
through Jeremiah the prophet was fulfilled, saying,

"They took the thirty pieces of silver,
the price of him upon whom a price had been set,
whom some of the children of Israel priced,
10 and they gave them for the potter's field,
as the Lord commanded me."

JUDAS

"I have sinned in that I betrayed innocent blood." Matthew 27:3-4

It starts with "borrowing" a few coins now and then from the group's money bag. Nothing big—and Judas figures he deserves a little something for his work as treasurer. Before long, he's helping himself to a bigger share. He needs the money, and nobody seems to miss it. Eventually, he gets so used to it that it upsets him when a friend of Jesus spends money without first running it past Judas. He doesn't want to miss any chance to skim his percentage. And then, his big opportunity—a one-time payoff to assist in a secret arrest. They'll eventually get Jesus anyway, with or without his help, so Judas might as well get something out of it.

Now it finally hits him. What started with just pinching a few coins has now made him a traitor and an accessory to murder. The victim is a man who treated him with nothing but perfect kindness and friendship for three years, who called him "friend" even when Judas kissed him off. The money Judas once loved suddenly disgusts him. He cries, "I have sinned, for I have betrayed innocent blood." But the men who paid him couldn't care less.

Judas wants to undo the results of his sin, but it's too late. The damage is done. Judas doesn't think of repenting and pleading for God's mercy. Regret and remorse, yes, but not repentance. If the friend he betrayed is going to hang on a tree, Judas will hang himself on a tree.

Godly sorrow brings repentance that leads to salvation and leaves no regret, but worldly sorrow brings death (2 Corinthians 7:10).

PRAYER

Father, we start with small sins and end up committing horrors. Through Jesus, transform our self-destructive remorse to God-centered repentance. We pray in his name, Amen.

Luke 23:1-12

1 The whole company of them rose up and brought him
before Pilate. 2 They began to accuse him, saying, “We found
this man perverting the nation, forbidding paying taxes to
Caesar, and saying that he himself is Christ, a king.”

3 Pilate asked him, “Are you the King of the Jews?”

He answered him, “So you say.”

4 Pilate said to the chief priests and the multitudes, “I find
no basis for a charge against this man.”

5 But they insisted, saying, “He stirs up the people, teaching throughout all Judea, beginning from Galilee even to this
place.” 6 But when Pilate heard Galilee mentioned, he asked
if the man was a Galilean. 7 When he found out that he was
in Herod’s jurisdiction, he sent him to Herod, who was also
in Jerusalem during those days.

8 Now when Herod saw Jesus, he was exceedingly glad,
for he had wanted to see him for a long time, because he had
heard many things about him. He hoped to see some miracle
done by him. 9 He questioned him with many words, but he
gave no answers. 10 The chief priests and the scribes stood,
vehemently accusing him. 11 Herod with his soldiers humili-
ated him and mocked him. Dressing him in luxurious clothing, they sent him back to Pilate. 12 Herod and Pilate became
friends with each other that very day, for before that they
were enemies with each other.

HERODANTIPAS

Now when Herod saw Jesus, he was exceedingly glad, for he had wanted to see him for a long time, because he had heard many things about him. He hoped to see some miracle done by him. Luke 23:8

At last! Herod finally gets to see this Jesus face to face. Herod has a love/hate relationship with preachers. A few years earlier, that strange hermit John the Baptizer publicly embarrassed Herod by scolding him for stealing his brother's wife. Herod had John arrested, of course, but, in spite of himself, he found the man fascinating and often talked with him. At least until the drunken night his shapely stepdaughter bewitched him with that dance of hers and then asked for John's head on a platter.

For a while now, Herod's been wondering if the Nazarene has any connection to John (Luke 9:7-9). At the same time, his instincts have been telling him he'd be wisest to eliminate anybody causing such a stir (Luke 13:31). Smart politics, that's all. Herod remembers how his father once slaughtered all the baby boys in Bethlehem just to squelch a rumor that one of those babies was born to be king.

But this is perfect. Pilate has sent Jesus to him. Herod can satisfy his curiosity, and still let Pilate worry about solving the problem. What if the man really can do miracles and magic tricks like the rumors say? That would be fun to watch. No miracles? Well, he's supposed to be an even more dynamic speaker than John. How about answering some questions? Don't want to say anything? Hah! What a joke this Jesus is! Get him out of here. Send him back to Pilate.

You know, Pilate seemed like a jerk at first, but once you get to know him, he's not so bad after all.

PRAYER

Lord, curiosity isn't enough. Sometimes we demand miracles or seek answers to all our questions, when we really need simple faith in you, dear Jesus. Help us believe. Amen.

John 18:33-40

33 Pilate therefore entered again into the Praetorium,
called Jesus, and said to him, "Are you the King of the
Jews?"
34 Jesus answered him, "Do you say this by yourself, or
did others tell you about me?"
35 Pilate answered, "I'm not a Jew, am I? Your own nation and the chief priests delivered you to me. What have
you done?"
36 Jesus answered, "My Kingdom is not of this world. If
my Kingdom were of this world, then my servants would
fight, that I wouldn't be delivered to the Jews. But now my
Kingdom is not from here."
37 Pilate therefore said to him, "Are you a king then?"

Jesus answered, "You say that I am a king. For this reason I have been born, and for this reason I have come into the world, that I should testify to the truth. Everyone who is of the truth listens to my voice."

38 Pilate said to him, "What is truth?"

When he had said this, he went out again to the Jews, and
said to them, "I find no basis for a charge against him. 39 But
you have a custom, that I should release someone to you at
the Passover. Therefore do you want me to release to you the
King of the Jews?"
40 Then they all shouted again, saying, "Not this man, but
Barabbas!" Now Barabbas was a robber.

Matthew 27:19

19 While Pilate was sitting on the judgment seat, his wife sent to him, saying, "Have nothing to do with that righteous man, for I have suffered many things today in a dream because of him."

MRS. PILATE

"Have nothing to do with that righteous man, for I have suffered many things today in a dream because of him." Matthew 27:19

There it is again—that face. She's been running from something terrifying, but no matter what direction she flees, that face looms up in front of her. She stops running and shrinks back from the face. The world seems to be collapsing in on her. A single word booms and then echoes: "Innocent, innocent, innocent, innocent..."

She screams, then finds herself lying in bed. What a relief! Just a nightmare. She rolls over and reaches across the bed toward her husband. Where is he? Oh, that's right. She vaguely recalls whispers in the dark: her husband's assistant calling Pontius out of bed. An emergency session with those bothersome priests. Something about a dangerous prisoner. That's when she drifted off again and the nightmare began.

The prisoner! That's it! The face in the dream belongs to the prisoner. The nightmare echoes again in her mind, "Innocent, innocent..." The nightmare is over, yet it's not over. Mrs. Pilate throws on a robe and hastily scribbles a message.

Pontius Pilate looks up in irritation. Can't the servant see he's busy? Oh, a message from his wife—something urgent. Pilate scans the note: "Have nothing to do with that righteous man, for I have suffered many things today in a dream because of him." He glances over at the prisoner and scowls. Then he crumples the note. A superstitious wife and a prisoner who talks in riddles. What is truth, anyway?

The crowd is getting louder.

PRAYER

Father, you reveal truth and warn us in many ways, yet we, like Pilate, often refuse to listen. Move us to trust your sinless Son as the Way, the Truth, and the Life. Amen.

Matthew 27:22-26

22 Pilate said to them, "What then shall I do with Jesus,
who is called Christ?"
They all said to him, "Let him be crucified!"
23 But the governor said, "Why? What evil has he done?"
But they cried out exceedingly, saying, "Let him be crucified!"
24 So when Pilate saw that nothing was being gained, but
rather that a disturbance was starting, he took water, and
washed his hands before the multitude, saying, "I am innocent of the blood of this righteous person. You see to it."
25 All the people answered, "May his blood be on us, and
on our children!"
26 Then he released to them Barabbas, but Jesus he
flogged and delivered to be crucified.

PONTIUS PILATE

Pilate took water, and washed his hands before the multitude, saying, "I am innocent of the blood of this righteous person. You see to it." Matthew 27:24

Pilate weighs the various factors. He knows the religious leaders have handed Jesus over because of their envy. He knows Jesus hasn't committed any crime under Roman law. And he knows there's more to Jesus than meets the eye, though he can't figure out what it is. On the other hand, Pilate can't simply buck the wishes of his constituents. He's got to consider his popularity ratings, or he might be removed from office.

At last, Pilate figures it out. He'll let the people kill Jesus, if that's what they want, but he washes his hands of the whole mess. Pilate blazes a trail followed by many a politician since: "I'm personally opposed to the destruction of this innocent life, but I'm not going to force my convictions on you. It's your choice." Pilate isn't pro-crucifixion—not at all! He's simply pro-choice.

At first, Pilate asks, "What shall *I* do with Jesus?" (Matthew 27:22) "I" —not somebody else. Only Pilate can make Jesus' crucifixion legal. And yet, a moment later, he tries to pretend it's not his responsibility at all. But even as he scrubs his hands, he gives the execution order. Legalized murder is still murder, and Pilate the politician is responsible.

One day, all of us will join Pilate before the judgment seat of Christ. At that point, we won't be asking "What shall I do with Jesus?" but "What will Jesus do with me?" And the King will say, "Whatever you did not do for one of the least of these, you did not do for me" (Matthew 25:45).

PRAYER

Lord, in your presence all our excuses ring hollow. Forgive us, and grant us and our leaders the courage to stand up for Christ and defend the helpless. In Jesus' name, Amen.

Mark 15:6-15

6 Now at the feast he used to release to them one prisoner, whom they asked of him. 7 There was one called Barabbas, bound with his fellow insurgents, men who in the insurrection had committed murder. 8 The multitude, crying aloud,
began to ask him to do as he always did for them. 9 Pilate
answered them, saying, “Do you want me to release to you
the King of the Jews?” 10 For he perceived that for envy the
chief priests had delivered him up. 11 But the chief priests
stirred up the multitude, that he should release Barabbas to
them instead. 12 Pilate again asked them, “What then should I
do to him whom you call the King of the Jews?”

13 They cried out again, “Crucify him!”

14 Pilate said to them, “Why, what evil has he done?”

But they cried out exceedingly, “Crucify him!”

15 Pilate, wishing to please the multitude, released Barabbas to them, and handed over Jesus, when he had flogged
him, to be crucified.

BARABBAS

There was one called Barabbas, bound with his fellow insurgents, men who in the insurrection had committed murder. Mark 15:7

Barabbas is bracing himself. He knows the penalty under Roman law for revolution and murder. He's watched more than one crucifixion. It's gruesome, and Barabbas always knew his day might come. That's the chance you take when you're a terrorist. But it's one thing to consider the distant thought of being crucified someday. It's another to be staring it in the face, locked in prison with no way out, just waiting for the executioners to come.

Barabbas hears footsteps clicking on stone and someone fumbling at the door of his cell. The door groans open, and two soldiers pull him to his feet. Barabbas finds himself hoping that he can stifle his screams when they drive in the nails. He wants to give the hated Romans as little satisfaction as possible.

As they lead him out of the building, Barabbas blinks in the bright sunlight. And then the impossible happens. Someone is fumbling at his wrists and ankles. The chains come off. A gruff voice tells him he's free to go. He's been granted release and unconditional pardon.

The strangest thing has happened. Some harmless rabbi is about to be crucified on the garbage heap outside the city, even though no charge against him would stick. And Barabbas, a murderer, finds himself alive and absolutely free.

God made him who had no sin to be sin for us, so that in him we might become the righteousness of God (2 Corinthians 5:21 NIV).

PRAYER

Lord, when we were condemned and helpless, you suffered the fate we deserved. "Amazing love! How can it be that you my Lord would die for me?" Thank you, Lord Jesus. Amen.

John 19:5-16

5 ...Pilate said to them, “Behold, the man!”
6 When therefore the chief priests and the officers saw
him, they shouted, saying, “Crucify! Crucify!”
Pilate said to them, “Take him yourselves, and crucify
him, for I find no basis for a charge against him.”
7 The Jews answered him, “We have a law, and by our
law he ought to die, because he made himself the Son of
God.”
8 When therefore Pilate heard this saying, he was more
afraid. 9 He entered into the Praetorium again, and said to
Jesus, “Where are you from?” But Jesus gave him no answer. 10 Pilate therefore said to him, “Aren’t you speaking to
me? Don’t you know that I have power to release you, and
have power to crucify you?”
11 Jesus answered, “You would have no power at all
against me, unless it were given to you from above. Therefore he who delivered me to you has greater sin.”
12 At this, Pilate was seeking to release him, but the Jews
cried out, saying, “If you release this man, you aren’t Caesar’s friend! Everyone who makes himself a king speaks
against Caesar!”
13 When Pilate therefore heard these words, he brought
Jesus out, and sat down on the judgment seat at a place
called “The Pavement”, but in Hebrew, “Gabbatha.” 14 Now
it was the Preparation Day of the Passover, at about the sixth
hour. He said to the Jews, “Behold, your King!”
15 They cried out, “Away with him! Away with him!
Crucify him!”
Pilate said to them, “Shall I crucify your King?”
The chief priests answered, “We have no king but Caesar!”
16 So then he delivered him to them to be crucified. So
they took Jesus and led him away.

CAESAR

"If you release this man, you aren't Caesar's friend! Everyone who makes himself a king speaks against Caesar!" John 19:12

Rome is always in the headlines. Every day Tiberius Caesar is page 1 news. As for Judea, who cares what's happening in one of Rome's more backward and bothersome colonies? It's more important to know Caesar's latest edict, or even what he's been doing for fun at his sunny retreat on the island of Capri. When Caesar sneezes, the world catches a cold.

What will Caesar think? That's the ultimate question. Off in Jerusalem, Pilate knows all too well that he would have no power if it were not given to him from above. Of course his power comes from higher up—from Caesar! Caesar rules the world. He's the ultimate power. If Caesar hears even a rumor that Pilate is disloyal, Pilate will be finished.

If one Nazarene peasant dies, within a few days nobody but his closest friends will remember him. True, the peasant seems like an unusual man; he's got a mysterious way of talking, and it's a little spooky to hear that he claims to be the Son of God. But good sense prevails. Everybody knows that Caesar is lord. Everybody knows Caesar controls the destiny of people and nations. History will remember the emperor Tiberius, not the peasant Jesus.

God chose the weak things of the world to shame the strong. He chose the lowly things of this world and the despised things... None of the rulers of this age understood it, for if they had, they would not have crucified the Lord of glory (1 Corinthians 1:27-28, 2:8).

PRAYER

Father, when we're intimidated by famous people and power politics, remind us that "the weakness of God is stronger than men's strength" and that Jesus reigns supreme. Amen.

Mark 15:21-24

[21] They compelled one passing by, coming from the
country, Simon of Cyrene, the father of Alexander and
Rufus, to go with them, that he might bear his cross. [22] They
brought him to the place called Golgotha, which is, being
interpreted, "The place of a skull." [23] They offered Jesus
wine mixed with myrrh to drink, but he didn't take it.
[24] Crucifying him, they parted his garments among them,
casting lots on them, what each should take.

SIMON OF CYRENE

They compelled one passing by, coming from the country, Simon of Cyrene, the father of Alexander and Rufus, to go with them, that he might bear his cross. Mark 15:21

Simon's pilgrimage is almost over. He's travelled all the way from Cyrene in North Africa for the Passover celebration in Jerusalem. Coming up the road from the countryside on his way into the city, he runs into a gaper's delay. The road is jammed with people staring. Three men carrying stout wooden beams are being nudged along at sword-point. Headed for crucifixion, apparently. One looks like he should be dead already. His back is bloody, his face beaten to a pulp, his eyes swollen nearly shut. Some sadist has even jammed a wreath of thorns into his scalp. Too bad, but not much Simon can do about it. He starts to move on.

A rough hand grabs his shoulder. A gruff voice barks an order. Simon turns to see the prisoner lying prone beneath the heavy beam. He can't carry it another step. The soldiers want Simon to carry it. Of all the people there, why him? He's made the long journey from Cyrene to be at the temple for a sacred feast, and he ends up lugging a cross away from the city, with an exhausted prisoner staggering along in front of him. Not what Simon had planned.

And Simon's life is never the same again. The troublesome task forced upon him turns out to be the greatest privilege any man ever had. The bloody stranger whose cross he carried turns out to be the Son of God, the risen and living Lord. Simon's sons Alexander and Rufus become well known Christians. They know better than most that "anyone who does not carry his cross and follow me cannot be my disciple" (Luke 14:27).

PRAYER

Lord, we have our own plans and preferences. When you interrupt us with challenges and hardships, help us to take up our cross and follow Jesus wherever he leads. Amen.

Luke 23:27-31

27 A great multitude of the people followed him, including women who also mourned and lamented him. 28 But Jesus, turning to them, said, “Daughters of Jerusalem, don’t weep for me, but weep for yourselves and for your children. 29 For behold, the days are coming in which they will say, ‘Blessed are the barren, the wombs that never bore, and the breasts that never nursed.’ 30 Then they will begin to tell the mountains, ‘Fall on us!’ and tell the hills, ‘Cover us.’ 31 For if they do these things in the green tree, what will be done in the dry?”

DAUGHTERS OF JERUSALEM

"Daughters of Jerusalem, don't weep for me, but weep for yourselves and for your children." Luke 23:28

Not everyone in Jerusalem is gloating. Many are crying. True, Jesus' enemies managed to gather enough anti-Jesus demonstrators and stage a rally loud enough to sway Pilate. But these noisy activists don't represent everyone. There are a great many of Jesus' fellow Jews, especially women, who love Jesus. Their tears are many; their wailing is loud.

And Jesus' love for them is so great, his identification with them so complete, that he is concerned more about them than himself. If this is how the Romans treat an innocent man like him, what will happen when someone really does lead a rebellion against Caesar? Jesus sees forty years into the future: Roman legions rampaging, houses in flames, temple reduced to rubble, men slaughtered, women raped, children carried off into slavery.

So don't waste too much pity on Jesus. Weep for yourself. In rejecting your Messiah, Jerusalem, you are bringing terror and judgment upon yourself and all your inhabitants. Tender and terrifying words from the heart of someone who cares, "not wanting anyone to perish, but everyone to come to repentance" (2 Peter 3:9). Even on his way to the cross, Jesus wants not pity but repentance.

"O Jerusalem, Jerusalem, you who kill the prophets and stone those sent to you, how often I have longed to gather your children together, as a hen gathers her chicks under her wings, but you were not willing! Look, your house is left to you desolate" (Luke 13:34-35).

PRAYER

As we think of your suffering, dear Jesus, move us beyond pity and sentiment to real repentance. Give us faith in you and save us from the wrath to come. Amen.

John 19:2, 16-24

2 The soldiers twisted thorns into a crown, and put it on his head, and dressed him in a purple garment. 3 They kept saying, “Hail, King of the Jews!” and they kept slapping him…

16 So then Pilate delivered him to them to be crucified. So they took Jesus and led him away. 17 He went out, bearing his cross, to the place called “The Place of a Skull”, which is called in Hebrew, “Golgotha”, 18 where they crucified him, and with him two others, on either side one, and Jesus in the middle. 19 Pilate wrote a title also, and put it on the cross. There was written, “JESUS OF NAZARETH, THE KING OF THE JEWS.” 20 Therefore many of the Jews read this title, for the place where Jesus was crucified was near the city; and it was written in Hebrew, in Latin, and in Greek. 21 The chief priests of the Jews therefore said to Pilate, “Don’t write, ‘The King of the Jews,’ but, ‘he said, I am King of the Jews.’”

22 Pilate answered, “What I have written, I have written.”

23 Then the soldiers, when they had crucified Jesus, took his garments and made four parts, to every soldier a part; and also the coat. Now the coat was without seam, woven from the top throughout. 24 Then they said to one another, “Let’s not tear it, but cast lots for it to decide whose it will be,” that the Scripture might be fulfilled, which says, “For my cloak they cast lots.” Therefore the soldiers did these things.

SOLDIERS

Then the soldiers, when they had crucified Jesus, took his garments and made four parts, to every soldier a part. John 19:23

You get used to it after a while. The first crucifixion is always the hardest. The naked flesh, the oozing blood, the buzzing flies, those first shrieks of pain followed by gasping hours of slow suffocation—the first time, it turns your stomach. But after doing a few, you can handle it. Sometimes, in fact, you can have a little fun at it, and if you're lucky, you might even get a little something extra for yourself.

Most of the time, you don't really know the people you crucify. You're a soldier, you've got your orders, and you do what you're told. But this one is different. When you get a fellow labeled "The King of the Jews," it's too good to resist. You might as well have a little fun before you nail him up. Give him a stick for a scepter, a crown made of thorns, rough him up a bit, then bow down to "the king." More entertaining than your average execution.

And in this case, there's something for everybody. All four get a piece of his clothing. Ought to be worth at least a little something in the pawnshop. But what about that seamless tunic? Looks expensive—a shame to cut it up and ruin it. Good idea! A game! It will help pass the time while he's hanging there. Winner gets the tunic. Calvary Casino.

See? It's not so hard. Doing crucifixions is tough at first. But if you're a soldier long enough, nothing shocks you. If you can get used to letting people starve or seeing babies dismembered, you can probably handle crucifixions too. You get used to it after a while.

PRAYER

Lord, we shudder at the soldiers' casual brutality, yet we've become hard to the plight of the oppressed, the hungry, and the aborted. Forgive us and change us. Amen.

Luke 2:16-35

16 The shepherds came with haste, and found both Mary
and Joseph, and the baby, who was lying in the manger.
17 When they saw it, they spread the word which was spoken
to them about this child. 18 All who heard it marveled at the
things which were spoken to them by the shepherds. 19 But
Mary kept all these sayings, pondering them in her heart…
25 Behold, there was a man in Jerusalem whose name was
Simeon… 26 It had been revealed to him by the Holy Spirit
that he should not see death before he had seen the Lord's
Christ. 27 He came in the Spirit into the temple. When the
parents brought in the child, Jesus… 28 Simeon received him
into his arms, and blessed God, and said,

29 "Now you are releasing your servant, Master,
according to your word, in peace;
30 for my eyes have seen your salvation,
31 which you have prepared before the face of all peoples;
32 a light for revelation to the nations,
and the glory of your people Israel."

33 Joseph and Jesus' mother were marveling at the things
which were spoken concerning him, 34 and Simeon blessed
them, and said to Mary, his mother, "Behold, this child is set
for the falling and the rising of many in Israel, and for a sign
which is spoken against. 35 Yes, a sword will pierce through
your own soul, that the thoughts of many hearts may be revealed."

John 19:25-27

25 But there were standing by the cross of Jesus his mother, and his mother's sister, Mary the wife of Clopas, and
Mary Magdalene. 26 Therefore when Jesus saw his mother,
and the disciple whom he loved standing there, he said to his
mother, "Woman, behold your son!" 27 Then he said to the
disciple, "Behold, your mother!" From that hour, the disciple
took her to his own home.

MARY

He said to his mother, "Woman, behold your son!" Then he said to the disciple, "Behold, your mother!" John 19:26-27

The prophecy has echoed often in Mary's ears: "A sword will pierce through your own soul" (Luke 2:35). An old man named Simeon said that to her when her son was just a baby, being dedicated at the temple. Over the years, those words have come back to Mary time and again. What could they possibly mean? Now she knows. She sees her miraculous firstborn nailed to a cross. Her soul shudders.

Beside her stands young John, weighed down by sorrow of his own. Several years ago John left everything to follow the young rabbi. He's been awed by his miracles, transfixed by his teaching, and over the years, he's also become unusually close to Jesus as a friend. Oh, how they love each other! And now the Friend above all friends is dying.

Mother and friend stand near the cross, both staring blankly at the dirt, their world in ruins. And then the gentle voice they both love is speaking to them. Mary lifts her head and gazes through her tears into the tender eyes of Jesus. He is telling her to look at John: "Woman, behold your son!" Mary turns her head, and John's bloodshot eyes meet hers. "Behold, your mother!" Jesus tells his friend. And in that moment, the love Mary and John feel for Jesus becomes love for each other.

Their sorrow will become joy when Jesus rises again. Still, they must let him go when he returns to his heavenly throne. But Mary and John are not alone. Jesus has given them each other, and he will give them his Spirit.

PRAYER

Lord Jesus, we love because you first loved us. When our grief seems unbearable, comfort us and relieve our loneliness through the love of others in the family of God. Amen.

Matthew 27:39-49

[39] Those who passed by blasphemed him, wagging their heads, [40] and saying, "You who destroy the temple, and build it in three days, save yourself! If you are the Son of God, come down from the cross!"

[41] Likewise the chief priests were also mocking, with the scribes, the Pharisees, and the elders. They said, [42] "He saved others, but he can't save himself. If he is the King of Israel, let him come down from the cross now, and we will believe in him. [43] He trusts in God. Let God deliver him now, if he wants him; for he said, 'I am the Son of God.'" [44] The robbers also who were crucified with him cast on him the same reproach.

[45] Now from the sixth hour there was darkness over all the land until the ninth hour. [46] About the ninth hour Jesus cried with a loud voice, saying, "Eli, Eli, lama sabachthani?" That is, "My God, my God, why have you forsaken me?"

[47] Some of them who stood there, when they heard it, said, "This man is calling Elijah."

[48] Immediately one of them ran, and took a sponge, and filled it with vinegar, and put it on a reed, and gave him a drink. [49] The rest said, "Let him be. Let's see whether Elijah comes to save him."

SCOFFER

"He saved others, but he can't save himself. If he is the King of Israel, let him come down from the cross now, and we will believe in him... Let God deliver him now, if he wants him; for he said, 'I am the Son of God.'" Matthew 27:43

There is justice, after all. For a while there, I wondered. The Galilean had been misleading the people. He did miracles in the power of the devil, and the crowds kept getting bigger and bigger. But finally he's getting what he deserves.

That pitiful scream of his says it all. Some think he's calling for Elijah, but I was closer, and I could hear better what he really said. He didn't say, "Eli-jah.' He said, "*Eli lama sabachthani*: My God, why have you forsaken me?" Even now, at the end, this guy still doesn't get it.

Why did God forsake him? It's obvious. The man said that if the temple was destroyed, he could build it again in just three days. He claimed the authority to forgive sins. And he called himself the Son of the living God. This Galilean peasant goes around talking like he's God and acting like he's God, and then he wonders why God forsakes him.

If he was really the Almighty, he wouldn't be hanging helpless on a cross. God is showing beyond a doubt his wrath against the blasphemer. By subjecting him to crucifixion, the Lord puts him under the curse which the Law of Moses declares on anyone who is hung on a tree. And by hiding the light of the sun itself, God shows his utter rejection of this man.

We considered him plagued,
struck by God, and afflicted.
But he was pierced for our transgressions.
He was crushed for our iniquities. (Isaiah 53:4-5).

PRAYER

Father, we misjudge so many things. Your ways are so far beyond ours. Thank you that through the rejection of your Son, you've made a way to accept us. In Jesus' name, Amen.

Luke 23:32-39

32 There were also others, two criminals, led with him to
be put to death. 33 When they came to the place that is called
The Skull, they crucified him there with the criminals, one
on the right and the other on the left.
34 Jesus said, "Father, forgive them, for they don't know
what they are doing."
Dividing his garments among them, they cast lots. 35 The
people stood watching. The rulers with them also scoffed at
him, saying, "He saved others. Let him save himself, if this
is the Christ of God, his chosen one!"
36 The soldiers also mocked him, coming to him and offering him vinegar, 37 and saying, "If you are the King of the
Jews, save yourself!"
38 An inscription was also written over him in letters of
Greek, Latin, and Hebrew: "THIS IS THE KING OF THE
JEWS."
39 One of the criminals who was hanged insulted him,
saying, "If you are the Christ, save yourself and us!"

BITTER CRIMINAL

One of the criminals who was hanged insulted him, saying, "If you are the Christ, save yourself and us!" Luke 23:39

When the going gets tough, the tough don't get religion. They get mad. Repentance is for wimps. Why admit the mess is your own fault, when you can snarl at Jesus instead? This criminal gets himself crucified for his own crimes, and then he blames Jesus for his predicament.

He's not alone. A man neglects or abuses his wife and then screams at God for allowing his marriage to fall apart. Another person abuses alcohol or drugs, and then hates God for the disasters that come with addiction. Another catches a sexually transmitted disease and blames God. Another winds up in jail, and instead of repenting, becomes even more angry and bitter.

"If you're so great, Jesus, why am I hanging on this cross? Aren't you the Christ, the mighty Messiah? Then do something about it. Save yourself and us! Are you helpless, or what?"

"What's that idiot on the other cross saying? Oh, he's asking me, 'Don't you fear God?' Of course I don't fear God! Am I supposed to get religion just because I'm dying? No way! I've lived without God, and I'll die without him. Pitiful how the other guy is pleading for Jesus' help. Guess he's not as tough as I am."

In the horrible mystery of sin, some people are so addicted to rage and hatred that they shake their fist at God even as they dangle over the Abyss and are about to plunge into hell. They'd rather keep their pride and perish, than humble themselves and live.

PRAYER

Father in heaven, rescue us from the deadly grip of resentment. Forgive our sins, help us endure suffering, and grant us eternal life through Jesus Christ our Lord. Amen.

Luke 23:39-43 NIV

39 One of the criminals who hung there hurled insults at
him: “Aren’t you the Christ? Save yourself and us!”
40 But the other criminal rebuked him. “Don’t you fear
God,” he said, “since you are under the same sentence?
41 We are punished justly, for we are getting what our deeds
deserve. But this man has done nothing wrong.”
42 Then he said, “Jesus, remember me when you come into your kingdom.”
43 Jesus answered him, “I tell you the truth, today you
will be with me in paradise.”

CRIMINAL IN PARADISE

Jesus answered him, "I tell you the truth, today you will be with me in paradise." Luke 23:43

The man still can't get over the fact that he's in heaven. His life was a waste, a complete disaster. Society would have been better off without him, and, in the end, it did get rid of him. His crime and cruelty brought him to a well-deserved end. But here in heaven, nobody seems to remember that.

Amazing how it happened. At first he'd been cursing Jesus right along with the other criminal, but then it struck him. God is real, and before long, he would be facing him. He was on that cross because he deserved it, while Jesus was totally innocent. And then, another thought. Maybe, just maybe, this wouldn't be the end of Jesus. Hard to say where that idea came from, but he found himself increasingly convinced.

He gasps, "Jesus, remember me when you come into your kingdom."

"Today, you will be with me in paradise," Jesus replies.

Later, a sickening crunch and stabs of pain as they break his legs. Can't hold himself up. Can't breathe. And then...

Paradise. No more pain, just pleasure. No more sorrow, just joy. No more hatred, just love. No more guilt, just acceptance. The Man from the middle cross is there too, of course, no longer bloody and haggard, but radiant beyond description. And the former criminal is with him forever.

When we were still powerless, Christ died for the ungodly. Very rarely will anyone die for a righteous man, though for a good man someone might possibly dare to die. But God demonstrates his own love for us in this: While we were still sinners, Christ died for us (Romans 5:6-8).

PRAYER

Dear God, we can't understand your love for undeserving sinners like us. But we praise you for it, and for opening the way to paradise through Jesus our Lord. Amen.

Matthew 27:50-54

50 Jesus cried again with a loud voice, and yielded up his
spirit. 51 Behold, the veil of the temple was torn in two from
the top to the bottom. The earth quaked and the rocks were
split. 52 The tombs were opened, and many bodies of the
saints who had fallen asleep were raised; 53 and coming out
of the tombs after his resurrection, they entered into the holy
city and appeared to many.

54 Now the centurion, and those who were with him
watching Jesus, when they saw the earthquake, and the
things that were done, feared exceedingly, saying, "Truly
this was the Son of God."

CENTURION

And when the centurion heard his cry and saw how he died, he said, "Surely this man was the Son of God!" Mark 15:39

Never saw anything like it. Nine o'clock. He's offered wine mixed with myrrh to dope him up and ease the pain, but he turns it down. Seems he'd rather suffer the worst with a clear head than take the easy way out. The men strip him naked, spread him out, hammer spikes into his wrists and heels, hoist him up—and what does he say? "Father, forgive them, for they do not know what they are doing." There's something unearthly about him.

Then at noon, everything turns dark. It stays that way for three solid hours. The sun is nowhere to be seen. Around three o'clock, after six hours of hanging there, when you'd expect him to have no energy left, he suddenly shouts in a loud, triumphant voice, "Finished!" (John 19:30) It's like he's in control somehow, and he decides when enough is enough. Then quietly: "Father, into your hands I commit my spirit." The moment he says that, he dies (Luke 23:46).

That's when the earthquake hits. It's like God himself is reacting. People staggering, rocks shattering—it's like his death has shifted the structure of the entire universe. Surely this man was the Son of God!

God so loved the world, that he gave his one and only Son, that whoever believes in him should not perish, but have eternal life. For God did not send his Son into the world to judge the world, but that the world should be saved through him. He who believes in him is not judged. He who does not believe has been judged already, because he has not believed in the name of God's one and only Son (John 3:16-18).

PRAYER

Savior, you are the Son of God! Were the whole realm of nature mine, that were a present far too small. Love so amazing, so divine, demands my soul, my life, my all. Amen.

John 19:31-37

31 Therefore the Jews, because it was the Preparation Day, so that the bodies wouldn't remain on the cross on the Sabbath (for that Sabbath was a special one), asked of Pilate that their legs might be broken, and that they might be taken away. 32 Therefore the soldiers came, and broke the legs of the first, and of the other who was crucified with him; 33 but when they came to Jesus, and saw that he was already dead, they didn't break his legs. 34 However one of the soldiers pierced his side with a spear, and immediately blood and water came out. 35 He who has seen has testified, and his testimony is true. He knows that he tells the truth, that you may believe. 36 For these things happened, that the Scripture might be fulfilled, "A bone of him will not be broken." 37 Again another Scripture says, "They will look on him whom they pierced."

JOHN

He who has seen has testified, and his testimony is true. He knows that he tells the truth, that you may believe. John 19:35

John has been an eyewitness to all the major happenings. At the Last Supper, John was beside his Lord. At the cross, John was there watching. Later, John saw for himself the empty tomb, the discarded grave clothes, and best of all, the sight of his risen Master eating fish. What's more, John has been the Lord's dearest friend, his closest confidant. After Jesus' ascension, John shares his home with Jesus' blessed mother Mary and adds her memories of Jesus to his own. As eyewitness to all the major events, confidant of Jesus' most intimate thoughts, and, with the Spirit's help, knowledgeable about prophetic Scripture, John tells the truth. Believe it.

John noted the timing of Jesus' death: during Passover, the festival of deliverance when a lamb's blood had to be spilled without breaking any bones. John saw the criminals' legs shatter under the soldier's club. He saw the soldier walk over to Jesus, only to find him already dead. John saw the club tossed aside, and then a spear plunging into Jesus' abdomen, bringing a strange flow of blood and water. No doubt about it. Jesus is the ultimate Passover Lamb. He's the one the ancient scriptures predicted would be pierced. He's the Savior foretold by the prophets.

John tells the truth. Believe it.

That which was from the beginning, which we have heard, which we have seen with our eyes, which we have looked at and our hands have touched—this we proclaim concerning the Word of life (1 John 1:1-2).

PRAYER

God of truth, thank you for revealing Christ to us through reliable witnesses. By your Spirit, help us understand and believe the truth of salvation in Jesus. Amen.

John 19:38-42

38 After these things, Joseph of Arimathaea, being a disciple of Jesus, but secretly for fear of the Jews, asked of Pilate that he might take away Jesus' body. Pilate gave him
permission. He came therefore and took away his body.
39 Nicodemus, who at first came to Jesus by night, also came
bringing a mixture of myrrh and aloes, about a hundred Roman pounds. 40 So they took Jesus' body, and bound it in lin-
en cloths with the spices, as the custom of the Jews is to
bury. 41 Now in the place where he was crucified there was a
garden. In the garden was a new tomb in which no man had
ever yet been laid. 42 Then because of the Jews' Preparation
Day (for the tomb was near at hand) they laid Jesus there.

JOSEPH AND NICODEMUS

Joseph of Arimathaea, being a disciple of Jesus, but secretly for fear of the Jews, asked of Pilate that he might take away Jesus' body... Nicodemus, who at first came to Jesus by night, also came... So they took Jesus' body. John 19:38-40

Joseph of Arimathea has been waiting eagerly for the kingdom of God. For some time he's believed in Jesus, though secretly due to fear of certain powerful people. Ironically, though, the more grim Jesus' situation becomes, the less Joseph hides his loyalty. When Jesus comes to trial, Joseph begins to show his true colors by refusing to support the Council's decision and action (Luke 23:50-51). And at the cross, Joseph comes right out into the open. It was risky to identify with Jesus in any way, but Joseph "went *boldly* to Pilate and asked for Jesus' body" (Mark 15:43).

Same story with Nicodemus. At first he doesn't want to be seen talking with Jesus, so he visits him under the cover of night (John 3:2). Later, when the Pharisees are saying bad things about Jesus, Nicodemus gets just a little bolder and says, "Does our law condemn anyone without first hearing him to find out what he is doing?" (John 7:51) And finally, at the cross, Nicodemus is willing to stand up and be counted.

It might be dangerous, and it's certainly not a good career move for two council members. But Joseph and Nicodemus have played it safe long enough. Time to step forward. No more of this secret admirer business. Better to die with Jesus than keep living a lie with their phony cronies. Come what may, they are going to give this prophet, this Messenger of God's kingdom, a decent burial. Strange, isn't it, how it's not in Jesus' miracles but in his death that they at last find the courage and resolve to overcome their fears?

PRAYER

Lord, we so often fear the worst and refuse to take risks. Help us find courage at the foot of the cross to identify with you no matter what. Through Jesus our Lord, Amen.

Luke 8:1-3

1 Soon afterwards, Jesus went about through cities and villages, preaching and bringing the good news of God's Kingdom. With him were the twelve, 2 and certain women who had been healed of evil spirits and infirmities: Mary who was called Magdalene, from whom seven demons had gone out; 3 and Joanna, the wife of Chuza, Herod's steward; Susanna; and many others; who served them from their possessions.

Mark 15:37-47

37 Jesus cried out with a loud voice, and gave up the spirit. 38 The veil of the temple was torn in two from the top to the bottom. 39 When the centurion, who stood by opposite him, saw that he cried out like this and breathed his last, he said, "Truly this man was the Son of God!"

40 There were also women watching from afar, among whom were both Mary Magdalene, and Mary the mother of James the less and of Joses, and Salome; 41 who, when he was in Galilee, followed him, and served him; and many other women who came up with him to Jerusalem.

42 When evening had now come, because it was the Preparation Day, that is, the day before the Sabbath, 43 Joseph of Arimathaea, a prominent council member who also himself was looking for God's Kingdom, came. He boldly went in to Pilate, and asked for Jesus' body. 44 Pilate marveled if he were already dead; and summoning the centurion, he asked him whether he had been dead long. 45 When he found out from the centurion, he granted the body to Joseph. 46 He bought a linen cloth, and taking him down, wound him in the linen cloth, and laid him in a tomb which had been cut out of a rock. He rolled a stone against the door of the tomb. 47 Mary Magdalene and Mary, the mother of Joses, saw where he was laid.

WOMEN WHO CARED

In Galilee these women had followed him and cared for his needs. Mark 15:41 NIV

Mary of Magdala starts following Jesus after he frees her from seven demons. Salome, Zebedee's wife, gets involved with Jesus' ministry about the same time as her sons James and John. One by one, for a variety of reasons, a sizeable group of women are drawn to the Teacher from Nazareth. He treats women with love, not lust; with respect, not condescension. Unlike most rabbis, Jesus is happy to teach women as well as men, and to discuss freely with them. The women become vital partners in his ministry. As he moves around Galilee, they travel with him, providing meals, arranging for lodging, paying bills out of their own pockets. When Jesus leaves for Jerusalem, these loyal women travel with him.

When they get there, however, they are in for a shock. The Teacher is seized, beaten, and then crucified. There he hangs, limp and lifeless. Most of his male disciples are in hiding, but the women are there at the cross, watching through their tears.

When it's over, they decide to do one last thing for him. They've cared for Jesus in life, and they will care for him in death. So the women take careful note of where he is buried, then hurry off to prepare spices for the body. Once Sabbath is over, they hurry to the tomb in order to anoint his lacerated corpse. When they get there, they are in for another shock. And the women's witness will shock the world.

PRAYER

Dear Jesus, you have done so much for women, and Christian women have done so much for you. Thank you for courageous women who love you and serve you. Amen.

Revelation 5 NIV

1 Then I saw in the right hand of him who sat on the throne a scroll with writing on both sides and sealed with seven seals. 2 And I saw a mighty angel proclaiming in a loud voice, "Who is worthy to break the seals and open the scroll?" 3 But no one in heaven or on earth or under the earth could open the scroll or even look inside it. 4 I wept and wept because no one was found who was worthy to open the scroll or look inside. 5 Then one of the elders said to me, "Do not weep! See, the Lion of the tribe of Judah, the Root of David, has triumphed. He is able to open the scroll and its seven seals."

6 Then I saw a Lamb, looking as if it had been slain, standing in the center of the throne, encircled by the four living creatures and the elders. He had seven horns and seven eyes, which are the seven spirits of God sent out into all the earth. 7 He came and took the scroll from the right hand of him who sat on the throne. 8 And when he had taken it, the four living creatures and the twenty-four elders fell down before the Lamb. Each one had a harp and they were holding golden bowls full of incense, which are the prayers of the saints.

9 And they sang a new song: "You are worthy to take the scroll and to open its seals, because you were slain, and with your blood you purchased men for God from every tribe and language and people and nation. 10 You have made them to be a kingdom and priests to serve our God, and they will reign on the earth." 11 Then I looked and heard the voice of many angels, numbering thousands upon thousands, and ten thousand times ten thousand. They encircled the throne and the living creatures and the elders. 12 In a loud voice they sang: "Worthy is the Lamb, who was slain, to receive power and wealth and wisdom and strength and honor and glory and praise!" 13 Then I heard every creature in heaven and on earth and under the earth … and all that is in them, singing: "To him who sits on the throne and to the Lamb be praise and honor and glory and power, for ever and ever!"

HEAVEN'S CHOIR

"Worthy is the Lamb, who was slain, to receive power and wealth and wisdom and strength and honor and glory and praise!" Revelation 5:12

This is the moment the choir has been waiting for. Who is worthy to open the scroll? Who can unfold God's plans and judgments and bring history to its appointed goal under his reign? Nobody. No one is worthy.

Wait a moment! There, at the center of the throne, is the Lamb who was slain. He is worthy. All of heaven falls at his feet and becomes one great mass choir. Because the Lamb is slain, he has the right to open the scroll and direct the unfolding of history. His blood has bought people of every kind for God, and he has made them worthy to reign with him. Heaven rings with hymn after hymn to the crucified Christ.

Back on earth, a great crowd also sang praise to Jesus once. He rode into Jerusalem at the head of a multitude of admirers, all with high hopes that he would conquer evil and establish the reign of God. "Hosanna to the Son of David! Blessed is he who comes in the name of the Lord" (Matthew 21:9). The Man riding the donkey accepted that Palm Sunday praise, but he knew that he must be slain before he could reign. In the words of a hymn, "Ride on, ride on in majesty as all the crowds 'Hosanna!' cry; through waving branches slowly ride, O Savior, to be crucified. Ride on, ride on in majesty, in lowly pomp ride on to die; bow your meek head to mortal pain, then take, O God, your power and reign!"

By his death, Jesus has redeemed people of every kind and directs the flow of history on his Father's behalf. No wonder heaven sings!

PRAYER

King Jesus, we sing with heaven's choir: "Worthy is the Lamb, who was slain, to receive power and wealth and wisdom and strength and honor and glory and praise." Amen.

Colossians 2:6-15 NIV

6 So then, just as you received Christ Jesus as Lord, continue to live your lives in him, 7 rooted and built up in him,
strengthened in the faith as you were taught, and overflowing
with thankfulness.

8 See to it that no one takes you captive through hollow
and deceptive philosophy, which depends on human tradition
and the elemental spiritual forces of this world rather than on
Christ.

9 For in Christ all the fullness of the Deity lives in bodily
form, 10 and in Christ you have been brought to fullness. He
is the head over every power and authority. 11 In him you
were also circumcised with a circumcision not performed by
human hands. Your whole self ruled by the flesh* was put
off when you were circumcised by Christ, 12 having been
buried with him in baptism, in which you were also raised
with him through your faith in the working of God, who
raised him from the dead.

13 When you were dead in your sins and in the uncircum-
cision of your flesh, God made you alive with Christ. He
forgave us all our sins, 14 having canceled the charge of our
legal indebtedness, which stood against us and condemned
us; he has taken it away, nailing it to the cross. 15 And having
disarmed the powers and authorities, he made a public spectacle of them, triumphing over them by the cross.

*In contexts like this, the Greek word for *flesh* (*sarx*) refers to the sinful state of human beings, often presented as a power in opposition to the Spirit.

Hebrews 2:14-15 NIV

14 Since the children have flesh and blood, he too shared
in their humanity so that by his death he might break the
power of him who holds the power of death—that is, the
devil— 15 and free those who all their lives were held in
slavery by their fear of death.

SATAN

Having disarmed the powers, he made a public spectacle of them, triumphing over them by the cross. Colossians 2:15

The terrorist is holding hostages. He wants to topple the government, and even if he can't, he intends at least to destroy the captives. But the leader of the government doesn't give in. Instead, he becomes a hostage himself. The terrorist is gleeful. He's got a chance to lay his hands on this person he hates so much. He's got the leader right where he wants him, trapped in his hideout with all the other hostages. But suddenly the terrorist finds himself disarmed. The leader parades the terrorist out of the building at the point of his own weapon, and the captives are set free.

When sinful people were trapped under Satan's power, the divine King joined them in their desperate situation. Jesus "shared in their humanity so that by his death he might destroy him who holds the power of death—that is, the devil—and free those who all their lives were held in slavery by their fear of death" (Hebrews 2:15).

Jesus took Satan's two deadliest weapons, sin and death, and used them against the enemy. There was never a greater sin than the crucifixion of Jesus, never a more awful death than the one Jesus endured. But Jesus used the worst of sins to overcome sin. He used the most awful of deaths "to destroy him who holds the power of death."

Jesus disarmed Satan the cosmic terrorist, defeated him with his own weapons, and made a public spectacle of him. We're hostages no longer. "The reason the Son of God appeared was to destroy the devil's work" (1 John 3:8).

PRAYER

Thank you, Jesus, for ending Satan's terror, for setting us free, and for establishing that you are the rightful King of the universe and the Savior of your people. Amen.

Romans 3:9-26 NIV

[9] What shall we conclude then? Do we have any advantage? Not at all! For we have already made the charge that Jews and Gentiles alike are all under the power of sin. [10] As it is written:

"There is no one righteous, not even one;
[11] there is no one who understands;
there is no one who seeks God.
[12] All have turned away,
they have together become worthless;
there is no one who does good,
not even one…."
[14] "Their mouths are full of cursing and bitterness."
[15] "Their feet are swift to shed blood;
[16] ruin and misery mark their ways,
[17] and the way of peace they do not know."
[18] "There is no fear of God before their eyes."

[19] Now we know that whatever the law says, it says to those who are under the law, so that every mouth may be silenced and the whole world held accountable to God. [20] Therefore no one will be declared righteous in God's sight by the works of the law; rather, through the law we become conscious of our sin.

[21] But now apart from the law the righteousness of God has been made known, to which the Law and the Prophets testify. [22] This righteousness is given through faith in Jesus Christ to all who believe. There is no difference between Jew and Gentile, [23] for all have sinned and fall short of the glory of God, [24] and all are justified freely by his grace through the redemption that came by Christ Jesus. [25] God presented Christ as a sacrifice of atonement, through the shedding of his blood—to be received by faith. He did this to demonstrate his righteousness, because in his forbearance he had left the sins committed beforehand unpunished— [26] he did it to demonstrate his righteousness at the present time, so as to be just and the one who justifies those who have faith in Jesus.

GOD

God presented Christ as a sacrifice of atonement, through the shedding of his blood—to be received by faith. He did this to demonstrate his righteousness. Romans 3:25

Here's how God sees it: "The Lord looks down from heaven on the sons of men to see if there are any who understand, any who seek God. All have turned aside, they have together become corrupt. There is no one who does good, not even one" (Psalm 14:2-3). How does God react? He is full of wrath. His eyes are too pure to look on evil; he cannot tolerate wrong (Habakkuk 1:13). When somebody sins, somebody pays, and "the wages of sin is death" (Romans 6:23). The evil must be punished.

But then, for no reason except his astonishing love, God decides to leave those sins unpunished. No, he doesn't compromise his justice. He doesn't set aside his law that "without the shedding of blood there is no forgiveness" (Hebrews 9:22). Instead, he devises a way to give sin the punishment it deserves and yet spare the sinners he loves.

He sees no one who can do it, so he does it all himself. In the person of his one and only Son, God becomes human and lives the perfect life no one else could. Because Jesus is sinless, he does not have to pay for his own sins. Because he is fully human, he is linked to us so intimately that he can represent us and take responsibility for our sin. And because he is God's eternal Son, his death is more than sufficient to pay for the sins of the whole world. Thus God satisfies his own justice and yet justifies sinners, making them right with him.

This is love: not that we loved God, but that he loved us and sent his Son as an atoning sacrifice for our sins (1 John 4:10).

PRAYER

"Guilty, helpless, vile were we. Spotless Lamb of God was he. Full atonement, can it be? Hallelujah! What a Savior!" Thank you, Father, for sacrificing your Son. Amen.

Matthew 27:62-66 NIV

[62] The chief priests and the Pharisees went to Pilate.
[63] "Sir," they said, "we remember that while he was still alive
that deceiver said, 'After three days I will rise again.' [64] So
give the order for the tomb to be made secure until the third
day. Otherwise, his disciples may come and steal the body
and tell the people that he has been raised from the dead.
This last deception will be worse than the first."

[65] "Take a guard," Pilate answered. "Go, make the tomb
as secure as you know how." [66] So they went and made the
tomb secure by putting a seal on the stone and posting the
guard.

GRAVEYARD SHIFT

"Take a guard," Pilate answered. "Go, make the tomb as secure as you know how." Matthew 27:65

Jesus' enemies are the only ones who remember. "We remember that when he was still alive, that deceiver said, 'After three days I will rise again.'" Jesus' friends are too busy crying to recall what he said, but his enemies remember. What if there's a grave robbery and a hoax? Or even worse, what if...? Nah, can't consider that possibility.

These paranoid priests are nothing if not thorough. After pushing Pilate to have Jesus killed, they now ask the governor to make sure he stays dead. Wearily, Pilate says they can post a security detail and do anything else they can think of to keep things from getting lively in the cemetery.

To the men in the guard detail, it all seems boring and a little silly. Take turns sitting around guarding a tomb for the next several days? Not much of a challenge. Not exactly a thrill a minute. Oh well, orders are orders, and at least it's not hard. It's easy for heavily armed soldiers to scare off would-be grave robbers, when they're nothing but ragtag fishermen and frightened women. It's easy to smother false rumors of resurrection before they ever start. Just put an official government seal on the tomb, sit near it with weapons in plain sight, and nobody's going to mess with anything. That body isn't going anywhere. Right?

Except that this grave robbery is going to be an inside job: the man inside the tomb is the one who will pull it off. "Go, make the tomb as secure as you know how." And how secure is that? Can a bazooka stop the sunrise?

PRAYER

Lord God, nothing can stop your triumph of life. Thank you, Jesus, for being buried in order to rob the grave and win the final victory over death and evil. Amen.

Matthew 28:1-10

1 After the Sabbath, at dawn on the first day of the week,
Mary Magdalene and the other Mary went to look at the
tomb.

2 There was a violent earthquake, for an angel of the Lord
came down from heaven and, going to the tomb, rolled back
the stone and sat on it. 3 His appearance was like lightning,
and his clothes were white as snow. 4 The guards were so
afraid of him that they shook and became like dead men.

5 The angel said to the women, "Do not be afraid, for I
know that you are looking for Jesus, who was crucified. 6 He
is not here; he has risen, just as he said. Come and see the
place where he lay. 7 Then go quickly and tell his disciples:
'He has risen from the dead and is going ahead of you into
Galilee. There you will see him.' Now I have told you."

8 So the women hurried away from the tomb, afraid yet
filled with joy, and ran to tell his disciples. 9 Suddenly Jesus
met them. "Greetings," he said. They came to him, clasped
his feet and worshiped him. 10 Then Jesus said to them, "Do
not be afraid. Go and tell my brothers to go to Galilee; there
they will see me."

STONE MOVER

There was a violent earthquake, for an angel of the Lord came down from heaven and, going to the tomb, rolled back the stone and sat on it. Matthew 28:2

When the angel came down and rolled away the stone, he wasn't letting Jesus out of the tomb. He was letting others in so that they could see Jesus was already gone. How that angel must have enjoyed his job! A few days earlier, the angel armies had been ordered to stand back while Jesus was tortured and murdered. But now all that was finished. Jesus had overcome death and emerged from the tomb, leaving his burial wrappings behind and going out through the stone as though it wasn't even there.

The angel flashed down from heaven with earthshaking power and dazzling brightness. He saw on the tomb a seal of officials who thought themselves powerful, and he shattered that silly seal in the name of the all-powerful Lord. The angel saw a massive stone the shape of a giant hockey puck, standing on edge in its groove, blocking the entrance to the tomb. He seized that heavy stone as though it were a feather and flung it away from the entrance with such force that it came out of its groove and landed flat on the ground. Then the angel sat on it. That huge barrier for keeping Jesus in and his friends out of the tomb had become a handy chair.

What a turnaround! Jesus, the dead man, was alive and unstoppable, while the big, strong soldiers who were supposed to keep him in the tomb lay as though dead. The tough guys trembled and fainted, but the women, astonished and frightened but still standing, heard the good news from the stone mover. Then they met the living Christ himself.

PRAYER

Lord Jesus, thank you for defeating death and for making sure we could know the good news. Help us to rejoice in you and to keep spreading the good news to others. Amen.

Matthew 28:11-15

[11] While the women were on their way, some of the guards went into the city and reported to the chief priests everything that had happened. [12] When the chief priests had met with the elders and devised a plan, they gave the soldiers a large sum of money, [13] telling them, "You are to say, 'His disciples came during the night and stole him away while we were asleep.' [14] If this report gets to the governor, we will satisfy him and keep you out of trouble." [15] So the soldiers took the money and did as they were instructed.

COVERUP COMMITTEE

When the chief priests had met with the elders and devised a plan, they gave the soldiers a large sum of money, telling them, "You are to say, 'His disciples came during the night and stole him away while we were asleep.'" Matt. 28:12-13

Those poor religious leaders! They had killed Jesus, they had taken measures to keep him dead and buried, but now their flunkies came straggling back with the news that Jesus' body was gone. Did the leaders instantly believe in Jesus? No, they did what many religious leaders typically do: they held a meeting, appointed a committee, and devised a plan.

The options were limited. Their best option, of course, was to produce Jesus' dead body and put it on display. That would surely stop the rumors that he was alive again. But the body was gone, and they couldn't find it anywhere. If they couldn't come up with the body, they would have to come up with a story. The best they could do was to have the guards say they fell asleep and Jesus' disciples stole the body.

The story had huge problems, of course. How could the guards all have slept through an earthquake and the sound of that huge stone crashing on its side? And if they were sleeping so soundly, how did they know Jesus' disciples stole the body? Did they see through their eyelids as they slept? The story got even flimsier as time went on, for Jesus' disciples were willing to go to prison or be killed rather than deny they'd seen Jesus alive. If they were just grave robbers, why die for a lie? The story about disciples stealing the body was full of holes, but it was the best the coverup committee could do. When people are determined not to believe in the risen Lord, they will believe almost any other story, no matter how ridiculous.

PRAYER

Dear Jesus, save us from religious leaders who are skilled in meetings, committees, and plans, but don't know you as the living Lord. Fill us with your life. Amen.

John 20:3-18

3 Peter and the other disciple [John] started for the tomb.
4 Both were running, but the other disciple outran Peter and
reached the tomb first. 5 He bent over and looked in at the
strips of linen lying there but did not go in. 6 Then Simon Peter came along behind him and went straight into the tomb.
He saw the strips of linen lying there, 7 as well as the cloth
that had been wrapped around Jesus' head. The cloth was
still lying in its place, separate from the linen. 8 Finally the
other disciple, who had reached the tomb first, also went inside. He saw and believed. 9 (They still did not understand
from Scripture that Jesus had to rise from the dead.) 10 Then
the disciples went back to where they were staying.

11 Now Mary stood outside the tomb crying. As she wept,
she bent over to look into the tomb 12 and saw two angels in
white, seated where Jesus' body had been, one at the head
and the other at the foot.

13 They asked her, "Woman, why are you crying?"

"They have taken my Lord away," she said, "and I don't
know where they have put him." 14 At this, she turned around
and saw Jesus standing there, but she did not realize that it
was Jesus.

15 He asked her, "Woman, why are you crying? Who is it
you are looking for?"

Thinking he was the gardener, she said, "Sir, if you have carried him away, tell me where you have put him, and I will get him."

16 Jesus said to her, "Mary."

She turned toward him and cried out in Aramaic, "Rabboni!" (which means "Teacher").

17 Jesus said, "Do not hold on to me, for I have not yet ascended to the Father. Go instead to my brothers and tell them, 'I am ascending to my Father and your Father, to my God and your God.'"

18 Mary Magdalene went to the disciples with the news: "I have seen the Lord!" And she told them that he had said these things to her.

MARY MAGDALENE

Mary said, "Sir, if you have carried him away, tell me where you have put him, and I will get him." Jesus said to her, "Mary." John 20:15-16

Mary Magdalene was so busy looking for a dead body that she didn't recognize the living Jesus. She was so focused on memories from the past that she didn't expect to find her Lord in the present. It was not the sight of Jesus but his voice speaking her name that finally made Mary recognize him.

It's easy to miss Jesus if you don't expect him to come to you. If you think only about memories from the past, you can miss out on the joy of the living Lord here in the present. Sometimes religion can be like an embalmed corpse. The focus is on dead heroes, old traditions and patterns that must be honored and preserved. But don't get stuck in the past. Jesus is not just someone who lived long ago. He lives right now. He may come to you at any moment.

What does it take to recognize that Christ is near? Not the sight of his face but the sound of his voice, calling your name. When Mary Magdalene heard Jesus call her by name, she recognized him even before she turned to look at him. The Good Shepherd "calls his own sheep by name... My sheep listen to my voice" (John 10:3,27). Though your eyes don't see him, your heart hears him and leaps with joy in the certainty that Jesus lives and loves you.

Mary Magdalene saw Jesus physically, which you can't do. But even Mary had to move beyond counting on Jesus' physical nearness. Jesus told her not to hang on to him. He would soon return to his Father in heaven, and Mary would no longer see his face. But she would always hear his voice through the Spirit in her heart. And she would tell others that Jesus lives and reigns.

PRAYER

Dear Jesus, let me always sense the nearness of your Spirit and hear your voice of love speaking my name, until the day comes when I see you face to face. Amen.

Luke 24:13-32 NIV

[13] Now that same day two of them were going to a village called Emmaus, about seven miles from Jerusalem… [15] Jesus himself came up and walked along with them; [16] but they were kept from recognizing him. [17] He asked them, "What are you discussing together as you walk along?"

They stood still, their faces downcast. [18] One of them, named Cleopas, asked him, "Are you the only one visiting Jerusalem who does not know the things that have happened there in these days?"

19 "What things?" he asked.

"About Jesus of Nazareth," they replied. "He was a prophet, powerful in word and deed before God and all the people. [20] The chief priests and our rulers handed him over to be sentenced to death, and they crucified him… [22] In addition, some of our women amazed us. They went to the tomb early this morning [23] but didn't find his body. They came and told us that they had seen a vision of angels, who said he was alive. [24] Then some of our companions went to the tomb and found it just as the women had said, but they did not see Jesus."

[25] He said to them, "How foolish you are, and how slow to believe all that the prophets have spoken! [26] Did not the Messiah have to suffer these things and then enter his glory?" [27] And beginning with Moses and all the Prophets, he explained to them what was said in all the Scriptures concerning himself.

[28] As they approached the village to which they were going, Jesus continued on as if he were going farther. [29] But they urged him strongly, "Stay with us, for it is nearly evening; the day is almost over." So he went in to stay with them.

[30] When he was at the table with them, he took bread, gave thanks, broke it and began to give it to them. [31] Then their eyes were opened and they recognized him, and he disappeared from their sight. [32] They asked each other, "Were not our hearts burning within us while he talked with us on the road and opened the Scriptures to us?"

CLEOPAS

"Were not our hearts burning within us while he talked with us on the road and opened the Scriptures to us?" Luke 24:32

Various people who met the risen Jesus didn't know him right away. "They were kept from recognizing him" (Luke 24:16). Jesus wanted them to sense him with their hearts before they recognized him with their eyes. Jesus wanted it that way not just for their sake, but for ours. He wants us to know that seeing and recognizing aren't the same thing. It was possible to see the risen Lord without recognizing him. It's also possible to recognize the risen Lord without seeing him.

Cleopas and his companion didn't recognize Jesus' face at first, but as Jesus explained what the Bible said about himself, they sensed a fire being lit inside them, and they didn't want it to stop. So too, when the Holy Spirit's fire touches your heart as you hear the Bible revealing the suffering Savior and his victory over death, you are hearing the voice of Christ himself. Jesus is walking beside you. Like Cleopas, invite Jesus to stay with you. Open your door to him. Jesus says, "Here I am! I stand at the door and knock. If anyone hears my voice and opens the door, I will come in and eat with him, and he with me" (Revelation 3:20).

Cleopas recognized Jesus in the breaking of the bread. Still today, whenever bread is broken in holy communion, the bread comes to us from the nail-scarred hands of Jesus himself. Even though we don't see him, we recognize him.

If the biblical words of Christ are burning in your heart and the bread of holy communion is in your mouth, then Christ is with you as surely as if he were physically sitting across the table from you. Recognize him and rejoice!

PRAYER

Lord Jesus, though we do not see you, we believe in you and love you and rejoice in you. Set our hearts aflame with your truth, and nourish our souls with yourself. Amen.

John 20:19-31 NIV

19 On the evening of that first day of the week, when the
disciples were together, with the doors locked for fear of the
Jewish leaders, Jesus came and stood among them and said,
"Peace be with you!" 20 After he said this, he showed them
his hands and side. The disciples were overjoyed when they
saw the Lord.

21 Again Jesus said, "Peace be with you! As the Father
has sent me, I am sending you." 22 And with that he breathed
on them and said, "Receive the Holy Spirit. 23 If you forgive
anyone's sins, their sins are forgiven; if you do not forgive
them, they are not forgiven."

24 Now Thomas (also known as Didymus [the twin]), one
of the Twelve, was not with the disciples when Jesus came.
25 So the other disciples told him, "We have seen the Lord!"

But he said to them, "Unless I see the nail marks in his hands and put my finger where the nails were, and put my hand into his side, I will not believe."

26 A week later his disciples were in the house again, and
Thomas was with them. Though the doors were locked, Jesus
came and stood among them and said, "Peace be with you!"
27 Then he said to Thomas, "Put your finger here; see my
hands. Reach out your hand and put it into my side. Stop
doubting and believe."

28 Thomas said to him, "My Lord and my God!"

29 Then Jesus told him, "Because you have seen me, you
have believed; blessed are those who have not seen and yet
have believed."

30 Jesus performed many other signs in the presence of
his disciples, which are not recorded in this book. 31 But
these are written that you may believe that Jesus is the Messiah, the Son of God, and that by believing you may have life
in his name.

THOMAS

Thomas said to him, "My Lord and my God!" John 20:28

Thomas is often remembered as "doubting Thomas" because he doubted Jesus' resurrection. But don't forget *believing* Thomas. He made the supreme statement of faith in Jesus recorded in the Bible: "My Lord and my God."

Believing Thomas can teach us a thing or two. Sure, Thomas was hard to persuade, but once the Lord convinced him, Thomas didn't just say, "I guess Jesus really did rise after all." Thomas embraced the full meaning of what the resurrection showed about Jesus. Thomas honored the risen Christ as Lord of all things and God of the universe, and he declared his personal commitment: "*My* Lord and *my* God."

Do you adore the divine glory of Jesus and commit yourself to him? The resurrection is not just an event that happened long, long ago, and Jesus is not just someone who lives in a galaxy far, far away. The resurrection displays God's glory in Christ, the Lord of life. God's glory in Christ matters here and now, and you must believe, worship, and commit to the Lord Jesus here and now.

When the Bible tells us of Jesus, the purpose is not just to provide information about what happened back then, but to lead us into a living relationship with the living Lord right now. "These are written that you may believe that Jesus is the Christ, the Son of God, and that by believing you may have life in his name" (John 20:31).

PRAYER

Jesus Christ, my Lord and my God, forgive my doubts, increase my faith, and fill me with love for you, for your Father, and for the blessed Holy Spirit. Amen.

John 21:1-14

1 Afterward Jesus appeared again to his disciples, by the Sea of Galilee. It happened this way: 2 Simon Peter, Thomas (also known as Didymus), Nathanael from Cana in Galilee, the sons of Zebedee, and two other disciples were together. 3 "I'm going out to fish," Simon Peter told them, and they said, "We'll go with you." So they went out and got into the boat, but that night they caught nothing.

4 Early in the morning, Jesus stood on the shore, but the disciples did not realize that it was Jesus.

5 He called out to them, "Friends, haven't you any fish?"

"No," they answered.

6 He said, "Throw your net on the right side of the boat and you will find some." When they did, they were unable to haul the net in because of the large number of fish.

7 Then the disciple whom Jesus loved said to Peter, "It is the Lord!" As soon as Simon Peter heard him say, "It is the Lord," he wrapped his outer garment around him (for he had taken it off) and jumped into the water. 8 The other disciples followed in the boat, towing the net full of fish, for they were not far from shore, about a hundred yards. 9 When they landed, they saw a fire of burning coals there with fish on it, and some bread.

10 Jesus said to them, "Bring some of the fish you have just caught." 11 So Simon Peter climbed back into the boat and dragged the net ashore. It was full of large fish, 153, but even with so many the net was not torn. 12 Jesus said to them, "Come and have breakfast." None of the disciples dared ask him, "Who are you?" They knew it was the Lord. 13 Jesus came, took the bread and gave it to them, and did the same with the fish. 14 This was now the third time Jesus appeared to his disciples after he was raised from the dead.

FISHERMEN

They were unable to haul the net in because of the large number of fish. Then the disciple whom Jesus loved said to Peter, "It is the Lord!" (John 21:6-7)

The fishermen didn't recognize the man on the shore right away, but suddenly they knew it was Jesus. What made them so sure? It was the fact that after their own efforts failed, they suddenly got more blessings than they could handle—153 fish—simply by doing what he told them to do.

Does Jesus seem like a distant stranger to you? If so, perhaps you've been too busy fishing on your own, depending on your own efforts. Stop doing everything your own way. Get help from Jesus. Do what he says, and see amazing things happen. He may help with an urgent need, renew your spirit, change your family, empower you to win others to salvation, or pour out some other blessing on you. Whatever form it takes, when you experience a big blessing, you recognize that the risen Lord is the one doing it.

We've learned that it's possible to see without believing and that it's equally possible to believe without seeing. If, like Mary Magdalene, you sense the Lord calling your name; if, like Cleopas, you find that Jesus sets your heart afire with the Bible and reveals himself in the Lord's Supper; if, like the fishermen, you are challenged to do something different and get a huge blessing, then you don't need to see Jesus to recognize the risen Lord. As Peter wrote, "Though you have not seen him, you love him; and even though you do not see him now, you believe in him and are filled with an inexpressible and glorious joy, for you are receiving the goal of your faith, the salvation of your souls" (1 Peter 1:8).

PRAYER

Praise be to you, God and Father of our Lord Jesus Christ! In your great mercy you have given us new birth into a living hope through the resurrection of Jesus (1 Peter 1:3). Amen.

Romans 6:1-11 NIV

1 What shall we say, then? Shall we go on sinning so that
grace may increase? 2 By no means! We are those who have
died to sin; how can we live in it any longer? 3 Or don't you
know that all of us who were baptized into Christ Jesus were
baptized into his death? 4 We were therefore buried with him
through baptism into death in order that, just as Christ was
raised from the dead through the glory of the Father, we too
may live a new life.

5 For if we have been united with him in a death like his,
we will certainly also be united with him in a resurrection
like his. 6 For we know that our old self was crucified with
him so that the body ruled by sin might be done away with,
that we should no longer be slaves to sin— 7 because anyone
who has died has been set free from sin.

8 Now if we died with Christ, we believe that we will also
live with him. 9 For we know that since Christ was raised
from the dead, he cannot die again; death no longer has mas-
tery over him. 10 The death he died, he died to sin once for
all; but the life he lives, he lives to God.

11 In the same way, count yourselves dead to sin but alive
to God in Christ Jesus.

1 Peter 2:20-25 NIV

20 If you suffer for doing good and you endure it, this is
commendable before God. 21 To this you were called, because Christ suffered for you, leaving you an example, that
you should follow in his steps. 22 "He committed no sin, and
no deceit was found in his mouth." 23 When they hurled their
insults at him, he did not retaliate; when he suffered, he
made no threats. Instead, he entrusted himself to him who
judges justly. 24 "He himself bore our sins" in his body on the
cross, so that we might die to sins and live for righteousness;
"by his wounds you have been healed." 25 For "you were like
sheep going astray," but now you have returned to the Shepherd and Overseer of your souls.

WERE YOU THERE?

I have been crucified with Christ and I no longer live, but Christ lives in me. Galatians 2:20

An old song asks, "Were you there when they crucified my Lord?"

If you believe in Jesus Christ as your Savior, you are there. The Holy Spirit lives in you and connects you to Christ. With him you die to sin; with him you rise to new life. "He himself bore our sins in his body on the tree, so that we might die to sins and live for righteousness; by his wounds you have been healed. For you were like sheep going astray, but now you have returned to the Shepherd and Overseer of your souls" (1 Peter 2:24-25).

During Holy Communion, you are there. By his Spirit, Jesus is present in the Supper whenever it is celebrated. As you chew bread and sip wine, your soul feasts on the body and blood of Christ. "Is not the cup of thanksgiving ...a participation in the blood of Christ? And is not the bread that we break a participation in the body of Christ?" (1 Corinthians 10:16)

When you suffer righteously, you are there. "The sufferings of Christ flow over into our lives" (2 Corinthians 1:5), and we experience "the fellowship of sharing in his sufferings" (Philippians 3:10). "To this you were called, because Christ suffered for you, leaving you an example, that you should follow in his steps" (1 Peter 2:21).

"I have been crucified with Christ and I no longer live, but Christ lives in me. The life I live in the body, I live by faith in the Son of God, who loved me and gave himself for me" (Galatians 2:20).

Sometimes it causes me to tremble.

PRAYER

Lord, we want to know you and the power of your resurrection and the fellowship of sharing in your sufferings (Philippians 3:10). Thank you for uniting us to yourself. Amen.

Part Three

RICHES IN CHRIST

The readings and meditations in Part Three focus on some of the riches that become ours through knowing Jesus. These few meditations cannot cover *all* his benefits—even eternity will not be long enough to know the fullness of God's riches. But we will sample some of the treasures.

Everyone needs to know the benefits of belonging to Jesus. If you don't yet belong to Jesus, you need to know what you are missing. Once you understand the riches available in Christ, you won't want to spend another day without him.

If you already have a living, firsthand relationship with Jesus, you still need to keep listening to what the Bible says about his riches. This will prevent you from taking them for granted. It may also help you to discover and enjoy some blessings that are rightfully yours in Christ but which you have not yet experienced. If you trust Jesus, "all things are yours, and you are of Christ, and Christ is of God" (1 Corinthians 3:22-23).

We count our blessings for our own good but also to honor God. "Praise be to the God and Father of our Lord Jesus Christ, who has blessed us in the heavenly realms with every spiritual blessing in Christ" (Ephesians 1:3).

Romans 8:28-39 ESV

28 And we know that for those who love God all things
work together for good, for those who are called according to
his purpose. 29 For those whom he foreknew he also predestined to be conformed to the image of his Son, in order that
he might be the firstborn among many brothers. 30 And those
whom he predestined he also called, and those whom he
called he also justified, and those whom he justified he also
glorified.

31 What then shall we say to these things? If God is for
us, who can be against us? 32 He who did not spare his own
Son but gave him up for us all, how will he not also with him
graciously give us all things? 33 Who shall bring any charge
against God's elect? It is God who justifies. 34 Who is to
condemn? Christ Jesus is the one who died—more than that,
who was raised—who is at the right hand of God, who indeed is interceding for us. 35 Who shall separate us from the
love of Christ? Shall tribulation, or distress, or persecution,
or famine, or nakedness, or danger, or sword? 36 As it is written, "For your sake we are being killed all the day long; we
are regarded as sheep to be slaughtered."

37 No, in all these things we are more than conquerors
through him who loved us. 38 For I am sure that neither death
nor life, nor angels nor rulers, nor things present nor things
to come, nor powers, 39 nor height nor depth, nor anything
else in all creation, will be able to separate us from the love
of God in Christ Jesus our Lord.

OVERCOMING THE VICTIM MENTALITY

No, in all these things we are more than conquerors through him who loved us. Romans 8:37

Sometimes it is comfortable to be a victim. You get to feel sorry for yourself. You get to throw yourself a pity party and invite others to join. "You poor thing! You really have it rough." We all enjoy a little pity once in a while.

Being a victim also comes in handy when you don't feel like changing. Your troubled childhood, your emotional wounds, your alcoholic spouse, your nasty boss, your painful illness—surely no one should expect much from you, not even God. Who can expect you to move ahead in life? Don't you have every right to wallow in self-pity?

Jesus shatters the victim mentality. We're tempted to think of ourselves as helpless lambs being dragged to the slaughter. But faith in Jesus makes us "more than conquerors through him who loved us." Nothing, no matter how painful or powerful, can separate us from God's love in Christ Jesus. That makes us victorious, no matter what.

One of my greatest joys as a pastor has been seeing God's love overcome the victim mentality. People paralyzed by pain and self-pity discover how much God loves them. They find that Christ's riches are greater than their problems, that a victory celebration is more fun than a pity party. They stop using their troubles as an excuse. Instead, they overcome their troubles. Through God's love, they become more than conquerors. And so can you.

PRAYER

Show me, Lord Jesus, the riches of your salvation. Then help me to receive your benefits, enjoy each one, and give you all praise. Amen.

Ephesians 2:1-10 ESV

[1] And you were dead in the trespasses and sins [2] in which you once walked, following the course of this world, following the prince of the power of the air, the spirit that is now at work in the sons of disobedience— [3] among whom we all once lived in the passions of our flesh, carrying out the desires of the body and the mind, and were by nature children of wrath, like the rest of mankind. [4] But God, being rich in mercy, because of the great love with which he loved us, [5] even when we were dead in our trespasses, made us alive together with Christ—by grace you have been saved— [6] and raised us up with him and seated us with him in the heavenly places in Christ Jesus, [7] so that in the coming ages he might show the immeasurable riches of his grace in kindness toward us in Christ Jesus. [8] For by grace you have been saved through faith. And this is not your own doing; it is the gift of God, [9] not a result of works, so that no one may boast. [10] For we are his workmanship, created in Christ Jesus for good works, which God prepared beforehand, that we should walk in them.

FROM DEATH TO LIFE

But God, being rich in mercy, because of the great love with which he loved us, even when we were dead in our trespasses, made us alive together with Christ—by grace you have been saved. Ephesians 2:4-5

According to the Bible, every person without Christ is spiritually dead. But when we look around us, this doesn't ring true. Some people might seem totally corrupt, but many others look like decent people and appear to be very much alive. Isn't it too extreme to say that all people without Jesus are dead in sin?

A carefully embalmed body is less shocking than a badly mangled or decaying corpse. In the same way, one person's sinful condition may be much less obvious and offensive than another's. But a corpse is still a corpse, no matter what cosmetics are used. In the same way, there may be different degrees of spiritual decay, but all are equally dead in sin.

Once a person is dead, the degree of decay makes little difference. Dead is dead. That's why believers talk like this: "On my own, I would ignore the Bible and be indifferent to Christ. But because God's Spirit has breathed new life into my soul, I trust in Jesus and I believe his Word. It is by grace I have been saved."

"You see, at just the right time, when we were still powerless, Christ died for the ungodly... While we were still sinners, Christ died for us" (Romans 5:6, 8). When we were dead and decaying, Jesus overcame sin and death. Then he breathed the life of his Spirit into our souls and created in us the faith to accept him. We did nothing. God has done it all.

PRAYER

Thank you, Father, for your love. Thank you, Jesus, for dying our death and raising us to life with you. Thank you, Holy Spirit, for bringing this life into our hearts. Amen.

1 Thessalonians 5:1-11 ESV

Now concerning the times and the seasons, brothers, you
have no need to have anything written to you. 2 For you
yourselves are fully aware that the day of the Lord will come
like a thief in the night. 3 While people are saying, "There is
peace and security," then sudden destruction will come upon
them as labor pains come upon a pregnant woman, and they
will not escape. 4 But you are not in darkness, brothers, for
that day to surprise you like a thief. 5 For you are all children
of light, children of the day. We are not of the night or of the
darkness. 6 So then let us not sleep, as others do, but let us
keep awake and be sober. 7 For those who sleep, sleep at
night, and those who get drunk, are drunk at night. 8 But
since we belong to the day, let us be sober, having put on the
breastplate of faith and love, and for a helmet the hope of
salvation. 9 For God has not destined us for wrath, but to obtain salvation through our Lord Jesus Christ, 10 who died for
us so that whether we are awake or asleep we might live with
him. 11 Therefore encourage one another and build one another up, just as you are doing.

RESCUED FROM HELL

For God has not destined us for wrath, but to obtain salvation through our Lord Jesus Christ, who died for us so that ... we might live with him. 1 Thessalonians 5:9-10

No one can escape hell by pretending it is not real. Those who comfort themselves with sweet sayings about peace and safety are in for a dreadful disappointment. God's wrath against sin is fierce, and it lasts forever. The second coming of Jesus will be sudden and terrifying for those who do not believe in him as Savior. They will face an eternity of horror.

In God's great plan, however, not every sinner is destined for hell. Jesus was forsaken by his heavenly Father on the cross. He suffered the awful torments of God's wrath against sin, enduring the agony of hell. Jesus did this so that sinners could be shielded from the wrath of God. Jesus paid the penalty of sin so that his people would not have to.

Jesus died so that we might live through him. No one who trusts in the saving power of Jesus' sacrifice will ever have to endure God's wrath. God does not appoint his chosen people for wrath but for salvation through Jesus. Therefore, we who trust in Jesus do not have to fear the sudden return of Jesus to judge the living and the dead.

What a relief to know that God has not appointed me for wrath but for salvation in Jesus! I have been spared an eternity of suffering by the infinite suffering of God's Son on the cross. Jesus suffered hell in my place. Such sacrificial love staggers my imagination, and I will never be able to thank him enough.

PRAYER

Thank you, Lord, for rescuing me from the wrath to come. Please touch the hearts of many who do not yet know you, so that they too may rejoice in your salvation. Amen.

1 Kings 18:25-39

[25] Elijah said to the prophets of Baal, "Choose one bull for yourselves, and dress it first; for you are many; and call on the name of your god, but put no fire under it."

[26] They took the bull which was given them, and they dressed it, and called on the name of Baal from morning even until noon, saying, "Baal, hear us!" But there was no voice, and nobody answered. They leaped about the altar which was made. [27] At noon, Elijah mocked them, and said, "Cry aloud; for he is a god. Either he is deep in thought, or he has gone somewhere, or he is on a journey, or perhaps he sleeps and must be awakened." [28] They cried aloud, and cut themselves in their way with knives and lances, until the blood gushed out on them. [29] When midday was past, they prophesied until the time of the evening offering; but there was no voice, no answer, and nobody paid attention.

[30] Elijah said to all the people, "Come near to me!"; and all the people came near to him. He repaired the altar of Yahweh that had been thrown down… [33] He put the wood in order, and cut the bull in pieces, and laid it on the wood. He said, "Fill four jars with water, and pour it on the burnt offering, and on the wood." [34] He said, "Do it a second time"; and they did it the second time. He said, "Do it a third time"; and they did it the third time. [35] The water ran around the altar; and he also filled the trench with water.

[36] At the time of the evening offering, Elijah the prophet came near, and said, "Yahweh, the God of Abraham, of Isaac, and of Israel, let it be known today that you are God in Israel, and that I am your servant, and that I have done all these things at your word. [37] Hear me, Yahweh, hear me, that this people may know that you, Yahweh, are God, and that you have turned their heart back again."

[38] Then Yahweh's fire fell, and consumed the burnt offering, the wood, the stones, and the dust, and licked up the water that was in the trench. [39] When all the people saw it, they fell on their faces. They said, "Yahweh, he is God! Yahweh, he is God!"

GETTING GOD'S ATTENTION

The Lord is far from the wicked but he hears the prayer of the righteous. Proverbs 15:29

God does not listen to everyone. If you trust any god but Yahweh, you can pray all day, you can dance around in worship, you can even make yourself bleed, but God pays no attention. You are crying out to the wrong god. Also, if you pray to the true God but persist in pride and sin, prayer is a waste of breath. God says, "When you spread out your hands in prayer, I will hide my eyes from you; even if you offer many prayers, I will not listen" (Isaiah 1:14-15).

Christians do not pray to just any god. We pray to the Father of our Lord Jesus. And, wonder of wonders, he listens! The ruler of the universe pays careful attention to tiny humans who speak to him in faith. Jesus gives his followers unlimited access to God by removing the barrier of sin between us and God. "Let us then approach the throne of grace with confidence, so that we may receive mercy and find grace to help us in our time of need" (Hebrews 4:16).

When God's people talk, he listens. It's that simple. Elijah did not need wild rituals, or fancy words, or special methods, or vivid mental images to get God's attention. He prayed a simple prayer to the one true God. He spoke from a heart dedicated to God. And God paid attention. You and I can be sure that God pays attention to us, too. Jesus says, "I will do whatever you ask in my name, so that the Father may be glorified in the Son. You may ask me for anything in my name, and I will do it" (John 14:13-14 NIV).

PRAYER

Thank you, Lord, for listening to me. Keep me from sins that might hinder my prayers. Thank you, Jesus, for providing free access to God. In your name, Amen.

Matthew 12:22-37 NIV

22 Then they brought him a demon-possessed man who was blind and mute, and Jesus healed him, so that he could both talk and see. 23 All the people were astonished and said, "Could this be the Son of David?"

24 But when the Pharisees heard this, they said, "It is only by Beelzebul, the prince of demons, that this fellow drives out demons."

25 Jesus knew their thoughts and said to them, "Every kingdom divided against itself will be ruined, and every city or household divided against itself will not stand. 26 If Satan drives out Satan, he is divided against himself. How then can his kingdom stand? 27 And if I drive out demons by Beelzebul, by whom do your people drive them out? So then, they will be your judges. 28 But if it is by the Spirit of God that I drive out demons, then the kingdom of God has come upon you.

29 "Or again, how can anyone enter a strong man's house and carry off his possessions unless he first ties up the strong man? Then he can plunder his house.

30 "Whoever is not with me is against me, and whoever does not gather with me scatters. 31 And so I tell you, every kind of sin and slander can be forgiven, but blasphemy against the Spirit will not be forgiven. 32 Anyone who speaks a word against the Son of Man will be forgiven, but anyone who speaks against the Holy Spirit will not be forgiven, either in this age or in the age to come.

33 "Make a tree good and its fruit will be good, or make a tree bad and its fruit will be bad, for a tree is recognized by its fruit. 34 You brood of vipers, how can you who are evil say anything good? For the mouth speaks what the heart is full of. 35 A good man brings good things out of the good stored up in him, and an evil man brings evil things out of the evil stored up in him. 36 But I tell you that everyone will have to give account on the day of judgment for every empty word they have spoken. 37 For by your words you will be acquitted, and by your words you will be condemned."

BINDING THE STRONG MAN

"Or again, how can anyone enter a strong man's house and carry off his possessions unless he first ties up the strong man? Then he can plunder his house." Matthew 12:29

Many of our troubles involve sin. But there is more behind these sins than just a choice to do wrong. We face a deadly illness, an overwhelming bondage, a force stronger than we are. Spiritual sickness and slavery are Satan's specialties. He often uses methods much more subtle than outright demon possession. Every day, people find that they cannot escape alcoholism or fits of rage or sexual misbehavior in their own strength. Human effort cannot overcome the dread power of Satan. There is no use condemning ourselves for a lack of willpower. We can't help it if Satan is stronger than we are. Every attempt to change will only be frustrating until someone binds the power that is destroying us.

We need a power greater than ourselves, and greater than Satan, to free us and heal us. So we must admit our helplessness and entrust our lives to Jesus. Christ can overpower Satan, bind him, and set us free from every kind of sickness and slavery. Most bondage is not a case of actual possession by a particular demon, so deliverance does not always involve a dramatic exorcism. But the liberation is real.

In surrender to Christ, we find that destructive behavior is no longer dominating our lives. Each day our freedom grows and flourishes as we depend on God's power, in fellowship with other people he has liberated. Satan's reign of terror is over.

PRAYER

Lord Jesus, without you we are at Satan's mercy—and he has no mercy. Destroy the devil's power over us; free us from slavery and heal our sickness by your Spirit. Amen.

1 John 1:1-2:2 NIV

1 That which was from the beginning, which we have heard, which we have seen with our eyes, which we have looked at and our hands have touched—this we proclaim concerning the Word of life. 2 The life appeared; we have seen it and testify to it, and we proclaim to you the eternal life, which was with the Father and has appeared to us. 3 We proclaim to you what we have seen and heard, so that you also may have fellowship with us. And our fellowship is with the Father and with his Son, Jesus Christ. 4 We write this to make our joy complete.

5 This is the message we have heard from him and declare to you: God is light; in him there is no darkness at all. 6 If we claim to have fellowship with him and yet walk in the darkness, we lie and do not live out the truth. 7 But if we walk in the light, as he is in the light, we have fellowship with one another, and the blood of Jesus, his Son, purifies us from all sin.

8 If we claim to be without sin, we deceive ourselves and the truth is not in us. 9 If we confess our sins, he is faithful and just and will forgive us our sins and purify us from all unrighteousness. 10 If we claim we have not sinned, we make him out to be a liar and his word is not in us.

2:1 My dear children, I write this to you so that you will not sin. But if anybody does sin, we have an advocate with the Father—Jesus Christ, the Righteous One. 2 He is the atoning sacrifice for our sins, and not only for ours but also for the sins of the whole world.

COMING CLEAN

He who conceals his sins does not prosper, but whoever confesses and renounces them finds mercy. Proverbs 28:13

Do you know any child who willingly tells his sister "I'm sorry" without a nudge and perhaps a threat from his parents? "Tell your sister you're sorry—or else!" For that matter, when is the last time *you* said "I'm sorry" to anyone? Apologies don't come naturally. We seldom see how we have been wrong, and even if we do, we don't like admitting it to anyone else.

That's a serious problem. "He who conceals his sin does not prosper." Our relationships with other people do not prosper if we never admit we are wrong. Our relationship with God does not prosper unless we confess and renounce our sins. The longer we hide our sins, the more miserable we become (Psalm 32:3-4).

Confession does not come naturally. But it can come supernaturally. When God's light shines on us, we are able to come clean. We stop deceiving ourselves. We stop calling God a liar. "Therefore confess your sins to each other and pray for each other" (James 5:16). With God's help, make a list of the sins against God and others that you have not yet confessed. Then confess to God and to those you've wronged. Come clean. "If we confess our sins, he is faithful and just and will forgive us our sins and purify us from all unrighteousness" (1 John 1:9). As we bring our sins into the light, we experience God's mercy and forgiveness. "We have fellowship with one another, and the blood of Jesus, his Son, purifies us from all sin" (1 John 1:7).

PRAYER

Lord, show me how I have offended you and hurt others. Then move me to confess to you and to them. Thank you for the mercy and blessing that come through confession. Amen.

Ezekiel 1:4-28 NIV

4 I looked, and I saw a windstorm coming out of the north—an immense cloud with flashing lightning and surrounded by brilliant light. The center of the fire looked like glowing metal, 5 and in the fire was what looked like four living creatures. In appearance their form was human, 6 but each of them had four faces and four wings. 7 Their legs were straight; their feet were like those of a calf and gleamed like burnished bronze. 8 Under their wings on their four sides they had human hands. All four of them had faces and wings, 9 and the wings of one touched the wings of another. Each one went straight ahead; they did not turn as they moved…

13 The appearance of the living creatures was like burning coals of fire or like torches. Fire moved back and forth among the creatures; it was bright, and lightning flashed out of it. 14 The creatures sped back and forth like flashes of lightning…

22 Spread out above the heads of the living creatures was what looked something like a vault, sparkling like crystal, and awesome. 23 Under the vault their wings were stretched out one toward the other, and each had two wings covering its body. 24 When the creatures moved, I heard the sound of their wings, like the roar of rushing waters, like the voice of the Almighty, like the tumult of an army. When they stood still, they lowered their wings.

25 Then there came a voice from above the vault over their heads as they stood with lowered wings. 26 Above the vault over their heads was what looked like a throne of lapis lazuli, and high above on the throne was a figure like that of a man. 27 I saw that from what appeared to be his waist up he looked like glowing metal, as if full of fire, and that from there down he looked like fire; and brilliant light surrounded him. 28 Like the appearance of a rainbow in the clouds on a rainy day, so was the radiance around him.

This was the appearance of the likeness of the glory of the LORD. When I saw it, I fell facedown, and I heard the voice of one speaking.

GLORY

This was the appearance of the likeness of the glory of the Lord. When I saw it, I fell facedown. Ezekiel 1:28

Ezekiel did not see the Lord. He did not see even the glory of the Lord. He saw only "the appearance of the likeness of the glory of the Lord." Ezekiel caught just a glimpse of a glimmer of divine radiance, but that was enough to floor him.

The Lord is awesome. He is "God, the blessed and only Ruler, the King of kings and Lord of lords, who alone is immortal and who lives in unapproachable light, whom no one has seen nor can see. To him be honor and might forever. Amen." (1 Timothy 6:15-16)

God gave hints of his glory to his prophets, but his final revelation to us came in his Son, Jesus Christ. "The Word became flesh and made his dwelling among us. We have seen his glory, the glory of the One and Only, who came from the Father, full of grace and truth.... No one has ever seen God, but God the One and Only, who is at the Father's side, has made him known" (John 1:14, 18).

When we trust Jesus and receive his Spirit, our petty plans give way to awestruck reverence. "For God, who said, 'Let light shine out of darkness,' made his light shine in our hearts to give us the light of the knowledge of the glory of God in the face of Christ" (2 Corinthians 4:6). As his glory fills us and thrills us, we worship his majesty. What a privilege!

PRAYER

Our Father, who art in heaven, hallowed be thy name. "Now to the King eternal, immortal, invisible, the only God, be honor and glory for ever and ever. Amen." (1 Timothy 1:17)

Ezekiel 36:22-28

22 Therefore tell the house of Israel, Thus says the Lord Yahweh: I don't do this for your sake, house of Israel, but for my holy name, which you have profaned among the nations, where you went. 23 I will sanctify my great name, which has been profaned among the nations, which you have profaned among them; and the nations shall know that I am Yahweh, says the Lord Yahweh, when I shall be sanctified in you before their eyes. 24 For I will take you from among the nations, and gather you out of all the countries, and will bring you into your own land. 25 I will sprinkle clean water on you, and you shall be clean: from all your filthiness, and from all your idols, will I cleanse you. 26 I will also give you a new heart, and I will put a new spirit within you; and I will take away the stony heart out of your flesh, and I will give you a heart of flesh. 27 I will put my Spirit within you, and cause you to walk in my statutes, and you shall keep my ordinances, and do them. 28 You shall dwell in the land that I gave to your fathers; and you shall be my people, and I will be your God.

HEART TRANSPLANT

"I will also give you a new heart, and I will put a new spirit within you; and I will take away the stony heart out of your flesh, and I will give you a heart of flesh." Ezekiel 36:26

"I guess I was born that way—that's just the way I am." Some people use that statement to claim that any tendency is good so long as you were born with it. You can't help the way God made you. If you are stubborn or hot-tempered, that's just a family trait. If you grew up having homosexual desires, God must want you to act on your impulses.

Such thinking ignores a basic truth of the Bible. There is more to each human being than divinely created innocence. We are created in God's image with many marvelous capabilities, but we have also been born with a sinful nature. Sin twists our identity and personality from our very first moments of life. The fact some of my desires and habits go back as far as I can remember does not make them right. I was born with a stone-cold heart, and my natural tendency is to center on what I want rather than on what God wants. If I'm born with a bad heart, then bad actions will come naturally to me unless I get a new heart. Jesus says, "An evil man brings evil things out of the evil stored up in his heart" (Luke 6:45).

I can't change the way I am. But God can change me. His Spirit has given me a heart transplant. I was born sinful, but through Jesus I have been born again. I started out with a bad heart, but after being born again, I have a good heart. Jesus says, "A good man brings good things out of the good stored up in his heart" (Luke 6:45). I have a new life and a new identity in Jesus Christ. Now I don't need to make excuses for the way I was born. Instead, I can live as someone who has been born again and has a good heart.

PRAYER

Lord, I have never been innocent. Help me to stop making excuses. I leave my hard heart at the foot of your cross and rejoice in the new heart you have given me. Amen.

Acts 16:16-34 NIV

16 Once when we were going to the place of prayer, we were met by a female slave who had a spirit by which she predicted the future. She earned a great deal of money for her owners by fortune-telling… Paul said to the spirit, "In the name of Jesus Christ I command you to come out of her!" At that moment the spirit left her.

19 When her owners realized that their hope of making money was gone, they seized Paul and Silas and dragged them into the marketplace to face the authorities… 22 The crowd joined in the attack against Paul and Silas, and the magistrates ordered them to be stripped and beaten with rods. 23 After they had been severely flogged, they were thrown into prison, and the jailer was commanded to guard them carefully. 24 When he received these orders, he put them in the inner cell and fastened their feet in the stocks.

25 About midnight Paul and Silas were praying and singing hymns to God, and the other prisoners were listening to them. 26 Suddenly there was such a violent earthquake that the foundations of the prison were shaken. At once all the prison doors flew open, and everyone's chains came loose. 27 The jailer woke up, and when he saw the prison doors open, he drew his sword and was about to kill himself because he thought the prisoners had escaped. 28 But Paul shouted, "Don't harm yourself! We are all here!"

29 The jailer called for lights, rushed in and fell trembling before Paul and Silas. 30 He then brought them out and asked, "Sirs, what must I do to be saved?"

31 They replied, "Believe in the Lord Jesus, and you will be saved—you and your household." 32 Then they spoke the word of the Lord to him and to all the others in his house. 33 At that hour of the night the jailer took them and washed their wounds; then immediately he and all his household were baptized. 34 The jailer brought them into his house and set a meal before them; he was filled with joy because he had come to believe in God—he and his whole household.

FROM DESPAIR TO DELIGHT

He drew his sword and was about to kill himself... He was filled with joy because he had come to believe in God—he and his whole household. Acts 16:27,34

The jailer thought suicide was the only way out. He had fallen asleep while a couple of odd prisoners were singing songs even after a terrible beating. When he was jolted awake, the prison doors were open. The jailer was all shook up. He was ashamed and afraid. He had failed miserably. His superiors would probably torture him and then kill him. Suicide seemed to make a lot of sense.

Soon, though, he learned that the situation was not as bad as he had thought. He had assumed that all the prisoners had escaped through the open doors, but all were still there. He had overreacted. He had nearly killed himself for nothing.

In that moment of crisis, the jailer realized that those two singing prisoners had something he didn't have. How could he be saved? Paul and Silas gave a simple answer: "Believe on the Lord Jesus, and you will be saved—you and your household."

Many people discover Jesus after a brush with suicidal thoughts. In many cases, they overreact to a situation which is not really as severe as they think. But at the time, everything seems bleak, and all hope is gone. Just in time, however, something stops them from destroying themselves.

Then something wonderful happens. They realize that they are missing something. They start asking questions. Like the jailer, they believe in Jesus. And like the jailer, they are filled with joy because they have come to believe in God. Jesus is the way from despair to delight.

PRAYER

Lord, you have saved many people whose despair nearly destroyed them. Now, Lord Jesus, replace all my dark and self-destructive thoughts with your joy and light. Amen.

Luke 19:1-9

1 Jesus entered and was passing through Jericho. 2 There was a man named Zacchaeus. He was a chief tax collector, and he was rich. 3 He was trying to see who Jesus was, and couldn't because of the crowd, because he was short. 4 He ran on ahead, and climbed up into a sycamore tree to see him, for he was going to pass that way. 5 When Jesus came to the place, he looked up and saw him, and said to him, "Zacchaeus, hurry and come down, for today I must stay at your house." 6 He hurried, came down, and received him joyfully. 7 When they saw it, they all murmured, saying, "He has gone in to lodge with a man who is a sinner."

8 Zacchaeus stood and said to the Lord, "Behold, Lord, half of my goods I give to the poor. If I have cheated anybody of anything, I restore four times as much."

9 Jesus said to him, "Today, salvation has come to this house, because he also is a son of Abraham."

MORE GOOD THAN HARM

"Behold, Lord, half of my goods I give to the poor. If I have cheated anybody of anything, I restore four times as much." Luke 19:8

Zaccheus got rich because he knew how to get more than his fair share of things. But when he met Jesus, Zaccheus changed. He wanted to repay those he had cheated, and he decided to help poor people rather than make them poorer. Zaccheus became a giver rather than a taker.

Still today, Jesus transforms villains into heroes. People who once sold drugs have met Jesus and are now helping victims of addiction to recover. Others were imprisoned for criminal activities, but through the power of Jesus, have become active in prison ministry. Others were hot tempered and cruel, but Jesus made them calm and kind. Still others were selfish and greedy, always taking and never giving. But through Jesus they have found that it is more blessed to give than to receive.

It is an amazing gift to be forgiven for a harmful past. But an equally splendid benefit is that Jesus gives you a new future of helping people rather than hurting them. So wherever it is possible and helpful, make restitution to those you have hurt or cheated. Then give of yourself to help other people.

God has given you resources and skills. He will give you the opportunity to use what you have in order to help others. Then, like Zaccheus, you can enjoy the rich satisfaction of doing more good than harm.

PRAYER

Lord, if I have hurt others, show me the best way to make amends. Thank you for forgiving my sins and helping me to become a force for good through Jesus our Lord. Amen.

Matthew 5:38-48

38 "You have heard that it was said, 'An eye for an eye,
and a tooth for a tooth.' 39 But I tell you, don't resist him who
is evil; but whoever strikes you on your right cheek, turn to
him the other also. 40 If anyone sues you to take away your
coat, let him have your cloak also. 41 Whoever compels you
to go one mile, go with him two. 42 Give to him who asks
you, and don't turn away him who desires to borrow from
you.

43 "You have heard that it was said, 'You shall love your
neighbor and hate your enemy.' 44 But I tell you, love your
enemies, bless those who curse you, do good to those who
hate you, and pray for those who mistreat you and persecute
you, 45 that you may be children of your Father who is in
heaven. For he makes his sun to rise on the evil and the
good, and sends rain on the just and the unjust. 46 For if you
love those who love you, what reward do you have? Don't
even the tax collectors do the same? 47 If you only greet your
friends, what more do you do than others? Don't even the tax
collectors do the same? 48 Therefore you shall be perfect, just
as your Father in heaven is perfect."

LOVING YOUR ENEMIES

"I tell you, love your enemies, bless those who curse you, do good to those who hate you, and pray for those who mistreat you and persecute you, that you may be children of your Father who is in heaven." Matthew 5:44-45

Life without forgiveness is torture. When people have sinned, they often suffer from guilt. When people have been sinned against, they are often tormented by anger and hatred. The gospel of Jesus brings relief to both situations: to sinners and to those who have been sinned against.

If you have been abused or deeply offended, the memories can be as devastating as what actually happened. You may consciously carry a grudge and wish the worst upon the person you hate. Or the memory may be so frightening that you can't even bear to think about what happened. But when you trust in Jesus, you receive power to forgive sins committed against you. Jesus enables you to stop suppressing memories, and he helps you face the awful truth about how deeply you have been hurt. That person who hurt you has been your enemy in a terribly painful way, but you are going to love and pray for him anyway.

Loving your enemies is not a burden but a blessing. You begin to experience new freedom. Your enemy no longer controls your feelings toward him. Hatred is no longer your automatic reflex to a painful memory. Loving your enemies is a gift of God that helps you to experience God's love for you in a deeper and more powerful way. Every time you love an enemy, you realize again that while you were God's enemy, Jesus loved you and died for you (Romans 5:10).

PRAYER

Lord, thank you for freedom from resentment. If I harbor unresolved anger, help me to let go of it. Give my enemy the same joy and blessing that you give me in Christ. Amen.

Ephesians 4:17-32

[17] This I say therefore, and testify in the Lord, that you no longer walk as the rest of the Gentiles also walk, in the futility of their mind, [18] being darkened in their understanding, alienated from the life of God, because of the ignorance that is in them, because of the hardening of their hearts; [19] who having become callous gave themselves up to lust, to work all uncleanness with greediness. [20] But you did not learn Christ that way; [21] if indeed you heard him, and were taught in him, even as truth is in Jesus: [22] that you put away, as concerning your former way of life, the old man, that grows corrupt after the lusts of deceit; [23] and that you be renewed in the spirit of your mind, [24] and put on the new man, who in the likeness of God has been created in righteousness and holiness of truth.

[25] Therefore putting away falsehood, speak truth each one with his neighbor. For we are members of one another. [26] "Be angry, and don't sin." Don't let the sun go down on your wrath, [27] and don't give place to the devil. [28] Let him who stole steal no more; but rather let him labor, producing with his hands something that is good, that he may have something to give to him who has need. [29] Let no corrupt speech proceed out of your mouth, but only what is good for building others up as the need may be, that it may give grace to those who hear. [30] Don't grieve the Holy Spirit of God, in whom you were sealed for the day of redemption. [31] Let all bitterness, wrath, anger, outcry, and slander, be put away from you, with all malice. [32] And be kind to one another, tender hearted, forgiving each other, just as God also in Christ forgave you.

TRIMMING LOOSE ENDS

Don't let the sun go down on your wrath, and don't give place to the devil... And be kind to one another, tender hearted, forgiving each other, just as God also in Christ forgave you. Ephesians 4:26-27, 32

Once upon a time, a couple went to a marriage counselor. The husband complained, "Whenever we disagree, my wife becomes historical."

The counselor interrupted, "You mean she becomes *hysterical*?"

"No," replied the man. "I mean she becomes historical. Any time we argue, she brings up everything I ever did."

When people get historical, relationships unravel. God's Word urges us to take off the old self and to put on the new self. The new life in Christ is like a new set of clothes. Things like honesty, hard work, kindness, and love form the fabric of this clothing. We need to take good care of our new clothes.

When you notice a loose end on a garment, you must deal with it. You don't want to leave the thread dangling, but it is seldom wise simply to grab a loose end and keep pulling on it. You might unravel a lot more material and ruin your clothing. Rather than keep yanking on the thread, you trim the loose end in order to prevent further damage.

Constantly tugging at a grievance can damage our new clothing in Christ and reduce us to the condition of the old, tattered self. However, when we cut our anger short at sundown each day, we prevent the devil from causing our new way of life to unravel. Instead, our relationships flourish, and our new self in Christ remains like new.

PRAYER

Lord, your anger lasts only a moment, but your favor lasts a lifetime (Psalm 30:5). Make me like you. Help me not to stay angry but to begin each day anew. Amen.

Jeremiah 10:2-16 ESV

2 Thus says the LORD:
"Learn not the way of the nations,
nor be dismayed at the signs of the heavens
because the nations are dismayed at them,
3 for the customs of the peoples are vanity.
A tree from the forest is cut down
and worked with an axe by the hands of a craftsman.
4 They decorate it with silver and gold;
they fasten it with hammer and nails
so that it cannot move.
5 Their idols are like scarecrows in a cucumber field,
and they cannot speak;
they have to be carried,
for they cannot walk.
Do not be afraid of them,
for they cannot do harm,
neither is it in them to do good."
6 There is none like you, O LORD;
you are great, and your name is great in might.
7 Who would not fear you, O King of the nations?
For this is your due;
for among all the wise ones of the nations
and in all their kingdoms
there is none like you.
8 They are both stupid and foolish;
the instruction of idols is but wood!
10 But the LORD is the true God;
he is the living God and the everlasting King.
At his wrath the earth quakes,
and the nations cannot endure his indignation.
11 Thus shall you say to them: "The gods who did not make
the heavens and the earth shall perish from the earth and
from under the heavens."
12 It is he who made the earth by his power,
who established the world by his wisdom,
and by his understanding stretched out the heavens.

NOT SCARED OF SCARECROWS

"Their idols are like scarecrows in a cucumber field... Do not be afraid of them, for they cannot do harm, neither is it in them to do good." Jeremiah 10:5

Throughout history, people have depended on various gods to make them happy and successful. Anytime something good happened, the gods were smiling. Whenever disaster came, the gods were angry. People have agonized, prayed, and even sacrificed their children to keep the gods happy. All this religion has been a waste of time and emotion. "The LORD is the true God; he is the living God and the everlasting King" (Jeremiah 10:10). Everything else is just a scarecrow. The living God, the Holy Trinity of Father, Son, and Holy Spirit, reigns supreme.

When we know that one great God created and controls all things, we are set free from superstition. Horoscopes are a hoax. The number 13 is harmless. Various tribal gods are garbage. "They cannot do harm, neither is it in them to do good" (Jeremiah 10:5). Their charms cannot help their worshippers. Their curses cannot hurt God's people. Many people who once followed traditional religious customs and feared gods, spirits, and witchcraft have been freed from fear by knowing the true Lord.

Jesus is real. He is no superstition. He will judge the world and save all who believe in him. Faith in Jesus restores us to true worship and frees us from false hopes and foolish fears. We take the true God seriously, and nothing else. When we revere "the true God, the living God, the everlasting King," we stop being scared of scarecrows.

PRAYER

"There is none like you, O LORD; you are great, and your name is great in might" (Jeremiah 10:6). We honor you, and we thank you for freeing us from superstition. Amen.

John 4:7-29 NIV

7 When a Samaritan woman came to draw water, Jesus said to her, “Will you give me a drink?” 8 (His disciples had gone into the town to buy food.)

9 The Samaritan woman said to him, “You are a Jew and I am a Samaritan woman. How can you ask me for a drink?” (For Jews do not associate with Samaritans.)

10 Jesus answered her, “If you knew the gift of God and who it is that asks you for a drink, you would have asked him and he would have given you living water.... Whoever drinks the water I give them will never thirst. Indeed, the water I give them will become in them a spring of water welling up to eternal life.”

15 The woman said to him, “Sir, give me this water so that I won’t get thirsty and have to keep coming here to draw water.”

16 He told her, “Go, call your husband and come back.”

17 “I have no husband,” she replied.

Jesus said to her, “You are right when you say you have no husband. 18 The fact is, you have had five husbands, and the man you now have is not your husband. What you have just said is quite true.”

19 “Sir,” the woman said, “I can see that you are a prophet. 20 Our ancestors worshiped on this mountain, but you Jews claim that the place where we must worship is in Jerusalem.”

21 “Woman,” Jesus replied, “believe me, a time is coming when you will worship the Father neither on this mountain nor in Jerusalem... 24 God is spirit, and his worshipers must worship in the Spirit and in truth.”

25 The woman said, “I know that Messiah” (called Christ) “is coming. When he comes, he will explain everything to us.” 26 Then Jesus declared, “I, the one speaking to you—I am he.” ...

28 Then, leaving her water jar, the woman went back to the town and said to the people, 29 “Come, see a man who told me everything I ever did. Could this be the Messiah?”

JESUS KNOWS

"Come, see a man who told me everything I ever did. Could this be the Messiah?" John 4:29

Even the most harmless small talk can poke into areas we would rather not talk about. When someone asks, "How are you?" what do you say if you feel rotten? Often you force a smile and say, "I'm fine. How are you?" When someone asks what you do for a living, you might just say, "Oh, I'm in construction." You'd rather not mention the fact that you've been out of work for three months.

When a total stranger says, "Hey, I'd like to meet your husband," what do you say? If you've been divorced five times and are now living with somebody else, nobody can blame you for simply saying, "I don't have a husband." You don't feel like explaining. Why give a stranger all the details of the broken promises and shattered dreams? Your shame and pain are none of his business, and he wouldn't understand anyway.

But this man already knows your hurts, your failures, and your sins. He knows every dark corner of your life, and yet he has not rejected you. Instead, he is still talking to you, offering you living water. When Jesus says he can quench your thirst and empower you to live forever, you begin to believe him. He knows every mess you've made, every embarrassment you've caused or suffered, yet he is inviting you to be one of the worshipers God is seeking. If he knows you so thoroughly and still cares about you so deeply, he just might be the Messiah you have been looking for. This is too good to keep to yourself. "Come, see a man who told me everything I ever did. Could this be the Messiah?" (John 4:29)

PRAYER

Lord Jesus, with you we have no secrets. Thank you for probing our painful areas and cleansing our guilt. Refresh us with the living water of your Holy Spirit. Amen.

Ephesians 2:11-22 NIV

[11] Therefore, remember that formerly you who are Gentiles by birth and called "uncircumcised" by those who call themselves "the circumcision" (which is done in the body by human hands)— [12] remember that at that time you were separate from Christ, excluded from citizenship in Israel and foreigners to the covenants of the promise, without hope and without God in the world. [13] But now in Christ Jesus you who once were far away have been brought near by the blood of Christ.

[14] For he himself is our peace, who has made the two groups one and has destroyed the barrier, the dividing wall of hostility, [15] by setting aside in his flesh the law with its commands and regulations. His purpose was to create in himself one new humanity out of the two, thus making peace, [16] and in one body to reconcile both of them to God through the cross, by which he put to death their hostility. [17] He came and preached peace to you who were far away and peace to those who were near. [18] For through him we both have access to the Father by one Spirit.

[19] Consequently, you are no longer foreigners and strangers, but fellow citizens with God's people and also members of his household, [20] built on the foundation of the apostles and prophets, with Christ Jesus himself as the chief cornerstone. [21] In him the whole building is joined together and rises to become a holy temple in the Lord. [22] And in him you too are being built together to become a dwelling in which God lives by his Spirit.

A PLACE TO BELONG

You are no longer foreigners and strangers, but fellow citizens with God's people and also members of his household. Ephesians 2:19

People tend to be tribal. We associate with others like us but avoid those who are different.

Jesus breaks down walls of tribalism. He brings into his church people who are otherwise very different. Jesus calls Jews and Gentiles. Jesus calls people from every racial and national background. Jesus calls women and men, boys and girls. Jesus calls rich and poor. Jesus calls people who have very different political convictions. Among his first disciples, Matthew was a collaborator with the Romans who occupied Israel, while Simon the Zealot was an anti-Roman extremist. Jesus shatters every social barrier that divides us.

One of the supreme benefits of salvation is a sense of belonging: you belong to God, and you belong to his church. If you are from a background that is different from most people in your local church, you still belong to the fellowship of believers every bit as much as they do. If you are a brand new Christian, you are just as much a part of the church as long-time members. If you trust Jesus, you belong.

The church is not an elite social club but a spiritual fellowship. Our unity is not based on social similarity. We are united by Jesus Christ through the teaching of his prophets and apostles. We are all fellow citizens and members of God's household. We belong.

PRAYER

Thank you, Lord Jesus, for removing our divisions and making us part of your church. Help me to sense your welcome and to extend that same welcome to others. Amen.

Joshua 1:1-9

1 Now after the death of Moses the servant of Yahweh,
Yahweh spoke to Joshua the son of Nun, Moses' servant,
saying, 2 "Moses my servant is dead. Now therefore arise, go
across this Jordan, you, and all these people, to the land
which I am giving to them, even to the children of Israel. 3 I
have given you every place that the sole of your foot will
tread on, as I told Moses. 4 From the wilderness, and this
Lebanon, even to the great river, the river Euphrates, all the
land of the Hittites, and to the great sea toward the going
down of the sun, shall be your border. 5 No man will be able
to stand before you all the days of your life. As I was with
Moses, so I will be with you. I will not fail you nor forsake
you.

6 "Be strong and courageous; for you shall cause this
people to inherit the land which I swore to their fathers to
give them. 7 Only be strong and very courageous. Be careful
to observe to do according to all the law, which Moses my
servant commanded you. Don't turn from it to the right hand
or to the left, that you may have good success wherever you
go. 8 This book of the law shall not depart from your mouth,
but you shall meditate on it day and night, that you may observe to do according to all that is written in it; for then you
shall make your way prosperous, and then you shall have
good success. 9 Haven't I commanded you? Be strong and
courageous. Don't be afraid. Don't be dismayed, for Yahweh
your God is with you wherever you go."

NEVER ALONE

"I will be with you. I will not fail you nor forsake you... Be strong and courageous. Don't be afraid. Don't be dismayed, for Yahweh your God is with you wherever you go." Joshua 1:5, 9

Moses was dead. Joshua's friend and mentor for more than forty years was gone. The whole nation mourned the passing of Moses for an entire month (Deuteronomy 34:8). Long after that time of intense grief, Joshua would continue to miss Moses. But he had to move on without Moses and take up his responsibilities as leader of the nation. It would be lonely and difficult.

But the Lord showed Joshua that his future peace of mind and success did not depend on Moses. The man of God was dead, but God himself remained very near. He promised Joshua, "I will not fail you nor forsake you."

If you have lost a loved one, you may not be able to imagine a future without someone who meant so much to you. But the Bible shows us that there is life after death, not just for the person who died but for those who must go on living. "Don't be afraid. Don't be dismayed, for Yahweh your God is with you wherever you go."

This benefit of salvation is priceless. When you are lonely, you are not alone. When you feel afraid, divine comfort is nearby. When the task ahead seems impossible, divine power will strengthen you. When you wonder what to do next, God's Word will nourish and guide you. Jesus says, "Surely I am with you always, to the very end of the age" (Matthew 28:20).

PRAYER

Thank you, Father, that you are always near, that nothing can separate me from your love in Christ Jesus. Walk with me wherever I go, and help me to sense your presence. Amen.

Romans 8:9-17

[9] But you are not in the flesh but in the Spirit, if the Spirit of God dwells in you. But if any man doesn't have the Spirit of Christ, he is not his. [10] If Christ is in you, the body is dead because of sin, but the spirit is alive because of righteousness. [11] But if the Spirit of him who raised up Jesus from the dead dwells in you, he who raised up Christ Jesus from the dead will also give life to your mortal bodies through his Spirit who dwells in you. [12] So then, brothers, we are debtors, not to the flesh, to live after the flesh. [13] For if you live after the flesh, you must die; but if by the Spirit you put to death the deeds of the body, you will live. [14] For as many as are led by the Spirit of God, these are children of God. [15] For you didn't receive the spirit of bondage again to fear, but you received the Spirit of adoption, by whom we cry, "Abba! Father!"

[16] The Spirit himself testifies with our spirit that we are children of God; [17] and if children, then heirs; heirs of God, and joint heirs with Christ; if indeed we suffer with him, that we may also be glorified with him.

Galatians 3:26-28, 4:4-7

[3:26] For you are all children of God, through faith in Christ Jesus. [27] For as many of you as were baptized into Christ have put on Christ. [28] There is neither Jew nor Greek, there is neither slave nor free man, there is neither male nor female; for you are all one in Christ Jesus.

[4:4] … when the fullness of the time came, God sent out his Son, born to a woman, born under the law, [5] that he might redeem those who were under the law, that we might receive the adoption of children. [6] And because you are children, God sent out the Spirit of his Son into your hearts, crying, "Abba, Father!" [7] So you are no longer a bondservant, but a son; and if a son, then an heir of God through Christ.

CHILDREN OF GOD

The Spirit himself testifies with our spirit that we are children of God. Romans 8:16

Every Christian is a servant of Christ, subject to his orders. But we are much more than servants—we have been adopted as God's children.

Adoption means *security*. A boss might fire an employee who fails, but a loving father cannot get rid of his own child. "There is no fear in love. But perfect love drives out fear, because fear has to do with punishment" (1 John 4:18). When God adopts us as his children through faith in Christ, we need not fear that he will reject us.

Adoption means *closeness*. Bosses and workers may settle for a businesslike relationship, but a father and child long for warmth and intimacy. God wants his children to obey him, but he also wants us to draw close to him simply because we love him, and he loves us. The Spirit of adoption moves us to call God "Abba," an ancient word for "Daddy." It is a word full of respect and love.

Adoption means *inheritance*. "Now if we are children, then we are heirs—heirs of God and co-heirs with Christ" (Romans 8:17). Everything that belongs to him belongs also to his children. Since our Father is the King, we his children are princes and princesses, and we "will reign forever and ever" (Revelation 22:5). "Do you not know that the saints will judge the world? ...Do you not know that we will judge the angels?" (1 Corinthians 6:2,3).

PRAYER

Father, how great is the love you have lavished upon us, that we should be called children of God! We thank you, Father, for the astonishing privileges of adoption. Amen.

Proverbs 3:1-12

1 My son, don't forget my teaching;
but let your heart keep my commandments:
2 for length of days, and years of life,
and peace, will they add to you.
3 Don't let kindness and truth forsake you.
Bind them around your neck.
Write them on the tablet of your heart.
4 So you will find favor,
and good understanding in the sight of God and man.
5 Trust in Yahweh with all your heart,
and don't lean on your own understanding.
6 In all your ways acknowledge him,
and he will make your paths straight.
7 Don't be wise in your own eyes.
Fear Yahweh, and depart from evil.
8 It will be health to your body,
and nourishment to your bones.
9 Honor Yahweh with your substance,
with the first fruits of all your increase:
10 so your barns will be filled with plenty,
and your vats will overflow with new wine.
11 My son, don't despise Yahweh's discipline,
neither be weary of his reproof:
12 for whom Yahweh loves, he reproves;
even as a father reproves the son in whom he delights.

DISCIPLINE

My son, don't despise Yahweh's discipline, neither be weary of his reproof: for whom Yahweh loves, he reproves; even as a father reproves the son in whom he delights. Proverbs 3:12

If you're an athlete, you need a coach to discipline you. You might rather avoid hard workouts, but a coach pushes you to the limit and drives you to excel: "No pain, no gain."

If you're a child, you need parents to discipline you. If no one makes you do your homework or punishes you for breaking rules, you will not develop into a responsible person. The firm discipline of loving parents can bring out the best in you.

If you are a child of God, you need his discipline. You may prefer all happy times, but God uses disappointment and suffering to cultivate character (Romans 5:3-4). God disciplines you because he cares. Your Father in heaven does not want to raise a spoiled brat; he wants you to grow up to maturity.

"Endure hardship as discipline ... God disciplines us for our good, that we may share in his holiness. No discipline seems pleasant at the time, but painful. Later on, however, it produces a harvest of righteousness and peace for those who have been trained by it" (Hebrews 12:7, 10-11 NIV).

Discipline is painful. You don't have to pretend to enjoy it. But you can still thank God for what he is teaching you, and you can look forward to the end result. Your Father is working to give you not just better self-esteem but a better self. He is shaping you to be like Jesus.

PRAYER

Father, thank you for Jesus, who "learned obedience from what he suffered" (Hebrews 5:8). Teach me that same obedience, and make me more and more like Jesus. Amen.

Numbers 9:15-23

[15] On the day that the tabernacle was raised up, the cloud
covered the tabernacle, even the Tent of the Testimony: and
at evening it was over the tabernacle as it were the appearance of fire, until morning. [16] So it was continually. The
cloud covered it, and the appearance of fire by night.
[17] Whenever the cloud was taken up from over the Tent, then
after that the children of Israel traveled; and in the place
where the cloud remained, there the children of Israel encamped. [18] At the commandment of Yahweh, the children of
Israel traveled, and at the commandment of Yahweh they
encamped. As long as the cloud remained on the tabernacle
they remained encamped. [19] When the cloud stayed on the
tabernacle many days, then the children of Israel kept Yahweh's command, and didn't travel. [20] Sometimes the cloud
was a few days on the tabernacle; then according to the
commandment of Yahweh they remained encamped, and according to the commandment of Yahweh they traveled.
[21] Sometimes the cloud was from evening until morning; and
when the cloud was taken up in the morning, they traveled:
or by day and by night, when the cloud was taken up, they
traveled. [22] Whether it was two days, or a month, or a year
that the cloud stayed on the tabernacle, remaining on it, the
children of Israel remained encamped, and didn't travel; but
when it was taken up, they traveled. [23] At the commandment
of Yahweh they encamped, and at the commandment of
Yahweh they traveled. They kept Yahweh's command, at the
commandment of Yahweh by Moses.

GUIDED BY GOD

For this God is our God for ever and ever; he will be our guide even to the end. Psalm 48:14

The ancient Israelites had little trouble knowing where God wanted them to go next. They just kept an eye on the cloud and followed it. God is still God today, and he has promised to guide his people always. Being guided by God is a tremendous privilege. But he no longer uses a cloud to lead us. So how can we understand God's will for choosing a career, buying a house, finding a marriage partner, or any other decision?

First, before we commit to a career or marriage or make other major choices, we must make a commitment to Jesus. This commitment shapes all other decisions, so we must put it first.

Next, we must be sure that the choices we are considering are within the Bible's guidelines. This will eliminate certain options. The Bible clearly prohibits believers marrying non-Christians, choosing a sleazy career, or spending all their money on extravagant homes while giving nothing to God's work. It is never God's will to violate clear biblical teaching.

However, even if we commit ourselves to Christ and study the Bible, certain decisions are still not clear. The Bible does not print out your spouse's name or your job or the address of the home you should buy. In making such decisions, get advice from wise people, pray for God's leading, and be open to the inner promptings of his Spirit. Then trust him to guide and bless the decisions you make.

PRAYER

Thank you, Father, for guiding me. Lead me by your Spirit in the way of Jesus. Help me to know your plan for me in the decisions that I face and to follow wherever you lead. Amen.

Acts 18:24-28

24 Now a certain Jew named Apollos, an Alexandrian by race, an eloquent man, came to Ephesus. He was mighty in the Scriptures. 25 This man had been instructed in the way of the Lord; and being fervent in spirit, he spoke and taught accurately the things concerning Jesus, although he knew only the baptism of John. 26 He began to speak boldly in the synagogue. But when Priscilla and Aquila heard him, they took him aside, and explained to him the way of God more accurately.

27 When he had determined to pass over into Achaia, the brothers encouraged him, and wrote to the disciples to receive him. When he had come, he greatly helped those who had believed through grace; 28 for he powerfully refuted the Jews, publicly showing by the Scriptures that Jesus was the Christ.

THE DELIGHT OF DISCOVERY

But when Priscilla and Aquila heard him, they took him aside, and explained to him the way of God more accurately. Acts 18:26

Nobody could preach like Apollos. He was bright. He was eloquent. He knew his Bible. His messages were accurate and dynamic. But Priscilla and Aquila knew something Apollos didn't know, and they decided to tell him. Apollos was more talented than Priscilla and Aquila. He may have been tempted to ignore them. Great speakers are not always good listeners. But Apollos realized that these people of lesser talent had greater insight. So he listened and learned.

Learning is one of the great thrills of the Christian life. You not only gain fresh insights into the Bible, but you also enjoy a deeper awareness of the majesty and love of Jesus Christ through his Spirit. You are never too talented or too advanced to learn. As long as you are willing to listen to other Christians, God will lead you to new discoveries.

Sometimes you learn from Christians of ordinary ability but extraordinary insight. In a group discussion or in a personal conversation, you hear powerful truths you did not grasp before, and you rejoice at the discovery. At other times, God uses specially gifted communicators. Apollos, with his powerful talent and vast learning, "was a great help to those who by grace had believed" (Acts 18:27). Getting to know God better is always a delight, whether it happens through a powerful and persuasive communicator or through ordinary Christians.

PRAYER

Lord, I want to know you better. Thank you, Holy Spirit, for special people you use in my life to teach me the Way more adequately. Help me enrich others too. Amen.

Isaiah 8:11-22

11 For Yahweh spoke thus to me with a strong hand, and instructed me not to walk in the way of this people, saying, 12 "Don't say, 'A conspiracy!' concerning all about which this people say, 'A conspiracy!' neither fear their threats, nor be terrorized. 13 Yahweh of Armies is who you must respect as holy. He is the one you must fear. He is the one you must dread. 14 He will be a sanctuary, but for both houses of Israel, he will be a trap and a snare for the inhabitants of Jerusalem. 15 Many will stumble over it, fall, be broken, be snared, and be captured."

16 Wrap up the testimony. Seal the law among my disciples. 17 I will wait for Yahweh, who hides his face from the house of Jacob, and I will look for him. 18 Behold, I and the children whom Yahweh has given me are for signs and for wonders in Israel from Yahweh of Armies, who dwells in Mount Zion.

19 When they tell you, "Consult with those who have familiar spirits and with the wizards, who chirp and who mutter," shouldn't a people consult with their God? Should they consult the dead on behalf of the living? 20 Turn to the law and to the testimony! If they don't speak according to this word, surely there is no morning for them. 21 They will pass through it, very distressed and hungry; and it will happen that when they are hungry, they will worry, and curse their king and their God. They will turn their faces upward, 22 and look to the earth, and see distress, darkness, and the gloom of anguish. They will be driven into thick darkness.

SOMETHING TO BELIEVE IN

Turn to the law and to the testimony! If they don't speak according to this word, surely there is no morning for them. Isaiah 8:20

Religious gurus seem to be everywhere. A host of preachers claim to receive visions and messages directly from God. But their messages are very different. As a broadcaster, I received letters from several people claiming to be the last true prophet on earth. Obviously, they couldn't all be right!

God gave us a tremendous gift when he gave us the Bible. Otherwise we would live in hopeless confusion. With so many ideas floating around, we need something as our standard. God has not left us guessing. We can use a test: if an idea contradicts the Bible, it does not come from the Lord. "Turn to the law and to the testimony! If they don't speak according to this word, surely there is no morning for them" (Isaiah 8:20).

This test does not solve every dispute. The pages of the Bible "contain some things that are hard to understand" (2 Peter 3:16). But even if we struggle to understand some things, we can remain certain of the essential truths about God, about salvation through Jesus, and about Christian living.

When God gave us the Bible, he gave us something to believe in. The Bible teaches truth. The Bible teaches everything God wants us to know about him. We can safely ignore the gurus, and believe the Word.

PRAYER

Father, "your word is a lamp to my feet and a light for my path" (Psalm 119:105). Protect me from lies and confusion. Help me believe and live according to your Word. Amen.

Acts 1:1-11 ESV

1 In the first book, O Theophilus, I have dealt with all
that Jesus began to do and teach, 2 until the day when he was
taken up, after he had given commands through the Holy
Spirit to the apostles whom he had chosen. 3 He presented
himself alive to them after his suffering by many proofs, ap-
pearing to them during forty days and speaking about the
kingdom of God.

4 And while staying with them he ordered them not to
depart from Jerusalem, but to wait for the promise of the Father, which, he said, "you heard from me; 5 for John baptized
with water, but you will be baptized with the Holy Spirit not
many days from now."

6 So when they had come together, they asked him,
"Lord, will you at this time restore the kingdom to Israel?"
7 He said to them, "It is not for you to know times or seasons
that the Father has fixed by his own authority. 8 But you will
receive power when the Holy Spirit has come upon you, and
you will be my witnesses in Jerusalem and in all Judea and
Samaria, and to the end of the earth." 9 And when he had said
these things, as they were looking on, he was lifted up, and a
cloud took him out of their sight. 10 And while they were
gazing into heaven as he went, behold, two men stood by
them in white robes, 11 and said, "Men of Galilee, why do
you stand looking into heaven? This Jesus, who was taken up
from you into heaven, will come in the same way as you saw
him go into heaven."

REIGNING AND RETURNING

"This Jesus, who was taken up from you into heaven, will come in the same way as you saw him go into heaven." Acts 1:11

When Jesus went up into the air and disappeared in a cloud, his followers kept gazing upward, wondering what had happened. They soon got the answer: Jesus had gone into heaven. Heaven isn't just a nicer planet in a distant galaxy. Heaven is the realm of the eternal, the place of direct, unclouded contact with the Father. Jesus entered heaven in his glorified body and will remain there until he comes again and brings heaven to earth.

By ascending to heaven, Jesus took charge of all things. Shortly before he left earth, he said, "All authority in heaven and on earth has been given to me" (Matthew 28:18). God "seated him at his right hand in the heavenly realms, far above all rule and authority, power and dominion, and every title that can be given, not only in the present age but in the one to come. And God placed all things under his feet" (Ephesians 1:20-22).

All things! Every moment you live, every relationship you have, every decision you make, every dollar you spend, every subject you study, every job you do, every game you play, belongs under the rule of Christ. There is not one square inch of your life of which Jesus does not say, "Mine!" Jesus reigns on the throne of heaven. Do you honor him on the throne of your life? If so, you can enjoy his riches now and gladly welcome him when he returns.

PRAYER

King Jesus, all authority is yours! Reign over all things, and reign over me. Thank you that you are preparing a heavenly home for us. Come quickly, Lord. Amen.

John 17 NIV

1 After Jesus said this, he looked toward heaven and
prayed:

"Father, the hour has come. Glorify your Son, that your
Son may glorify you. 2 For you granted him authority over all
people that he might give eternal life to all those you have
given him. 3 Now this is eternal life: that they know you, the
only true God, and Jesus Christ, whom you have sent. 4 I
have brought you glory on earth by finishing the work you
gave me to do. 5 And now, Father, glorify me in your presence with the glory I had with you before the world began…

13 "I am coming to you now, but I say these things while I
am still in the world, so that they may have the full measure
of my joy within them. 14 I have given them your word and
the world has hated them, for they are not of the world any
more than I am of the world. 15 My prayer is not that you
take them out of the world but that you protect them from the
evil one… Sanctify them by the truth; your word is truth.
18 As you sent me into the world, I have sent them into the
world...

20 "My prayer is not for them alone. I pray also for those
who will believe in me through their message, 21 that all of
them may be one, Father, just as you are in me and I am in
you. May they also be in us so that the world may believe
that you have sent me. 22 I have given them the glory that you
gave me, that they may be one as we are one— 23 I in them
and you in me—so that they may be brought to complete
unity. Then the world will know that you sent me and have
loved them even as you have loved me.

24 "Father, I want those you have given me to be with me
where I am, and to see my glory, the glory you have given
me because you loved me before the creation of the world.

25 "Righteous Father, though the world does not know
you, I know you, and they know that you have sent me. 26 I
have made you known to them, and will continue to make
you known in order that the love you have for me may be in
them and that I myself may be in them."

SEEING HIS GLORY

"Father, I want those you have given me to be with me where I am and to see my glory." John 17:24

Years after Jesus ascended to heaven, he appeared to his old friend John and gave him a glimpse of his glory. "His face was like the sun shining in all its brilliance." It was too much for John to take, and he fell at Jesus' feet as though dead. Jesus touched his friend and said, "Do not be afraid" (Revelation 1:16-17).

A long, direct look at the sun would blind us, and a long, direct look at the glory of Jesus would be too much for us in our present condition. But that will change. Jesus wants his Father to give us a place in heaven that we may see Jesus' glory and enjoy his splendor forever. The Holy Spirit promises, "They will see his face... They will not need the light of a lamp or the light of the sun, for the Lord God will give them light. And they will reign for ever and ever" (Revelation 22:4-5).

I will see God's glory in Christ and won't have to shield my eyes. I will reign with Jesus and feel at home on a throne. It sounds outrageous—but this is the Father's will, this is the Holy Spirit's work, this is what Jesus wants. This will happen because God lives in me and loves me with the same love that the Father has for Jesus (John 17:23,26). God glorifies himself not by keeping his glory to himself but by sharing his glory and making us "partakers of the divine nature" (2 Peter 1:4).

PRAYER

Lord, give us faith to share in your sufferings that we may also share in your glory. Unite us to fellow believers and to yourself in eternal love. Amen.

2 Corinthians 4:13-5:10 ESV

13 Since we have the same spirit of faith according to
what has been written, “I believed, and so I spoke,” we also
believe, and so we also speak, 14 knowing that he who raised
the Lord Jesus will raise us also with Jesus and bring us with
you into his presence. 15 For it is all for your sake, so that as
grace extends to more and more people it may increase
thanksgiving, to the glory of God.

16 So we do not lose heart. Though our outer self is wast-
ing away, our inner self is being renewed day by day. 17 For
this light momentary affliction is preparing for us an eternal
weight of glory beyond all comparison, 18 as we look not to
the things that are seen but to the things that are unseen. For
the things that are seen are transient, but the things that are
unseen are eternal.

5:1 For we know that if the tent that is our earthly home is
destroyed, we have a building from God, a house not made
with hands, eternal in the heavens. 2 For in this tent we
groan, longing to put on our heavenly dwelling, 3 if indeed
by putting it on we may not be found naked. 4 For while we
are still in this tent, we groan, being burdened—not that we
would be unclothed, but that we would be further clothed, so
that what is mortal may be swallowed up by life. 5 He who
has prepared us for this very thing is God, who has given us
the Spirit as a guarantee.

6 So we are always of good courage. We know that while
we are at home in the body we are away from the Lord, 7 for
we walk by faith, not by sight. 8 Yes, we are of good courage, and we would rather be away from the body and at
home with the Lord. 9 So whether we are at home or away,
we make it our aim to please him. 10 For we must all appear
before the judgment seat of Christ, so that each one may receive what is due for what he has done in the body, whether
good or evil.

TO DIE IS GAIN

For to me, to live is Christ and to die is gain. Philippians 1:21

Paul "would rather be away from the body and at home with the Lord." The great missionary loved living in his body, working for Jesus and helping others. But Paul knew that when death destroyed his body, Jesus would be waiting to welcome his soul home. That thought thrilled him.

After Paul died, his spirit would exist without a body ("this tent") until he got a glorified body on resurrection day ("a building from God"). The thought of not having a body for awhile didn't appeal to Paul ("we do not wish to be unclothed"). But his misgivings about leaving his body behind were overwhelmed by his eagerness to be at home with his dear Lord.

If you trust and love Jesus, you can't lose. You spend your time in the body gladly living for him on earth. When you die and leave your body, your spirit will instantly be at home with the Lord in heaven. "To live is Christ, and to die is gain." Eventually, when Jesus returns, your body will be raised to life again, no longer a weak tent but a glorious building from God that is splendid and immortal. Your perfect spirit and splendid body, joined together, will be the true you forever.

Does this mean that once you are a Christian, you will like the thought of dying? No, the possible pain of it may frighten you. The thought of existing without a body for awhile may trouble you. Fears of the unknown may nag you. But despite all that, dying is still gain. The instant you die, your spirit will be with Jesus. Your suffering will be over. You will be enjoying something too magnificent for words.

PRAYER

Lord Jesus, I rejoice in you. Fill my life in this earthly body with fruitful service to you and others. Help me see the great gain in dying and going home to you. Amen.

Revelation 21:9-27

9 One of the seven angels … came, and he spoke with me, saying, "Come here. I will show you the wife, the Lamb's bride." 10 He carried me away in the Spirit to a great and high mountain, and showed me the holy city, Jerusalem, coming down out of heaven from God, 11 having the glory of God. Her light was like a most precious stone, as if it were a jasper stone, clear as crystal; 12 having a great and high wall; having twelve gates, and at the gates twelve angels; and names written on them, which are the names of the twelve tribes of the children of Israel... 14 The wall of the city had twelve foundations, and on them twelve names of the twelve Apostles of the Lamb. 15 He who spoke with me had for a measure, a golden reed, to measure the city, its gates, and its walls. 16 The city is square, and its length is as great as its width. He measured the city with the reed, twelve thousand twelve stadia. Its length, width, and height are equal. 17 Its wall is one hundred forty-four cubits, by the measure of a man, that is, of an angel. 18 The construction of its wall was jasper. The city was pure gold, like pure glass. 19 The foundations of the city's wall were adorned with all kinds of precious stones… 21 The twelve gates were twelve pearls. Each one of the gates was made of one pearl. The street of the city was pure gold, like transparent glass. 22 I saw no temple in it, for the Lord God, the Almighty, and the Lamb, are its temple. 23 The city has no need for the sun, neither of the moon, to shine, for the very glory of God illuminated it, and its lamp is the Lamb. 24 The nations will walk in its light. The kings of the earth bring the glory and honor of the nations into it. 25 Its gates will in no way be shut by day (for there will be no night there), 26 and they shall bring the glory and the honor of the nations into it so that they may enter. 27 There will in no way enter into it anything profane, or one who causes an abomination or a lie, but only those who are written in the Lamb's book of life.

A GLIMPSE OF HEAVEN

He carried me away in the Spirit to a great and high mountain, and showed me the holy city, Jerusalem, coming down out of heaven from God, having the glory of God. Revelation 21:10-11

The Bible pictures heavenly happiness in terms of good things we know on earth: banquets and music; rivers, fruit trees, and a paradise of animals living together in peace; mansions, massive walls, gates of pearl, and streets of gold. Some of these splendid pictures may be literal. Others may turn out not to be literal. They are God's way of giving us the nearest hint we can grasp in our present situation.

Imagine you had to describe the taste of ice cream to people who had never eaten anything but oatmeal. How would you do it? You could compare it to the best-tasting oatmeal they'd ever eaten, and their mouths might water. But no oatmeal comparison could prepare them for the delicious flavor of ice cream.

Or suppose you were from Paris and had to describe the Eiffel Tower to people who had never seen any building grander than a mud hut. What would you say? You could compare it to the biggest, most impressive mud hut of their most important chief, and that might impress them. But it still wouldn't capture the splendor of the Eiffel Tower.

How, then, can God describe heaven to earthlings who have never tasted or seen heavenly reality? He uses terms that earthlings can understand: banquets, music, gold, jewels, and so forth. But only when heaven comes to earth will we taste what it's really like. Heaven on earth will be all that Scripture pictures and much more.

PRAYER

Lord, "you will fill me with joy in your presence, with eternal pleasures at your right hand" (Psalm 16:11). Thank you for preparing such a splendid place for us, dear Jesus. Amen.

Revelation 21:1-7, 22:1-5

21:1 I saw a new heaven and a new earth: for the first
heaven and the first earth have passed away, and the sea is
no more. 2 I saw the holy city, New Jerusalem, coming down
out of heaven from God, prepared like a bride adorned for
her husband. 3 I heard a loud voice out of heaven saying,
“Behold, God’s dwelling is with people, and he will dwell
with them, and they will be his people, and God himself will
be with them as their God. 4 He will wipe away from them
every tear from their eyes. Death will be no more; neither
will there be mourning, nor crying, nor pain, any more. The
first things have passed away.”

5 He who sits on the throne said, “Behold, I am making
all things new.” He said, “Write, for these words of God are
faithful and true.” 6 He said to me, “It is done! I am the Al-
pha and the Omega, the Beginning and the End. I will give
freely to him who is thirsty from the spring of the water of
life. 7 He who overcomes, I will give him these things. I will
be his God, and he will be my son.”

22:1 He showed me a river of water of life, clear as crystal,
proceeding out of the throne of God and of the Lamb, 2 in the
middle of its street. On this side of the river and on that was
the tree of life, bearing twelve kinds of fruits, yielding its
fruit every month. The leaves of the tree were for the healing
of the nations. 3 There will be no curse any more. The throne
of God and of the Lamb will be in it, and his servants will
serve him. 4 They will see his face, and his name will be on
their foreheads. 5 There will be no night, and they need no
lamp light; for the Lord God will illuminate them. They will
reign forever and ever.

SEEING HIS FACE

The throne of God and of the Lamb will be in it, and his servants will serve him. They will see his face... They will reign forever and ever. Revelation 22:4

The best thing about heaven, the thing that *makes* it heaven, is the presence of God himself: no more uncertainty or lack of clarity, just clear vision and ravishing enjoyment of our Lord. The greatest joy in the crowns he gives us will be the joy of placing those crowns at his feet in worship. The ultimate pleasure of heaven is God himself. We don't know God very well yet, so our desires sometimes focus on other aspects of heaven. But when we get there, we will find that anything beautiful will pale by comparison to the Source of all beauty. Every pleasure will seem dry compared to the Fountain of delight. Even our reunion with loved ones will take second place to our encounter with Love himself. These other joys are droplets, but God is the ocean. These others are rays, but God is the sun.

There will be many marvelous sights in heaven, but no sight will compare to gazing at the face of Jesus and seeing that he is looking at me—and smiling! There will be many lovely sounds in heaven, but no celestial music or conversation with saints and angels can compare to the sound of the voice that brought the world into being, the voice that shakes mountains and directs galaxies, the voice that whispers faith into my cold heart, the voice that calls the dead from their tombs—nothing can compare to the sound of that voice saying to me, "Well done, good and faithful servant. Enter into your master's joy. Welcome home, my child. Come reign with me!"

PRAYER

"Father of Jesus, Love divine, great King upon your throne, what joy to see you as you are and worship you alone!" I adore you, Jesus. I long to see you face to face. Amen.

Psalm 49:5-20

5 Why should I fear in times of trouble,
when the iniquity of those who cheat me surrounds me,
6 those who trust in their wealth
and boast of the abundance of their riches?
7 Truly no man can ransom another,
or give to God the price of his life,
8 for the ransom of their life is costly
and can never suffice,
9 that he should live on forever
and never see the pit.
10 For he sees that even the wise die;
the fool and the stupid alike must perish
and leave their wealth to others.
11 Their graves are their homes forever,
their dwelling places to all generations,
though they called lands by their own names.
12 Man in his pomp will not remain;
he is like the beasts that perish.
13 This is the path of those who have foolish confidence;
yet after them people approve of their boasts.
14 Like sheep they are appointed for Sheol;
death shall be their shepherd,
and the upright shall rule over them in the morning.
Their form shall be consumed in Sheol, with no place to dwell.
15 But God will ransom my soul from the power of Sheol,
for he will receive me.
16 Be not afraid when a man becomes rich,
when the glory of his house increases.
17 For when he dies he will carry nothing away;
his glory will not go down after him…
19 his soul will go to the generation of his fathers,
who will never again see light.
20 Man in his pomp yet without understanding is like the beasts that perish.

PAYING THE PRICE

Truly no man can ransom another, or give to God the price of his life, for the ransom of their life is costly... But God will ransom my soul from the power of Sheol. Psalm 49:7-8, 15

When someone gives you a check, the value of the check does not depend on how much money you have. Even if you have nothing, even if you are in debt, the check is still good as long as the person who wrote it can afford to pay the full amount. The check depends on their wealth, not yours.

Salvation is precious. We can't pay for the right to eternal life. On the contrary, we are in debt and deserve hell. You and I cannot pay the ransom for our own life. You and I cannot pay the ransom for each other's life. No payment of ours is enough. The price is too costly for us to pay. But we don't have to pay. Eternal life is God's gift. The question isn't whether *we* can pay, but whether *God* can pay.

God has already paid. "For you know that it was not with perishable things such as silver or gold that you were redeemed from the empty way of life handed down to you from your forefathers, but with the precious blood of Christ" (1 Peter 1:18, 19 NIV). The debt of hell has been paid, and the riches of heaven have been purchased, because Jesus' blood has infinite value. No promise based on the blood of Jesus will ever fail.

A check begins to benefit you when you take it to the bank and endorse it. You don't have to cover the amount, but you do have to sign your own name, trusting that the one who wrote it is able to pay the full amount. Have you personally endorsed God's gift of eternal life? Can you say with confidence, "God will ransom my soul"?

PRAYER

Thank you, Father, for your infinite riches. Thank you, Jesus, for paying for my salvation with your blood. Thank you, Holy Spirit, for flooding me with your blessings. Amen.

Acts 10:33-48 NLT

[Cornelius said to Peter,] [33] "Now we are all here, waiting before God to hear the message the Lord has given you."

[34] Then Peter replied, "I see very clearly that God shows no favoritism. [35] In every nation he accepts those who fear him and do what is right. [36] This is the message of Good News for the people of Israel—that there is peace with God through Jesus Christ, who is Lord of all. [37] You know what happened throughout Judea, beginning in Galilee, after John began preaching his message of baptism. [38] And you know that God anointed Jesus of Nazareth with the Holy Spirit and with power. Then Jesus went around doing good and healing all who were oppressed by the devil, for God was with him.

[39] "And we apostles are witnesses of all he did throughout Judea and in Jerusalem. They put him to death by hanging him on a cross, [40] but God raised him to life on the third day. Then God allowed him to appear, [41] not to the general public, but to us whom God had chosen in advance to be his witnesses. We were those who ate and drank with him after he rose from the dead. [42] And he ordered us to preach everywhere and to testify that Jesus is the one appointed by God to be the judge of all—the living and the dead. [43] He is the one all the prophets testified about, saying that everyone who believes in him will have their sins forgiven through his name."

[44] Even as Peter was saying these things, the Holy Spirit fell upon all who were listening to the message. [45] The Jewish believers who came with Peter were amazed that the gift of the Holy Spirit had been poured out on the Gentiles, too. [46] For they heard them speaking in other tongues and praising God.

Then Peter asked, [47] "Can anyone object to their being baptized, now that they have received the Holy Spirit just as we did?" [48] So he gave orders for them to be baptized in the name of Jesus Christ. Afterward Cornelius asked him to stay with them for several days.

RECEIVING HIS RICHES

"Everyone who believes in him will have their sins forgiven through his name." Acts 10:43

We have been thinking about the riches that are found in a firsthand relationship with Jesus. Much more could be said, but this much is clear: anyone who belongs to God is truly wealthy, and anyone who does not have a relationship with Jesus is poor indeed. So it is of utmost urgency that you have a relationship with the Lord and receive his riches.

There is just one thing that keeps anyone from God: sin. And there is just one way to have a relationship with God: Jesus. Christ paid the price of sin on the cross, and now he lives and brings blessing to his people. If the Holy Spirit has given you a desire for Jesus and the riches found in him, take these basic but life-changing steps, as simple as ABC:

- **A**dmit to God that you are a sinner. Don't think you're good enough. You're not. Don't think you can make up for your sins. You can't. Give up on saving yourself.
- **B**elieve in Jesus as your Savior and Leader. Trust that God forgives you because of Jesus' blood and that he gives you eternal life through Jesus' resurrection. Trust him, obey him, and treasure him.
- **C**ommit your life to following Jesus. Declare your faith publicly. If you're not baptized, get baptized and join a church that exalts Jesus and teaches the Bible. Keep listening to God's voice in the Bible, and keep talking to him in prayer. Love God, and love others.

Then relish the amazing fact that "all things are yours, and you are of Christ, and Christ is of God" (1 Corinthians 3:22-23). Don't shortchange yourself. Discover and enjoy every spiritual blessing in Christ.

PRAYER

Father, I admit that I am a sinner. I believe that you have forgiven my sins for Jesus' sake. I commit my life to serving my Savior and relishing his riches. In Jesus, Amen.

Part Four

KING OF ANGELS

Angels are alive and active. The Bible often tells about angels in action. Finding out about angels reminds us that there's more to life than the things we can see, touch, and control. Material things are not the only reality.

We must be careful, though, how we picture angels. Our Christmas angels are often cute, and the angels we find on TV and in bookstores are often consumer-friendly. Some people think of Jesus and his angels in much the same way that they think of Santa Claus and his elves: Jesus' job is to give us stuff we want, and angels are Jesus' "little helpers." This makes angels (and Jesus) seem as unreal as a fairy tale. It does not do justice to the power and importance of real angels and their great King.

The Bible shows us who angels really are, and it tells us many things angels have done. As we meet real angels in this section of meditations, we'll find that they are sometimes comforting, sometimes frightening, and always fascinating. More important, we'll gain a better understanding of the Maker and King of angels, our Lord Jesus Christ.

Psalm 148

1 Hallelujah!
Praise Yahweh from the heavens!
Praise him in the heights!
2 Praise him, all his angels!
Praise him, all his army!
3 Praise him, sun and moon!
Praise him, all you shining stars!
4 Praise him, you heavens of heavens,
You waters that are above the heavens.
5 Let them praise Yahweh's name,
For he commanded, and they were created.
6 He has also established them forever and ever.
He has made a decree which will not pass away.
7 Praise Yahweh from the earth,
you great sea creatures, and all depths!
8 Lightning and hail, snow and clouds;
stormy wind, fulfilling his word;
9 mountains and all hills;
fruit trees and all cedars;
10 wild animals and all livestock;
small creatures and flying birds;
11 kings of the earth and all peoples;
princes and all judges of the earth;
12 both young men and maidens;
old men and children:
13 let them praise Yahweh's name,
for his name alone is exalted.
His glory is above the earth and the heavens.
14 He has lifted up the horn of his people,
the praise of all his saints;
even of the children of Israel, a people near to him.
Hallelujah!

AMAZING CREATURES

Praise him, all his angels! Praise him, all his army! ... Let them praise Yahweh's name, for he commanded, and they were created. Psalm 148:2,5

Is there life on other planets? Do aliens from other worlds ever visit earth? Many people wonder about these things. Even some scientists look for signals from space that might alert us to other intelligent beings.

It's okay to be curious about other life forms, but don't believe every story about UFOs and aliens. Instead, listen to the Bible. According to Scripture, humans are not the only form of intelligent life, and we are not the most advanced. There are beings far stronger and smarter than we are, millions of them, in fact (Revelation 5:11).

These beings are unlike anything in our physical world. Angels exist in another dimension, the spirit realm. They are not subject to earthly physics and biology. Our microscopes, telescopes, and radar devices won't find them. As spirits, angels can't be detected by human eyes and ears unless they choose to be seen and heard for some special reason. According to the Bible, angels are so mighty and magnificent that even when they were on friendly visits, they frightened and amazed people who saw them.

Amazing as they are, angels remain God's creatures, not his equals. Unlike God, they have not always existed. God made them. "He commanded, and they were created." Like every other creature, angels owe their existence to God. And like every other creature, the main reason these amazing creatures exist is to praise their much more amazing Creator.

PRAYER

Great God, we join the angel armies of heaven and the creatures of the earth in praising you, our Maker. Your splendor is above the earth and the heavens. Hallelujah! Amen.

Job 38:1-33 NLT

1 Then the LORD answered Job from the whirlwind:
2 "Who is this that questions my wisdom
with such ignorant words?
3 Brace yourself like a man,
because I have some questions for you,
and you must answer them.
4 Where were you when I laid the foundations of the earth?
Tell me, if you know so much.
5 Who determined its dimensions
and stretched out the surveying line?
6 What supports its foundations,
and who laid its cornerstone
7 as the morning stars sang together
and all the angels shouted for joy? …
12 Have you ever commanded the morning to appear
and caused the dawn to rise in the east? …
16 Have you explored the springs from which the seas come?
Have you explored their depths?
17 Do you know where the gates of death are located?
Have you seen the gates of utter gloom?
18 Do you realize the extent of the earth?
Tell me about it if you know!
19 Where does light come from,
and where does darkness go? …
21 But of course you know all this!
For you were born before it was all created,
and you are so very experienced!
24 Where is the path to the source of light?
Where is the home of the east wind?
31 Can you direct the movement of the stars…
32 Can you direct the sequence of the seasons
or guide the Bear with her cubs across the heavens?
33 Do you know the laws of the universe?
Can you use them to regulate the earth?"

CHEERING FOR THE CREATOR

"Where were you when I laid the foundations of the earth? Tell me, if you know so much... Who laid its cornerstone as the morning stars sang together and all the angels shouted for joy?" Job 38:4-7

At some point before God created the world we live in, he made a heavenly realm and created angels. What are angels like? There's much we don't know. We don't even know how God made the earth and stars, so how could we know everything about a spirit realm that existed even before the earth was formed? Our knowledge of angels is limited, but the Bible provides a glimpse.

Angels are personal beings, not impersonal forces. Each has a name, such as Michael or Gabriel. Not all angels are alike. The Bible uses various titles: angels, archangels, cherubim, seraphim, thrones, dominions, rulers, authorities, and powers. Some writers in the Middle Ages took these titles and described nine different angelic levels. That was mostly guesswork; the Bible doesn't offer many details. But Scripture does indicate that there are different types of angels with different responsibilities and levels of authority.

When God made our world, angels were there watching and cheering. The real work of creating was done not by angels but by the Word of God operating through the Spirit of God. The Word of God is a Person, the second Person of the Holy Trinity, whom we know as Jesus Christ. "For by him all things were created: things in heaven and on earth, visible and invisible, whether thrones or powers or rulers or authorities; all things were created by him and for him, and in him all things hold together" (Colossians 1:16-17).

PRAYER

"You are worthy, our Lord and God, to receive glory and honor and power, for you created all things, and by your will they were created and have their being" (Revelation 4:11). Amen.

Revelation 12:7-12 NIV

7 Then war broke out in heaven. Michael and his angels
fought against the dragon, and the dragon and his angels
fought back. 8 But he was not strong enough, and they lost
their place in heaven. 9 The great dragon was hurled down—
that ancient serpent called the devil, or Satan, who leads the
whole world astray. He was hurled to the earth, and his angels with him.

10 Then I heard a loud voice in heaven say:

"Now have come the salvation and the power
and the kingdom of our God,
and the authority of his Messiah.
For the accuser of our brothers and sisters,
who accuses them before our God day and night,
has been hurled down.
11 They triumphed over him
by the blood of the Lamb
and by the word of their testimony;
they did not love their lives so much
as to shrink from death.
12 Therefore rejoice, you heavens
and you who dwell in them!
But woe to the earth and the sea,
because the devil has gone down to you!
He is filled with fury,
because he knows that his time is short."

TUG OF WAR

Michael and his angels fought against the dragon, and the dragon and his angels fought back. Revelation 12:7

All angels were created good, but not all remained good. A number of angels decided they no longer wanted to worship God or be ruled by him. The leader of the rebels, brilliant and powerful, became proud and thought himself greater than God. This proud rebel lost his place in heaven. He lost his beauty and the name he once had. He is now Satan, a dragon-like horror. The angels who fell with him are now demons.

We must be aware of the great struggle in the spirit realm and how it affects us. We must also realize that the struggle of good against evil is not between two sides of equal power.

I will never forget a picture drawn on an envelope by a man in prison who had become a Christian. The drawing shows a tug of war. On one side of the rope are demons: gritting their teeth, gripping the rope with both hands, sweating, leaning and pulling with all their might. On the other side of the rope stand angels: calm, smiling, relaxed, each holding the rope with just one hand. How can angels hold their ground so easily against demons who are working so hard? Behind the angels is an enormous hand holding the angels' end of the rope, the hand of the Lord himself.

Satan's power (at most) compares to the power of Michael, the chief angel. Satan is strong, but his power compared to God's is less than a fly compared to an elephant. The key to the holy angels' victory over the fallen angels is the power and triumph of Jesus.

PRAYER

Glory to you, Lord, for giving Michael's angels victory over Satan's demons. When Satan, in angry frustration, attacks us, save us, O God, and help us share your triumph. Amen.

Genesis 3:8-24 ESV

8 And they heard the sound of the LORD God walking in
the garden in the cool of the day, and the man and his wife
hid themselves from the presence of the LORD God among
the trees of the garden. 9 But the LORD God called to the man
and said to him, "Where are you?" 10 And he said, "I heard
the sound of you in the garden, and I was afraid, because I
was naked, and I hid myself." 11 He said, "Who told you that
you were naked? Have you eaten of the tree of which I
commanded you not to eat?" 12 The man said, "The woman
whom you gave to be with me, she gave me fruit of the tree,
and I ate." 13 Then the LORD God said to the woman, "What
is this that you have done?" The woman said, "The serpent
deceived me, and I ate."

14 So the LORD God said to the serpent, "… 15 I will put
enmity between you and the woman, and between your offspring and hers; he will crush your head, and you will strike
his heel." 16 To the woman he said, "I will greatly increase
your pains in childbearing; with pain you will give birth to
children. Your desire will be for your husband, and he will
rule over you." 17 To Adam he said, "Because you listened to
your wife and ate from the tree about which I commanded
you, 'You must not eat of it,' cursed is the ground because of
you; through painful toil you will eat of it all the days of
your life. 18 It will produce thorns and thistles for you, and
you will eat the plants of the field. 19 By the sweat of your
brow you will eat your food until you return to the ground,
since from it you were taken; for dust you are and to dust
you will return." …

22 Then the LORD God said, "Behold, the man has become like one of us in knowing good and evil. Now, lest he
reach out his hand and take also of the tree of life and eat,
and live forever—" 23 therefore the LORD God sent him out
from the garden of Eden to work the ground from which he
was taken. 24 He drove out the man, and at the east of the
garden of Eden he placed the cherubim and a flaming sword
that turned every way to guard the way to the tree of life.

ACCESS DENIED

He drove out the man, and at the east of the garden of Eden he placed the cherubim and a flaming sword that turned every way to guard the way to the tree of life. Genesis 3:24

Some books about angels speak of having your own angel to rescue you from trouble, help you win games, and give you an emotional high. One author says angels "always try to give us what we want." Like Aladdin's genie, angels are eager to do whatever makes us happy. Our wish is their command.

How real are these people-pleasing, sugar-coated angels? When something suits our taste too well, it often means we've cooked it up ourselves. In the Bible, angels are sometimes scary. The Bible has the taste of truth, not the artificial sweetness of something we cooked up to suit ourselves. The Bible tells us the way things are, not the way we'd like them to be.

Scripture says that when our first parents sinned, God posted cherubim, angelic warriors with a flaming sword, to deny Adam and Eve access to the tree of life. Sinners who disobey God cannot sneak into paradise, grab what they want, and enjoy eternal life. Unless we get right with God, angels will block us from heaven and throw us into hell, not be our personal genies.

There's only one way to be saved from God's judgment, one way past the cherubim who guard the entrance to paradise. "I am the way," says Jesus (John 14:6). To those who trust and obey him, Jesus promises, "I will give the right to eat from the tree of life, which is in the paradise of God" (Revelation 2:7).

PRAYER

Holy God, we sinners have no right to paradise, no right to expect anything but punishment from you and your angels. Thank you for restoring access through Jesus. Amen.

Genesis 19:1-27 ESV

[1] The two angels came to Sodom in the evening, and Lot was sitting in the gate of Sodom. When Lot saw them, he rose to meet them and bowed himself with his face to the earth [2] and said, "My lords, please turn aside to your servant's house and spend the night..." They said, "No; we will spend the night in the town square." [3] But he pressed them strongly; so they turned aside to him and entered his house. And he made them a feast… and they ate.

[4] But before they lay down, the men of the city… surrounded the house. [5] And they called to Lot, "Where are the men who came to you tonight? Bring them out to us, that we may know them." [9] … Then they pressed hard against the man Lot, and drew near to break the door down. [10] But the men reached out their hands and brought Lot into the house with them and shut the door. [11] And they struck with blindness the men who were at the entrance of the house, both small and great, so that they wore themselves out groping for the door.

[12] Then the men said to Lot, "…[13] We are about to destroy this place, because the outcry against its people has become great before the LORD, and the LORD has sent us to destroy it." … [15] As morning dawned, the angels urged Lot, saying, "Up! Take your wife and your two daughters who are here, lest you be swept away in the punishment of the city." [16] But he lingered. So the men seized him and his wife and his two daughters by the hand, the LORD being merciful to him, and they brought him out and set him outside the city. [17] And as they brought them out, one said, "Escape for your life. Do not look back or stop anywhere in the valley..."

[24] Then the LORD rained on Sodom and Gomorrah sulfur and fire from the LORD out of heaven. [25] And he overthrew those cities, and all the valley, and all the inhabitants of the cities, and what grew on the ground. [26] But Lot's wife, behind him, looked back, and she became a pillar of salt… [27] The smoke of the land went up like the smoke of a furnace.

AVENGING ANGELS

"We are about to destroy this place." Genesis 19:13

In all of Sodom and Gomorrah and their suburbs, only one family had a shred of goodness: Lot's family. The two angels told Lot, "We are about to destroy this place, because the outcry against its people has become great before the LORD, and the LORD has sent us to destroy it" (19:12-13).

Just two angels, in just a few moments, wiped out the proud, prosperous cities. Nothing remained but smoke and ashes. Lot's sons-in-law, having laughed at urgent warnings, were charcoal. Lot's wife was also dead, a salt statue with its head turned back toward Sodom.

This judgment previewed God's final judgment. "Sodom and Gomorrah and the surrounding towns gave themselves up to sexual immorality and perversion. They serve as an example of those who suffer the punishment of eternal fire" (Jude 7). Later, plagues against brutal Egyptians gave another glimpse of eternal agonies. God "unleashed against them his hot anger, his wrath, indignation and hostility—a band of destroying angels" (Psalm 78:49).

Beware of offending God and ignoring his avenging angels. "The angels will come," warns Jesus, "and separate the wicked from the righteous and throw them into the fiery furnace, where there will be weeping and gnashing of teeth" (Matthew 13:42). Angels are terrific rescuers but terrifying enemies. So too, the King of angels is a great Savior but a grim Judge. "It is a dreadful thing to fall into the hands of the living God" (Hebrews 10:31).

PRAYER

May God arise, may his enemies be scattered. As smoke is blown away by the wind, may you blow them away. But may the righteous be glad and rejoice. Amen. (Psalm 68)

Genesis 28:10-22

[10] Jacob went out from Beersheba, and went toward
Haran. [11] He came to a certain place, and stayed there all
night, because the sun had set. He took one of the stones of
the place, and put it under his head, and lay down in that
place to sleep. [12] He dreamed. Behold, a stairway set upon
the earth, and its top reached to heaven. Behold, the angels
of God ascending and descending on it. [13] Behold, Yahweh
stood above it, and said, "I am Yahweh, the God of Abraham
your father, and the God of Isaac. The land whereon you lie,
to you will I give it, and to your offspring [14] Your offspring
will be as the dust of the earth, and you will spread abroad to
the west, and to the east, and to the north, and to the south. In
you and in your offspring will all the families of the earth be
blessed. [15] Behold, I am with you, and will keep you, wherever you go, and will bring you again into this land. For I
will not leave you, until I have done that which I have spoken of to you."

[16] Jacob awakened out of his sleep, and he said, "Surely
Yahweh is in this place, and I didn't know it." [17] He was
afraid, and said, "How dreadful is this place! This is none
other than God's house, and this is the gate of heaven."

[18] Jacob rose up early in the morning, and took the stone
that he had put under his head, and set it up for a pillar, and
poured oil on its top. [19] He called the name of that place
Bethel, but the name of the city was Luz at the first. [20] Jacob
vowed a vow, saying, "If God will be with me, and will keep
me in this way that I go, and will give me bread to eat, and
clothing to put on, [21] so that I come again to my father's
house in peace, and Yahweh will be my God, [22] then this
stone, which I have set up for a pillar, will be God's house.
Of all that you will give me I will surely give a tenth to you."

STAIRWAY TO HEAVEN

Behold, a stairway set upon the earth, and its top reached to heaven. Behold, the angels of God ascending and descending on it. Genesis 28:12

Alvin Plantinga, one of the world's leading philosophers, often used dazzling logic to show that belief in God is rational. As a young man, though, he wasn't so sure. When he left his Christian home to attend Harvard University, he met smart people who despised Christianity. "I began to wonder," recalled Professor Plantinga, "whether what I had always believed could really be true."

"One gloomy evening, I was returning from dinner. It was dark, windy, raining, nasty. But suddenly it was as if the heavens opened; I heard, so it seemed, music of overwhelming power and grandeur and sweetness; there was light of unimaginable splendor and beauty; it seemed as if I could see into heaven itself; and I suddenly saw or perhaps felt with great clarity and persuasion and conviction that the Lord was really there and was all I had thought. Afterward I was still caught up in arguments about the existence of God, but they often seemed to me merely academic." Logic is good; personal encounter is better.

Jacob, too, was far from home. In a strange place, resting on rocks, miserable and alone, Jacob saw God's angels and heard God's promises. Earth was somehow connected with heaven.

The stairway in Jacob's dream is Christ (John 1:51). Jesus links earth and heaven. Angels and their King may show up where you least expect them. Then you exclaim, "Surely the Lord is in this place, and I was not aware of it."

PRAYER

Lord, when we are in new places and strange situations, alone and doubting, give us the awesome awareness that you and your angels are with us, through Jesus Christ. Amen.

Exodus 33:1-23 ESV

1 The LORD said to Moses, "Depart; go up from here, you
and the people whom you have brought up out of the land of
Egypt, to the land of which I swore to Abraham, Isaac, and
Jacob, saying, 'To your offspring I will give it.' 2 I will send
an angel before you... 3 Go up to a land flowing with milk
and honey; but I will not go up among you, lest I consume
you on the way, for you are a stiff-necked people." 4 When
the people heard this disastrous word, they mourned…
12 Moses said to the LORD, "See, you say to me, 'Bring
up this people,' but you have not let me know whom you
will send with me. Yet you have said, 'I know you by name,
and you have also found favor in my sight.' 13 Now therefore, if I have found favor in your sight, please show me now
your ways, that I may know you in order to find favor in
your sight. Consider too that this nation is your people."
14 And he said, "My presence will go with you, and I will
give you rest." 15 And he said to him, "If your presence will
not go with me, do not bring us up from here. 16 For how
shall it be known that I have found favor in your sight, I and
your people? Is it not in your going with us, so that we are
distinct, I and your people, from every other people on the
face of the earth?"

17 And the LORD said to Moses, "This very thing that you
have spoken I will do, for you have found favor in my sight,
and I know you by name." 18 Moses said, "Please show me
your glory." 19 And he said, "I will make all my goodness
pass before you and will proclaim before you my name 'The
LORD.' [Yahweh] And I will be gracious to whom I will be
gracious, and will show mercy on whom I will show mercy.
20 But," he said, "you cannot see my face, for man shall not
see me and live." 21 And the LORD said, "Behold, there is a
place by me where you shall stand on the rock, 22 and while
my glory passes by I will put you in a cleft of the rock, and I
will cover you with my hand until I have passed by. 23 Then I
will take away my hand, and you shall see my back, but my
face shall not be seen."

AN ANGEL IS NOT ENOUGH

"I will send an angel before you... But I will not go up among you..." Exodus 33:2-3

If you could have an angel to guide and protect you, overcome every enemy and problem, and settle you in a land of luxury, wouldn't you rejoice? What more could anyone want? But when the Israelites were promised these things, "they mourned." Why? Because God said, "I will not go up among you." What good is an angel, protection, victory, and luxury if God keeps his distance?

God was angry at Israel for a grievous sin. He warned that if he stayed too close to them, he might destroy them. So he would pull back and have an angel do good things for them. But an angel is not enough. Nothing less than God himself will do. "If your Presence will not go with me," pleaded Moses, "do not bring us up from here." Moses would rather remain in the desert with an angry Lord nearby than enjoy prosperity with God at a distance.

God agreed to accompany Moses and his people. Assured of God's nearness, Moses asked for even more: "Please show me your glory." God agreed to show Moses as much goodness and glory as Moses could bear.

Do you hunger for God's nearness? Do you long for God to show you all the divine glory you can handle? If you know Jesus, you have access to even more glory than God showed Moses: "the light of the knowledge of the glory of God in the face of Christ" (1 Corinthians 4:6).

PRAYER

One thing I ask, Lord: that I may dwell in the house of the Lord all the days of my life, to gaze upon the beauty of the Lord. Your face, Lord, I will seek. Amen. (Psalm 27)

Psalm 91 ESV

1 He who dwells in the shelter of the Most High
will abide in the shadow of the Almighty.
2 I will say to the LORD, "My refuge and my fortress,
my God, in whom I trust."
3 For he will deliver you from the snare of the fowler
and from the deadly pestilence.
4 He will cover you with his pinions,
and under his wings you will find refuge;
his faithfulness is a shield and buckler.
5 You will not fear the terror of the night,
nor the arrow that flies by day,
6 nor the pestilence that stalks in darkness,
nor the destruction that wastes at noonday.
7 A thousand may fall at your side,
ten thousand at your right hand,
but it will not come near you.
8 You will only look with your eyes
and see the recompense of the wicked.
9 Because you have made the LORD your dwelling place—
the Most High, who is my refuge—
10 no evil shall be allowed to befall you,
no plague come near your tent.
11 For he will command his angels concerning you
to guard you in all your ways.
12 On their hands they will bear you up,
lest you strike your foot against a stone.
13 You will tread on the lion and the adder;
the young lion and the serpent you will trample underfoot.
14 "Because he holds fast to me in love, I will deliver him;
I will protect him, because he knows my name.
15 When he calls to me, I will answer him;
I will be with him in trouble;
I will rescue him and honor him.
16 With long life I will satisfy him
and show him my salvation."

UNDER HIS WINGS

Under his wings you will find refuge ... For he will command his angels concerning you to guard you in all your ways. Psalm 91:4,11

Moving into the future can be exciting. It can also be scary. But even if the future is scary, you don't have to be scared. Psalm 91 goes through a list of dangers such as tricky traps, dreadful diseases, war and violence, lions and snakes. You might face somewhat different dangers, but God's message is the same: Even if you have to *face* dangers, you don't have to *fear* them—not if you're under God's wings.

God provides the protection of his own wings and the protection of his winged workers, the angels. So don't try to face the future alone, shivering in the icy winds of fear. Make the Lord your refuge. Take comfort in the protection of God's angels, and take even greater comfort in knowing that the best wings of all belong not to angels but to the Almighty.

Wings mean swiftness and safety. Swifter than any bird, heaven's power flies instantly to your aid if you trust the Lord and call for his help. Safer and warmer than a baby bird under its mother's wing, you can rest in the shelter of the Most High.

As you look to the future, trust the Lord. Rest assured that no lasting harm will befall you. The angels "will lift you up in their hands," and Someone much mightier than angels will also carry you: "The eternal God is your refuge, and underneath are the everlasting arms" (Deuteronomy 33:27).

PRAYER

"Beneath the shadow of your wings, your saints have dwelt secure. Sufficient is your arm alone, and our defense is sure." Thank you, Almighty Lord, for your protection. Amen.

2 Kings 6:13-23

13 The king of Syria said, “Go and see where the prophet
Elisha is, that I may send and seize him.” It was told him,
“Behold, he is in Dothan.” 14 So he sent there horses and
chariots and a great army, and they came by night and surrounded the city.

15 When the servant of the man of God rose early in the
morning and went out, behold, an army with horses and
chariots was all around the city. And the servant said, “Alas,
my master! What shall we do?” 16 He said, “Do not be afraid,
for those who are with us are more than those who are with
them.” 17 Then Elisha prayed and said, “O LORD, please open
his eyes that he may see.” So the LORD opened the eyes of
the young man, and he saw, and behold, the mountain was
full of horses and chariots of fire all around Elisha. 18 And
when the Syrians came down against him, Elisha prayed to
the LORD and said, “Please strike this people with blindness.” So he struck them with blindness… 19 And Elisha said
to them, “This is not the way, and this is not the city. Follow
me, and I will bring you to the man whom you seek.” And he
led them to Samaria.

20 As soon as they entered Samaria, Elisha said, “O
LORD, open the eyes of these men, that they may see.” So the
LORD opened their eyes and they saw, and behold, they were
in the midst of Samaria. 21 As soon as the king of Israel saw
them, he said to Elisha, “My father, shall I strike them
down? Shall I strike them down?” 22 He answered, “You
shall not strike them down. Would you strike down those
whom you have taken captive with your sword and with your
bow? Set bread and water before them, that they may eat and
drink and go to their master.” 23 So he prepared for them a
great feast, and when they had eaten and drunk, he sent them
away, and they went to their master. And the Syrians did not
come again on raids into the land of Israel.

CHARIOTS OF FIRE

So the LORD opened the eyes of the young man, and he saw, and behold, the mountain was full of horses and chariots of fire all around Elisha. 2 Kings 6:17

Many modern angels are too cute for comfort. Plump ceramic cherubs can serve as decorations, but they can't comfort us. The cuddly angels of TV and popular books can offer pleasant self-help advice, but they can't defend against powerful enemies.

Real angels aren't as cute or cuddly as fake ones. Real angels can be stern and terrifying. But they can also be comforting. When we're assaulted by strong, evil forces, we don't need phony angels that are too cute for comfort; we need chariots of fire, angelic warriors equipped for battle.

The prophet Elisha and his assistant awoke one morning to find themselves surrounded by armed enemies with horses and chariots. The assistant panicked. But Elisha replied, "Don't worry. Our army is bigger and stronger than theirs."

"*Our* army?" the assistant wondered. "I see nothing but enemy horses and chariots." But when Elisha prayed, his assistant suddenly saw a vast heavenly army all over the place, with enough firepower to defeat any opponent. In short order, the enemy troops were struck blind, captured, shown kindness, and sent back to their own land.

The angels and their chariots of fire aren't cute, but they are comforting. Angels are mighty warriors. The mightiest warrior of all is the King of angels: "The Lord is a warrior" (Exodus 15:3). "Who is like the Lord among the heavenly beings? He is more awesome than all who surround him" (Psalm 89:6-7).

PRAYER

"The chariots of God are tens of thousands and thousands of thousands. You are a God who saves and rescues from death. You are awesome, O God." Amen. (Psalm 68)

Daniel 6:6-24

6 The administrators and high officers went to the king
and said, "Long live King Darius! 7 … Give orders that for
the next thirty days any person who prays to anyone, divine
or human—except to you, Your Majesty—will be thrown
into the den of lions…." 9 So King Darius signed the law.

10 But when Daniel learned that the law had been signed,
he went home and knelt down as usual in his upstairs room,
with its windows open toward Jerusalem. He prayed three
times a day, just as he had always done, giving thanks to his
God. 11 Then the officials went together to Daniel's house
and found him praying and asking for God's help… 13 Then
they told the king, "That man Daniel, one of the captives
from Judah, is ignoring you and your law. He still prays to
his God three times a day." …

16 So at last the king gave orders for Daniel to be arrested
and thrown into the den of lions. The king said to him, "May
your God, whom you serve so faithfully, rescue you." …

18 Then the king returned to his palace and spent the night
fasting. He refused his usual entertainment and couldn't
sleep at all that night. 19 Very early the next morning, the
king got up and hurried out to the lions' den. 20 When he got
there, he called out in anguish, "Daniel, servant of the living
God! Was your God, whom you serve so faithfully, able to
rescue you from the lions?"

21 Daniel answered, "Long live the king! 22 My God sent
his angel to shut the lions' mouths so that they would not
hurt me, for I have been found innocent in his sight. And I
have not wronged you, Your Majesty."

23 The king was overjoyed and ordered that Daniel be
lifted from the den. Not a scratch was found on him, for he
had trusted in his God.

24 Then the king gave orders to arrest the men who had
maliciously accused Daniel. He had them thrown into the
lions' den, along with their wives and children. The lions
leaped on them and tore them apart before they even hit the
floor of the den.

ANGEL IN THE LIONS' DEN

"My God sent his angel to shut the lions' mouths so that they would not hurt me." Daniel 6:22

A government decree banned prayer and threatened to make lion food of any praying person. Daniel prayed anyway. He would rather spend a night with lions than spend a day without God. When Daniel was thrown to the lions, God's angel entered the den and made even the hungriest lion lose its appetite. Daniel escaped without a scratch "because he trusted in his God."

With faith inside him and an angel beside him, Daniel "shut the mouths of lions." But what about others, believers who have been "tortured," "put in prison," and "put to death"? Did God fail to keep his promise? Did the angels blow their assignment? No, even Christians who are persecuted and murdered escape unharmed, for they "gain a better resurrection" (Hebrews 11:33-37). God's enemies "will put some of you to death," says Jesus. "But not a hair of your head will perish. By standing firm you will gain life" (Luke 21:16-19).

Psalm 91 promises that God "will command his angels concerning you to guard you in all your ways," even when facing "the great lion." Sometimes angels shut lions' mouths; at other times angels allow lions to devour Christians but then carry the believers to glory. Either way, whether Christians live or die, the outcome is for their good. God's promise stands firm: "Because he loves me," says the Lord, "I will rescue him... With long life [indeed, eternal life] will I satisfy him and show him my salvation" (Psalm 91:14-16).

PRAYER

"O God, you are my God. Because your love is better than life, my lips will glorify you. Because you are my help, I sing in the shadow of your wings." Amen. (Psalm 63).

Luke 1:7-25

7 Zechariah and Elizabeth had no child, because Elizabeth was barren, and both were advanced in years.

8 Now while he was serving as priest before God when
his division was on duty, 9 according to the custom of the
priesthood, he was chosen by lot to enter the temple of the
Lord and burn incense. 10 And the whole multitude of the
people were praying outside at the hour of incense. 11 And
there appeared to him an angel of the Lord standing on the
right side of the altar of incense. 12 And Zechariah was troubled when he saw him, and fear fell upon him. 13 But the angel said to him, "Do not be afraid, Zechariah, for your prayer
has been heard, and your wife Elizabeth will bear you a son,
and you shall call his name John. 14 And you will have joy
and gladness, and many will rejoice at his birth, 15 for he will
be great before the Lord. And he must not drink wine or
strong drink, and he will be filled with the Holy Spirit, even
from his mother's womb. 16 And he will turn many of the
children of Israel to the Lord their God, 17 and he will go before him in the spirit and power of Elijah, to turn the hearts
of the fathers to the children, and the disobedient to the wisdom of the just, to make ready for the Lord a people prepared."

18 And Zechariah said to the angel, "How shall I know
this? For I am an old man, and my wife is advanced in
years." 19 And the angel answered him, "I am Gabriel. I stand
in the presence of God, and I was sent to speak to you and to
bring you this good news. 20 And behold, you will be silent
and unable to speak until the day that these things take place,
because you did not believe my words, which will be fulfilled in their time." …

24 After these days his wife Elizabeth conceived, and for
five months she kept herself hidden, saying, 25 "Thus the
Lord has done for me in the days when he looked on me, to
take away my reproach among people."

GABRIEL'S GOOD NEWS

"I am Gabriel. I stand in the presence of God, and I was sent to speak to you and to bring you this good news." Luke 1:19

Gabriel told Zechariah his barren wife would have a baby, but the old priest didn't believe it. Great Gabriel was offended. How dare this human pipsqueak doubt a splendid angel, coming straight from the throne room of God the Almighty, bringing good news? If the silly little man could only talk about his doubts, he could just keep his mouth shut.

Gabriel left the old man and went to a young woman. He told her she would have a baby without an earthly father—something even less likely than an old couple having a child. But the Virgin Mary, unlike Zechariah, didn't ask how she could be sure. She simply asked how it would happen. Gabriel explained that her holy child would be "the Son of God... For nothing is impossible with God" (Luke 1:35,37).

Many people (even a godly priest like Zechariah) use circumstances to decide what's doubtful or impossible. But to Gabriel, who stands in God's presence and knows God's power firsthand, doubt is dumb; "impossible" is insulting.

Eventually Zechariah learned his lesson. He couldn't speak for months. When baby John was born and named, Zechariah's voice at last returned. Praise replaced doubt. He praised God for baby John, who would prepare the way for the Lord Jesus himself. Zechariah praised "the tender mercy of our God, by which the rising sun will come to us from heaven to shine on those living in darkness" (1:78-79). Zechariah saw beyond John to Jesus. And Gabriel smiled.

PRAYER

Great Father of Jesus Christ, when your good news sounds too good to be true, close our mouths and open our hearts. Show us that nothing is impossible for you. Amen.

Luke 1:26-38, 2:7-14

26 The angel Gabriel was sent from God… 27 to a virgin
betrothed to a man whose name was Joseph… And the virgin's name was Mary. 28 And he came to her and said,
"Greetings, O favored one, the Lord is with you!" … 30 And
the angel said to her, "Do not be afraid, Mary, for you have
found favor with God. 31 And behold, you will conceive in
your womb and bear a son, and you shall call his name Jesus.
32 He will be great and will be called the Son of the Most
High. And the Lord God will give to him the throne of his
father David, 33 and he will reign over the house of Jacob
forever, and of his kingdom there will be no end."

34 And Mary said to the angel, "How will this be, since I
am a virgin?"

35 And the angel answered her, "The Holy Spirit will
come upon you, and the power of the Most High will over-
shadow you; therefore the child to be born will be called holy—the Son of God... 37 For nothing will be impossible with
God." 38 And Mary said, "Behold, I am the servant of the
Lord; let it be to me according to your word." And the angel
departed from her…

2:7 And she gave birth to her firstborn son and wrapped
him in swaddling cloths and laid him in a manger, because
there was no place for them in the inn.

8 And in the same region there were shepherds out in the
field, keeping watch over their flock by night. 9 And an angel
of the Lord appeared to them, and the glory of the Lord
shone around them, and they were filled with great fear.
10 And the angel said to them, "Fear not, for behold, I bring
you good news of great joy that will be for all the people.
11 For unto you is born this day in the city of David a Savior,
who is Christ the Lord. 12 And this will be a sign for you: you
will find a baby wrapped in swaddling cloths and lying in a
manger." 13 And suddenly there was with the angel a multitude of the heavenly host praising God and saying, 14 "Glory
to God in the highest, and on earth peace among those with
whom he is pleased!"

MESSENGERS

"I bring you good news of great joy that will be for all the people. For unto you is born this day in the city of David a Savior, who is Christ the Lord." Luke 2:10-11

In the Bible's original languages, the word *angel* means "messenger." Angels have delivered many important messages. They spoke to Abraham and took part in giving God's commandments to Moses. They described future events recorded in the prophecies of Daniel. They announced the births of Samson and John the Baptist.

The greatest birth announcement the angels ever made was the birth of Jesus. How did the virgin Mary first learn that she would give birth to the Savior? The angel Gabriel told her. How did Joseph find out that the baby growing inside Mary was really the Son of God? An angel told him. How did the shepherds on that first Christmas find out about the Christ child? An angel told them, backed by an entire chorus of angels.

Angels told of Jesus' birth, and they continued to bring messages about Jesus. When Jesus rose from the dead, angels were the first to announce it. When Jesus ascended to heaven, angels appeared and told his followers that the Lord would return again someday. As the early church faced many challenges, angels continued to bring messages from God. Many of the visions recorded in the book of Revelation were communicated through an angel messenger.

Angels have communicated or confirmed many important messages, but they have never brought any messages on their own authority. They have always spoken the message God has given them. They are always heralds for Jesus.

PRAYER

Glory to God in the highest! Thank you for the good news of great joy announced by your angels. Thank you, dear Jesus, for being our Savior, Messiah, and Lord. Amen.

Matthew 26:47-56

47 While he was still speaking, behold, Judas, one of the twelve, came, and with him a great multitude with swords and clubs, from the chief priest and elders of the people. 48 Now he who betrayed him gave them a sign, saying, "Whoever I kiss, he is the one. Seize him." 49 Immediately he came to Jesus, and said, "Hail, Rabbi!" and kissed him.

50 Jesus said to him, "Friend, why are you here?" Then they came and laid hands on Jesus, and took him. 51 Behold, one of those who were with Jesus stretched out his hand, and drew his sword, and struck the servant of the high priest, and struck off his ear. 52 Then Jesus said to him, "Put your sword back into its place, for all those who take the sword will die by the sword. 53 Or do you think that I couldn't ask my Father, and he would even now send me more than twelve legions of angels? 54 How then would the Scriptures be fulfilled that it must be so?"

55 In that hour Jesus said to the multitudes, "Have you come out as against a robber with swords and clubs to seize me? I sat daily in the temple teaching, and you didn't arrest me. 56 But all this has happened, that the Scriptures of the prophets might be fulfilled."

WHEN ANGELS STOOD BACK

"Do you think that I couldn't ask my Father, and he would even now send me more than twelve legions of angels?" Mathew 26:53

A legion was a unit of 6,000 soldiers. Twelve legions would make 72,000 soldiers. So when Jesus said he could call for more than twelve legions of angels, he was saying he could instantly get more than 72,000 angels to fight in his defense. Think about that for a moment. One angel was enough to destroy an invading army of 185,000 soldiers in a night (2 Kings 19:35). Two angels were enough to wipe out the cities of Sodom and Gomorrah and the nearby towns (Genesis 19). Imagine what more than 72,000 heavenly warriors could do to a few thugs armed with swords and clubs!

Jesus could have called for far more than twelve legions. Millions of angels, "ten thousand times ten thousand," serve Jesus. They stood ready to fight for him at his command. But the command never came. The angels stood back, and the King of angels allowed his human enemies to seize him.

The angels had seen astounding things before. They had seen the splendor and beauty of their King on his throne. They had seen him create worlds and galaxies from nothing—an amazing display of power and wisdom. They had seen him crush the rebellion of Satan and his rebel angels. They had seen their Lord raise up kings and bring down empires. But the angels had never seen anything quite like the love and mercy Jesus displayed when he laid down his life for the sins of the world. Nobody took Jesus' life from him. He could have called in a vast army of angels, or he could have wiped out his enemies himself with one blast of his divine might. But Jesus came to save, not to destroy.

PRAYER

Lord Jesus, we sing with the angels, "Worthy is the Lamb, who was slain, to receive power and wealth and wisdom and strength and honor and glory and praise." Amen. (Rev. 5:11)

Acts 8:26-39

26 But an angel of the Lord spoke to Philip, saying,
"Arise, and go toward the south to the way that goes down
from Jerusalem to Gaza. This is a desert."
27 He arose and went; and behold, there was a man of
Ethiopia, a eunuch of great authority under Candace, queen
of the Ethiopians, who was over all her treasure, who had
come to Jerusalem to worship. 28 He was returning and sitting in his chariot, and was reading the prophet Isaiah.
29 The Spirit said to Philip, "Go near, and join yourself to
this chariot."
30 Philip ran to him, and heard him reading Isaiah the
prophet, and said, "Do you understand what you are reading?"
31 He said, "How can I, unless someone explains it to
me?" He begged Philip to come up and sit with him. 32 Now
the passage of the Scripture which he was reading was this,
"He was led as a sheep to the slaughter.
As a lamb before his shearer is silent,
so he doesn't open his mouth.
33 In his humiliation, his judgment was taken away.
Who will declare His generation?
For his life is taken from the earth."
34 The eunuch answered Philip, "Who is the prophet talking about? About himself, or about someone else?"
35 Philip opened his mouth, and beginning from this
Scripture, preached to him Jesus. 36 As they went on the way,
they came to some water, and the eunuch said, "Behold, here
is water. What is keeping me from being baptized?" …
38 He commanded the chariot to stand still, and they both
went down into the water, both Philip and the eunuch, and he
baptized him.
39 When they came up out of the water, the Spirit of the
Lord caught Philip away, and the eunuch didn't see him anymore, for he went on his way rejoicing.

ANGEL EVANGELISM

An angel of the Lord spoke to Philip, saying, "Arise, and go toward the south to the way that goes down from Jerusalem to Gaza." Acts 8:26

Angels are ambassadors. They don't speak their own opinions; they say only what their King tells them to say. Their message is the eternal gospel. It comes from God and addresses everyone on earth. Scripture shows an "angel flying in midair, and he had the eternal gospel to proclaim to those who live on earth—to every nation, tribe, language, and people" (Revelation 14:6).

The Secretary of the Treasury for Ethiopia was sitting in his limousine, reading the Scriptures. This important African official didn't see an angel flying in midair. He saw only a stranger who ran up, introduced himself as Philip, and joined him in the limousine. As the driver sped along, Philip explained the everlasting gospel, the good news about Jesus. The official believed, was baptized, and "went on his way rejoicing."

When two people meet somewhere, and one tells the other about Jesus, an angel may be involved. As angels fly in midair proclaiming the eternal gospel, people on the ground do the actual explaining. Like the angels, Christians are ambassadors who speak for someone else: "we do not preach ourselves but Jesus Christ as Lord" (2 Corinthians 4:5). With angels in the air, Christians on the ground, and Christ on the throne, the eternal gospel keeps spreading. It brings joy to all who believe and are baptized, in Ethiopia and in "every nation, tribe, language, and people."

PRAYER

Praise to you, Lord, for the eternal gospel, the good news of Christ crucified, risen, and reigning. With the angels, may we preach not ourselves but Jesus as Lord. Amen.

Acts 12:1-16

1 Now about that time, King Herod stretched out his hands to oppress some of the assembly. 2 He killed James, the brother of John, with the sword. 3 When he saw that it pleased the Jews, he proceeded to seize Peter also... 4 When he had arrested him, he put him in prison, and delivered him to four squads of four soldiers each to guard him... 5 Peter therefore was kept in the prison, but constant prayer was made by the assembly to God for him. 6 The same night when Herod was about to bring him out, Peter was sleeping between two soldiers, bound with two chains. Guards in front of the door kept the prison.

7 And behold, an angel of the Lord stood by him, and a light shone in the cell. He struck Peter on the side, and woke him up, saying, "Stand up quickly!" His chains fell off from his hands. 8 The angel said to him, "Get dressed and put on your sandals." He did so. He said to him, "Put on your cloak, and follow me." 9 And he went out and followed him. He didn't know that what was being done by the angel was real, but thought he saw a vision. 10 When they were past the first and the second guard, they came to the iron gate that leads into the city, which opened to them by itself. They went out, and went down one street, and immediately the angel departed from him.

11 When Peter had come to himself, he said, "Now I truly know that the Lord has sent out his angel and delivered me out of the hand of Herod, and from everything the Jewish people were expecting." 12 Thinking about that, he came to the house of Mary, the mother of John who was called Mark, where many were gathered together and were praying. 13 When Peter knocked at the door of the gate, a maid named Rhoda came to answer. 14 When she recognized Peter's voice, she didn't open the gate for joy, but ran in, and reported that Peter was standing in front of the gate. 15 They said to her, "You are crazy!" But she insisted that it was so. They said, "It is his angel." 16 But Peter continued knocking. When they had opened, they saw him, and were amazed.

MISSION IMPOSSIBLE

"Now I truly know that the Lord has sent out his angel and delivered me out of the hand of Herod." Acts 12:11

Peter had been jailed before. He and his fellow apostles preached and healed in Jesus' name with such power that some jealous leaders jailed them. "But during the night an angel of the Lord opened the doors of the jail and brought them out. 'Go, stand in the temple courts,' he said, 'and tell the people the full message of this new life'" (Acts 5:20).

Now Peter was in jail again, but this was different. Now he was targeted by King Herod himself. Peter's friend James had already been killed, and Peter was next on Herod's list. Kept in maximum security, bound with two chains, sandwiched between two soldiers with two more guarding the door, Peter appeared doomed. How could anyone, even an angel, rescue him?

It seemed so impossible that Peter thought it must be a vision when an angel rescued him. Peter's praying friends could believe Peter's angel was knocking on their door, but they couldn't believe the angel had opened the prison doors. Still, it was true. The impossible happened. Despite Herod, the chains, and the soldiers, the angel rescued Peter.

When God's people are chained, "God's word is not chained" (2 Timothy 2:9). If God lets them be killed and takes them to heaven, their blood makes the church flourish and grow. If God wants them to live and keep working, no weapon can kill them, and no jail can hold them. The only truly impossible mission is to try stopping God's mission.

PRAYER

Thank you, Father, that "the angel of the Lord encamps around those who fear him, and he delivers them." Continue to rescue your people, spread your gospel, and build your kingdom, Lord. Amen.

Acts 12:18-24

[18] Now as soon as it was day, there was no small stir
among the soldiers about what had become of Peter. [19] When
Herod had sought for him, and didn't find him, he examined
the guards, and commanded that they should be put to death.
He went down from Judea to Caesarea, and stayed there.
[20] Now Herod was very angry with the people of Tyre and
Sidon. They came with one accord to him, and, having made
Blastus, the king's personal aide, their friend, they asked for
peace, because their country depended on the king's country
for food. [21] On an appointed day, Herod dressed himself in
royal clothing, sat on the throne, and gave a speech to them.
[22] The people shouted, "The voice of a god, and not of a
man!" [23] Immediately an angel of the Lord struck him, because he didn't give God the glory, and he was eaten by
worms and died.

[24] But the word of God grew and multiplied.

PLAYING GOD

Immediately an angel of the Lord struck him, because he didn't give God the glory, and he was eaten by worms and died. But the word of God grew and multiplied. Acts 12:23-24

Herod cared about power, not justice. He didn't value human life; he murdered whomever he wanted. He killed James and tried to kill Peter, simply to score political points. After Peter's escape, Herod killed the soldiers who had guarded Peter.

What makes a person so evil? Pride: putting self in the place of God, answering to nobody. "In all his thoughts there is no room for God... He says to himself, 'Nothing will shake me; I'll always be happy and never have trouble.' ... he murders the innocent... He says to himself, 'God has forgotten; he covers his face and never sees'" (Psalm 10).

Herod had a captive audience. People from a neighboring land needed his food supply. They might starve unless they made him happy. Knowing proud Herod, they figured he would like being praised as a god. They were right. The king smiled. But the King of angels frowned, and an angel struck Herod down.

Pride was Satan's sin, and pride produces all sins. For those who want to play God, the message is, "Too bad! The job is already taken." Those who make self supreme, despise God, and damage others become worm food in hell forever. "Their worm will not die, nor will their fire be quenched" (Isaiah 66:24). "This will happen when the Lord Jesus is revealed from heaven in blazing fire with his powerful angels. He will punish those who do not know God and do not obey the gospel of our Lord Jesus" (2 Thessalonians 1:6-9).

PRAYER

"O Lord, the God who avenges, shine forth. Rise up, O Judge of the earth; pay back to the proud what they deserve. Your love, O Lord, supports me." Amen. (Psalm 94)

Joshua 5:13-15

13 When Joshua was by Jericho, he lifted up his eyes and looked, and behold, a man stood in front of him with his sword drawn in his hand. Joshua went to him and said to him, “Are you for us, or for our enemies?”
14 He said, “Neither; but I have come now as commander of Yahweh’s army.”

Joshua fell on his face to the earth, and worshiped, and asked him, “What does my lord say to his servant?”
15 The prince of Yahweh’s army said to Joshua, “Take your shoes off of your feet; for the place on which you stand is holy.” Joshua did so.

WHOSE SIDE ARE ANGELS ON?

Joshua went to him and said to him, "Are you for us, or for our enemies?" He said, "Neither; but I have come now as commander of Yahweh's army." Joshua 5:13-14

None of us can say, "We have the angels on our side. They have to help us and destroy our enemies." Not even God's chosen nation could say that. Angels aren't on any side but God's. They take orders only from him. They "obey *his* word" and "do *his* will" (Psalm 103:20-21).

General Joshua was preparing to lead God's people against Jericho. When he met an unknown warrior, Joshua asked, "Are you for us or for our enemies?" The warrior replied, "Neither." He said, "I have come now as commander of Yahweh's army." Then Joshua fell facedown to the ground in reverence.

This happened shortly before the armies of heaven would smash the walls of wicked Jericho and give the city to the Israelites. Joshua may have been tempted to think the angels were automatically on his side. But it became clear that angels don't follow any human plan; they obey their heavenly commander.

Never assume God and his angels are on your side; strive to be on their side. God warned his very own people, "If you will not listen to me ... I will set my face against you so that you will be defeated by your enemies" (Leviticus 26:14,17).

If God sends you help from heaven, don't gloat. Fall "facedown on the ground in reverence." Thank God for his help. Then do God's will.

PRAYER

"Our Father who art in heaven, hallowed be thy name. Thy kingdom come, thy will be done on earth as it is in heaven." May we never seek our own kingdom but only yours. Amen.

Matthew 18:1-14

1 In that hour the disciples came to Jesus, saying, "Who then is greatest in the Kingdom of Heaven?"

2 Jesus called a little child to himself, and set him in the middle of them, 3 and said, "Most certainly I tell you, unless you turn, and become as little children, you will in no way enter into the Kingdom of Heaven. 4 Whoever therefore humbles himself as this little child, he is the greatest in the Kingdom of Heaven. 5 Whoever receives one such little child in my name receives me, 6 but whoever causes one of these little ones who believe in me to stumble, it would be better for him that a huge millstone should be hung around his neck, and that he should be sunk in the depths of the sea.

7 "Woe to the world because of occasions of stumbling! For it must be that the occasions come, but woe to that person through whom the occasion comes! 8 If your hand or your foot causes you to stumble, cut it off, and cast it from you. It is better for you to enter into life maimed or crippled, rather than having two hands or two feet to be cast into the eternal fire. 9 If your eye causes you to stumble, pluck it out, and cast it from you. It is better for you to enter into life with one eye, rather than having two eyes to be cast into the Gehenna of fire. 10 See that you don't despise one of these little ones, for I tell you that in heaven their angels always see the face of my Father who is in heaven. 11 For the Son of Man came to save that which was lost.

12 "What do you think? If a man has one hundred sheep, and one of them goes astray, doesn't he leave the ninety-nine, go to the mountains, and seek that which has gone astray? 13 If he finds it, most certainly I tell you, he rejoices over it more than over the ninety-nine which have not gone astray. 14 Even so it is not the will of your Father who is in heaven that one of these little ones should perish."

POLICE

"See that you don't despise one of these little ones, for I tell you that in heaven their angels always see the face of my Father who is in heaven." Matthew 18:10

Do you like seeing a police officer nearby? It all depends. If you have car trouble or an accident and need help, you're glad to see a police car pulling up. But if you drive too fast or run a red light, you're not happy to see the police behind you. If you're being robbed and beaten, you're overjoyed to see an officer coming. But if you happen to be the robber, an officer is the last person you want to see.

Angels, like police, are good news for some but bad news for others. Angels are good news for oppressed people but bad news for oppressors. Angels are good news for those who trust and obey the Lord but bad news for those who break God's law.

It's comforting to think angels stand up for you when you face trouble. But remember, angels stand up for others too. When you meet someone who seems weak, small or unimportant, don't despise or harm that person. "See that you don't despise one of these little ones," says Jesus, "for I tell you that in heaven their angels always see the face of my Father who is in heaven" (Matthew 18:10). It is an awful crime to harm the weak or cause little ones to sin.

The angelic police and their King will catch up with the guilty, making them wish they were encased in cement at the bottom of the ocean (Matthew 18:6).

PRAYER

Thank you, Lord, for police officers who help people in crisis and stop criminals. Help us to respect earthly and heavenly police. May we do right and be kind to everyone. Amen.

Numbers 22:21-34

21 Balaam rose in the morning and saddled his donkey and went with the princes of Moab. 22 But God's anger was kindled because he went, and the angel of the LORD took his stand in the way as his adversary. Now he was riding on the donkey, and his two servants were with him. 23 And the donkey saw the angel of the LORD standing in the road, with a drawn sword in his hand. And the donkey turned aside out of the road and went into the field. And Balaam struck the donkey, to turn her into the road. 24 Then the angel of the LORD stood in a narrow path between the vineyards, with a wall on either side. 25 And when the donkey saw the angel of the LORD, she pushed against the wall and pressed Balaam's foot against the wall. So he struck her again. 26 Then the angel of the LORD went ahead and stood in a narrow place, where there was no way to turn either to the right or to the left. 27 When the donkey saw the angel of the LORD, she lay down under Balaam. And Balaam's anger was kindled, and he struck the donkey with his staff. 28 Then the LORD opened the mouth of the donkey, and she said to Balaam, "What have I done to you, that you have struck me these three times?" 29 And Balaam said to the donkey, "Because you have made a fool of me. I wish I had a sword in my hand, for then I would kill you." 30 And the donkey said to Balaam, "Am I not your donkey, on which you have ridden all your life long to this day? Is it my habit to treat you this way?" And he said, "No."

31 Then the LORD opened the eyes of Balaam, and he saw the angel of the LORD standing in the way, with his drawn sword in his hand. And he bowed down and fell on his face. 32 And the angel of the LORD said to him, "Why have you struck your donkey these three times? Behold, I have come out to oppose you because your way is perverse before me. 33 The donkey saw me and turned aside before me these three times. If she had not turned aside from me, surely just now I would have killed you and let her live." 34 Then Balaam said to the angel of the LORD, "I have sinned."

GUARDIAN DONKEY

"The donkey saw me and turned aside before me these three times. If she had not turned aside from me, surely just now I would have killed you and let her live." Numbers 22:33

We want guardian angels, but sometimes we need guardian donkeys!

Balaam was having a lousy day. His donkey was behaving badly. First she swerved off the road into a field. Then she pressed close to a wall, crushing Balaam's foot. Then she simply lay down. Each time Balaam angrily beat the dumb donkey.

But the donkey wasn't so dumb. She talked. And Balaam talked back! The only thing stranger than a donkey talking to a man is a man talking back to the donkey. Balaam griped, "You have made a fool of me!" But he made a fool of himself. Balaam wished there was a sword nearby to kill the donkey. Well, there *was* a sword nearby, but it was in the angel's hand and was poised to kill sinful Balaam. The only thing that saved Balaam from the sword of the angel was his guardian donkey.

Balaam was foolish to beat and snarl at a donkey, but how many of us swear at a computer or kick a car? We gripe about traffic, sickness, people problems, anything that delays us from getting where we're trying to go. But what if we're on the wrong road, headed for a heavenly sword?

If your "donkey" gives you grief, if trouble stops you in your tracks, don't curse your trouble. It may be telling you something. Are you traveling in the wrong direction? Are you disobeying God? If so, you don't need angels to guard you from troubles; you need troubles to guard you from angels!

PRAYER

"I know, O Lord, that your laws are righteous, and in faithfulness you have afflicted me. May your unfailing love be my comfort. I hate every wrong path." Amen. (Psalm 119)

Isaiah 6:1-8

[1] In the year that king Uzziah died, I saw the Lord sitting
on a throne, high and lifted up; and his train filled the temple. [2] Above him stood the seraphim. Each one had six
wings. With two he covered his face. With two he covered
his feet. With two he flew. [3] One called to another, and said,

"Holy, holy, holy, is Yahweh of Armies!
The whole earth is full of his glory!"

[4] The foundations of the thresholds shook at the voice of
him who called, and the house was filled with smoke. [5] Then
I said, "Woe is me! For I am undone, because I am a man of
unclean lips, and I dwell among a people of unclean lips: for
my eyes have seen the King, Yahweh of Armies!"

[6] Then one of the seraphim flew to me, having a live coal
in his hand, which he had taken with the tongs from off the
altar. [7] He touched my mouth with it, and said, "Behold, this
has touched your lips; and your iniquity is taken away, and
your sin forgiven."

[8] I heard the Lord's voice, saying, "Whom shall I send,
and who will go for us?"

Then I said, "Here I am. Send me!"

AWESTRUCK ANGELS

"Holy, holy, holy, is Yahweh of Armies! The whole earth is full of his glory!" Isaiah 6:2-3

Seraph means "burning one," but there is something so dazzling that even "burning ones" cover their faces: the holy glory of Yahweh, the glory of the Lord Jesus. In Isaiah's vision, he saw Jesus' glory and spoke about him (John 12:41).

Angels are so splendid that if you saw one, you might be tempted to bow in worship. The apostle John once fell at the feet of an angel who had revealed astonishing visions. But the angel told him, "Do not do it! I am a fellow servant with you ... Worship God!" (Revelation 22:9) Angels know that their blazing brilliance is just a small spark of their King's glory.

Of all the things angels do, their foremost and favorite activity is awestruck worship of Christ their King. If not a single human ever worshipped God or believed in Jesus, the Lord would still have millions of magnificent creatures who never stop praising him.

It's humbling to know this, but it's also thrilling to know that by faith in Jesus, we can join our voices with God's angels. Together we can praise the holy Lord whose glory fills earth and heaven: "Blessed be your glorious name, which is exalted above all blessing and praise! You are Yahweh, even you alone. You have made heaven, the heaven of heavens, with all their army, the earth and all things that are on it, the seas and all that is in them, and you preserve them all. The army of heaven worships you" (Nehemiah 9:5-6).

PRAYER

"'Holy, holy, holy,' hear the hymn ascending, angels, saints, their voices blending. Bow your ear to us here; hear, O Christ, the praises that your church now raises.'" Amen.

Psalm 103

1 Praise Yahweh, my soul!
All that is within me, praise his holy name!
2 Praise Yahweh, my soul,
and don't forget all his benefits;
3 who forgives all your sins;
who heals all your diseases;
4 who redeems your life from destruction;
who crowns you with loving kindness and tender mercies;
5 who satisfies your desire with good things,
so that your youth is renewed like the eagle's…
8 Yahweh is merciful and gracious,
slow to anger, and abundant in loving kindness.
9 He will not always accuse;
neither will he stay angry forever.
10 He has not dealt with us according to our sins,
nor repaid us for our iniquities.
11 For as the heavens are high above the earth,
so great is his loving kindness toward those who fear him.
12 As far as the east is from the west,
so far has he removed our transgressions from us.
13 Like a father has compassion on his children,
so Yahweh has compassion on those who fear him.
14 For he knows how we are made.
He remembers that we are dust…
19 Yahweh has established his throne in the heavens.
His kingdom rules over all.
20 Praise Yahweh, you angels of his,
who are mighty in strength, who fulfill his word,
obeying the voice of his word.
21 Praise Yahweh, all you armies of his,
you servants of his, who do his pleasure.
22 Praise Yahweh, all you works of his,
in all places of his dominion.
Praise Yahweh, my soul!

SUPERNATURAL SERVANTS

Are not all angels ministering spirits sent to serve those who will inherit salvation? Hebrews 1:14

Angels are supernatural servants who work for God. Scripture speaks of "angels of his, who are mighty in strength, who fulfill his word, obeying the voice of his word… servants of his, who do his pleasure." (Psalm 103:20-21). In serving God, angels also serve God's people, working in many ways for our good.

The greatest supernatural servant, however, is not an angel but the King of angels. The Lord does so much for people: he "forgives all your sins," "heals all your diseases," and "redeems your life." How does he do it? Not simply by reigning in power but by becoming human and serving human needs. Christ Jesus, "being in very nature God," took "the very nature of a servant" (Philippians 2:6-7) and even died on a cross in order to provide pardon and salvation.

What is true greatness? Willingness to serve. As Jesus puts it, "Whoever wants to be great among you must be your servant, and whoever wants to be first must be slave of all. For even the Son of Man did not come to be served, but to serve, and to give his life as a ransom for many" (Mark 10:43-45).

If "mighty ones" among the angels obey God's word and stoop to serve "little ones" among God's people (Matthew 18:10), surely we are not too important to serve the last and least among us. If our almighty Lord washed his friends' feet and laid down his life, surely we can do humble tasks and serve others.

PRAYER

Thank you, Lord, for your angel servants. Thank you above all for becoming a loving servant yourself. May we rejoice in you and serve one another in Jesus' name. Amen.

2 Corinthians 11:1-15

1 I wish that you would bear with me in a little foolish-
ness, but indeed you do bear with me. 2 For I am jealous over
you with a godly jealousy. For I married you to one husband,
that I might present you as a pure virgin to Christ. 3 But I am
afraid that somehow, as the serpent deceived Eve in his craft-
iness, so your minds might be corrupted from the simplicity
that is in Christ. 4 For if he who comes preaches another Jesus, whom we did not preach, or if you receive a different
spirit, which you did not receive, or a different "good news",
which you did not accept, you put up with that well enough.
5 For I reckon that I am not at all behind the very best apostles. 6 But though I am unskilled in speech, yet I am not unskilled in knowledge. No, in every way we have been revealed to you in all things. 7 Or did I commit a sin in humbling myself that you might be exalted, because I preached to
you God's Good News free of charge? 8 I robbed other as-
semblies, taking wages from them that I might serve you.
9 When I was present with you and was in need, I wasn't a
burden on anyone, for the brothers, when they came from
Macedonia, supplied the measure of my need. In everything I
kept myself from being burdensome to you, and I will continue to do so. 10 As the truth of Christ is in me, no one will
stop me from this boasting in the regions of Achaia. 11 Why?
Because I don't love you? God knows. 12 But what I do, that
I will do, that I may cut off occasion from them that desire
an occasion, that in which they boast, they may be found
even as we. 13 For such men are false apostles, deceitful
workers, masquerading as Christ's apostles. 14 And no wonder, for even Satan masquerades as an angel of light. 15 It is
no great thing therefore if his servants also masquerade as
servants of righteousness, whose end will be according to
their works.

DEVIL IN DISGUISE

Satan masquerades as an angel of light. 2 Corinthians 11:14

In the 1820s Joseph Smith said that an angel named Moroni appeared to him at the top of a hill in Palmyra, New York. According to Smith, Moroni said an ancient book written on gold plates was hidden near Smith's home nearby. The angel instructed Smith to translate the mysterious book into English. The result was the Book of Mormon, first published in 1830. Joseph Smith's new religion was different from historic, biblical Christianity. Smith said he was restoring the true church and preaching the true gospel.

In our own time, some New Age leaders offer messages that, they say, were given to them by angels. These messages speak of "life" and "light" in a stirring way, but they are at odds with the message of Jesus in the Bible.

What should we make of such things? Some of these stories about angels may have been made up to give new ideas a glow of supernatural authority. But just suppose Joseph Smith or some New Age author really saw and heard an angel? What then?

Then it would confirm that "Satan himself masquerades as an angel of light." The Bible warns us not to be fooled by anyone promoting "worship of angels, taking his stand on visions" (Colossians 2:18). Scripture says, "Even if ... an angel from heaven should preach a gospel other than the one we preached to you, let him be eternally condemned!" (Galatians 1:8) We must not fall for messages of "another Jesus" unlike the Jesus revealed in the Bible. Anything that contradicts the gospel of the Bible is invented by a human liar or by a demon disguised as an angel. Either way, it is false.

PRAYER

Father in heaven, deliver us from evil. Guard us from false teachers and phony angels. Keep us true to your Word revealed in the Bible and faithful to Jesus our Lord. Amen.

1 Kings 13:11-26 ESV

[11] Now an old prophet lived in Bethel... [14] And he went
after the man of God and found him sitting under an oak.
And he said to him, "Are you the man of God who came
from Judah?" And he said, "I am." [15] Then he said to him,
"Come home with me and eat bread." [16] And he said, "I may
not return with you, or go in with you, neither will I eat
bread nor drink water with you in this place, [17] for it was said
to me by the word of the LORD, 'You shall neither eat bread
nor drink water there, nor return by the way that you came.'"
[18] And he said to him, "I also am a prophet as you are, and an
angel spoke to me by the word of the LORD, saying, 'Bring
him back with you into your house that he may eat bread and
drink water.'" But he lied to him. [19] So he went back with
him and ate bread in his house and drank water.

[20] And as they sat at the table, the word of the LORD came
to the prophet who had brought him back. [21] And he cried to
the man of God who came from Judah, "Thus says the LORD,
'Because you have disobeyed the word of the LORD and have
not kept the command that the LORD your God commanded
you, [22] but have come back and have eaten bread and drunk
water in the place of which he said to you, "Eat no bread and
drink no water," your body shall not come to the tomb of
your fathers.'" [23] And after he had eaten bread and drunk, he
saddled the donkey for the prophet whom he had brought
back. [24] And as he went away a lion met him on the road and
killed him. And his body was thrown in the road, and the
donkey stood beside it; the lion also stood beside the body.
[25] And behold, men passed by and saw the body thrown in
the road and the lion standing by the body. And they came
and told it in the city where the old prophet lived.

[26] And when the prophet who had brought him back from
the way heard of it, he said, "It is the man of God who disobeyed the word of the LORD; therefore the LORD has given
him to the lion, which has torn him and killed him, according
to the word that the LORD spoke to him."

"AN ANGEL TOLD ME"

"An angel said to me by the word of the Lord: 'Bring him back with you to your house.'" 1 Kings 13:18

The man of God was brave: he spoke God's word to an evil king, despite the king's threats. The man of God was determined: he obeyed God's command to eat nothing in that wicked place, even when the king offered gifts. But the man of God was easily fooled: he fell for the stately voice of an old preacher saying "an angel told me." The result was disobedience and death.

For some churchgoers, the greatest danger comes not from outside the church but from within. They stand against pressures and temptations from non-religious people and yet fall for any spiritual-sounding religious authority. Some church leaders say people can be saved through other religions without Jesus, or they offer new views on sex and abortion. They speak of "love," "compassion," and "fresh insight from God." They sound scholarly, friendly, even angelic. "They come to you in sheep's clothing," warns Jesus, "but inwardly they are ferocious wolves" (Matthew 7:15).

When God gives a teaching, believe it. When God gives a command, obey it. Don't change just because someone, even an old preacher with silver hair and a silver tongue, claims to have a new word from God. Not everyone who claims "the Lord said to me" or "an angel told me" is telling the truth. "Beloved, do not believe every spirit, but test the spirits to see whether they are from God, for many false prophets have gone out into the world" (1 John 4:1).

PRAYER

Lord, make us wise in your Word. Help us not to believe everything which claims to be spiritual but to test all things in light of Scripture. In Jesus' name we pray. Amen.

Genesis 24:34-51

34 He said, "I am Abraham's servant. 35 Yahweh has blessed my master greatly. He has become great. He has given him flocks and herds, silver and gold, male servants and female servants, and camels and donkeys. 36 Sarah, my master's wife, bore a son to my master when she was old. He has given all that he has to him. 37 My master made me swear, saying, 'You shall not take a wife for my son from the daughters of the Canaanites, in whose land I live, 38 but you shall go to my father's house, and to my relatives, and take a wife for my son.' 39 I asked my master, 'What if the woman will not follow me?' 40 He said to me, 'Yahweh, before whom I walk, will send his angel with you, and prosper your way. You shall take a wife for my son from my relatives, and of my father's house… 42 I came today to the spring, and said, 'Yahweh, the God of my master Abraham, if now you do prosper my way which I go— 43 behold, I am standing by this spring of water. Let it happen, that the maiden who comes out to draw, to whom I will say, "Please give me a little water from your pitcher to drink," 44 and she will tell me, "Drink, and I will also draw for your camels,"—let her be the woman whom Yahweh has appointed for my master's son.' 45 Before I had finished speaking in my heart, behold, Rebekah came out with her pitcher on her shoulder. She went down to the spring, and drew. I said to her, 'Please let me drink.' 46 She hurried and let down her pitcher from her shoulder, and said, 'Drink, and I will also give your camels a drink.' So I drank, and she also gave the camels a drink… 48 I bowed my head, and worshiped Yahweh, and blessed Yahweh, the God of my master Abraham, who had led me in the right way…

50 Then Laban and Bethuel answered, "The thing proceeds from Yahweh. We can't speak to you bad or good. 51 Behold, Rebekah is before you. Take her, and go, and let her be your master's son's wife, as Yahweh has spoken."

MARRIAGE MADE IN HEAVEN

"Yahweh, the God of heaven... will send his angel before you, and you shall take a wife for my son." Genesis 24:7

To find the right marriage partner, we need God and his angels. People of faith want a marriage made in heaven. We must count on heavenly help and follow down-to-earth principles.

First, don't marry one of "the Canaanites," someone who doesn't know the Lord. If you pursue romance with someone who isn't devoted to Christ, and it seems an angel is guiding you, it's a fallen angel. Your future mate "must belong to the Lord" (1 Corinthians 7:39).

Second, never be so eager for marriage that you abandon a clear call from God to a special place or task. God called Abraham and Isaac to a new land, so Isaac could not move back to the old country and settle down with a wife there. Find a spouse who will support and strengthen you in the position God has called you to.

Third, pray for guidance. "O Lord, give me success," prayed Abraham's servant. "Let her be the one you have chosen" (Genesis 24:12, 14). It was during a quiet time with God that Isaac first saw his future wife (24:63).

Isaac waited till age forty for marriage, but the lovely virgin Rebekah was worth waiting for. "She became his wife, and he loved her" (Genesis 24:67).

Some customs have changed over the years, but the basic principles remain the same, and the result will be the same: a loving marriage made in heaven.

PRAYER

Father in heaven, help all of us, single or married, to obey your call and trust your care. For those seeking a spouse, send your angel and lead them to the right person. Amen.

2 Kings 2:1-12 ESV

Now when the LORD was about to take Elijah up to heaven by a whirlwind, Elijah and Elisha were on their way from Gilgal. 2 And Elijah said to Elisha, "Please stay here, for the LORD has sent me as far as Bethel." But Elisha said, "As the LORD lives, and as you yourself live, I will not leave you." So they went down to Bethel. 3 And the sons of the prophets who were in Bethel came out to Elisha and said to him, "Do you know that today the LORD will take away your master from over you?" And he said, "Yes, I know it; keep quiet."

4 Elijah said to him, "Elisha, please stay here, for the LORD has sent me to Jericho." But he said, "As the LORD lives, and as you yourself live, I will not leave you." So they came to Jericho. 5 The sons of the prophets who were at Jericho drew near to Elisha and said to him, "Do you know that today the LORD will take away your master from over you?" And he answered, "Yes, I know it; keep quiet."

6 Then Elijah said to him, "Please stay here, for the LORD has sent me to the Jordan." But he said, "As the LORD lives, and as you yourself live, I will not leave you." So the two of them went on. 7 Fifty men of the sons of the prophets also went and stood at some distance from them, as they both were standing by the Jordan. 8 Then Elijah took his cloak and rolled it up and struck the water, and the water was parted to the one side and to the other, till the two of them could go over on dry ground.

9 When they had crossed, Elijah said to Elisha, "Ask what I shall do for you, before I am taken from you." And Elisha said, "Please let there be a double portion of your spirit on me." 10 And he said, "You have asked a hard thing; yet, if you see me as I am being taken from you, it shall be so for you, but if you do not see me, it shall not be so." 11 And as they still went on and talked, behold, chariots of fire and horses of fire separated the two of them. And Elijah went up by a whirlwind into heaven. 12 And Elisha saw it and he cried, "My father, my father! The chariots of Israel and its horsemen!" And he saw him no more.

SWING LOW, SWEET CHARIOT

Chariots of fire and horses of fire separated the two of them. And Elijah went up by a whirlwind into heaven. 2 Kings 2:11

Elijah never died. He rode to heaven in a chariot of fire in a whirlwind. Unlike Elijah, we will die—unless Jesus returns first. But, like Elijah, we can travel to heaven, escorted by angels. If you belong to Christ, angels will welcome you the moment you die and carry your soul home to heaven (Luke 16:22). What joy to be met by such a dazzling welcome committee! What comfort to have such mighty protection on your journey to the next world! The chariots of fire surround us in life, and in death they carry us to heaven.

This journey with angels is so swift and sweet, and the destination so splendid, that death disappears. You never see it. "I tell you the truth," says Jesus, "if anyone keeps my word, he will never see death" (John 8:51). Jonathan Edwards explained, "Death was once a terrible enemy, but now he has become weak. He spent all his strength on Christ; in killing him, he killed himself and now has no power to hurt Jesus' followers."

Why do many Christians fear death? We are like children who fear the dark even when there's no real danger. In the valley of the shadow of death, the shadow may frighten us, but it can't harm us, thanks to angels and their King. Nothing remains of death but a shadow, and even the shadow will be swallowed up in the light of Christ when the blazing sweet chariot swings low to carry us home.

PRAYER

"I looked over Jordan, and what did I see? A band of angels coming after me. Swing low, sweet chariot, coming for to carry me home." Thank you, Lord, for eternal life. Amen.

Luke 15:1-10

1 Now all the tax collectors and sinners were coming
close to Jesus to hear him. 2 The Pharisees and the scribes
murmured, saying, “This man welcomes sinners, and eats
with them.”

3 He told them this parable. 4 “Which of you men, if you
had one hundred sheep, and lost one of them, wouldn’t leave
the ninety-nine in the wilderness, and go after the one that
was lost, until he found it? 5 When he has found it, he carries
it on his shoulders, rejoicing. 6 When he comes home, he
calls together his friends and his neighbors, saying to them,
‘Rejoice with me, for I have found my sheep which was
lost!’ 7 I tell you that even so there will be more joy in heav-
en over one sinner who repents, than over ninety-nine righteous people who need no repentance. 8 Or what woman, if
she had ten drachma coins, if she lost one drachma coin,
wouldn’t light a lamp, sweep the house, and seek diligently
until she found it? 9 When she has found it, she calls together
her friends and neighbors, saying, ‘Rejoice with me, for I
have found the drachma which I had lost.’ 10 Even so, I tell
you, there is joy in the presence of the angels of God over
one sinner repenting.”

ANGEL PARTY

"I tell you, there is joy in the presence of the angels of God over one sinner repenting." Luke 15:10

Angels love parties, and they have lots of them. Angels have a merry celebration every time a sinner turns to Jesus.

If angels throw a party when you start your journey of faith, just imagine the party when you complete the journey. Your arrival in heaven will gladden the angels, and the joy may be especially great among angels who carried out assignments to defend and help you in your journey. In this life you seldom see angels or sense what they do for you. But when you get to heaven, you may meet those angels firsthand and find out all they did to help you. You will enjoy knowing and thanking them, and they will enjoy your fellowship and the satisfaction of another mission accomplished: another person who was once lost but now found and brought home to unending delight in the Lord whom angels adore.

The joy of the angels when you first repent and when you finally arrive in glory can be surpassed only by the enormous joy of the Lord himself. "As a bridegroom rejoices over his bride, so will your God rejoice over you" (Isaiah 62:5). "He will take great delight in you, he will quiet you with his love, he will rejoice over you with singing" (Zephaniah 3:17). How amazing! You will be guest of honor at an angel party, and the King of angels himself will be the life of the party.

PRAYER

Thank you, Lord, for salvation that brings such joy to us, to angels, and to you. Move other sinners to repent, receive eternal life, and add to heaven's joy. Amen.

Ephesians 3:6-21 ESV

6 This mystery is that the Gentiles are fellow heirs, members of the same body, and partakers of the promise in Christ
Jesus through the gospel.

7 Of this gospel I was made a minister according to the
gift of God's grace, which was given me by the working of
his power. 8 To me, though I am the very least of all the
saints, this grace was given, to preach to the Gentiles the unsearchable riches of Christ, 9 and to bring to light for everyone what is the plan of the mystery hidden for ages in God
who created all things, 10 so that through the church the manifold wisdom of God might now be made known to the rulers
and authorities in the heavenly places. 11 This was according
to the eternal purpose that he has realized in Christ Jesus our
Lord, 12 in whom we have boldness and access with confidence through our faith in him. 13 So I ask you not to lose
heart over what I am suffering for you, which is your glory.

14 For this reason I bow my knees before the Father,
15 from whom every family in heaven and on earth is named,
16 that according to the riches of his glory he may grant you
to be strengthened with power through his Spirit in your inner being, 17 so that Christ may dwell in your hearts through
faith—that you, being rooted and grounded in love, 18 may
have strength to comprehend with all the saints what is the
breadth and length and height and depth, 19 and to know the
love of Christ that surpasses knowledge, that you may be
filled with all the fullness of God.

20 Now to him who is able to do far more abundantly than
all that we ask or think, according to the power at work within us, 21 to him be glory in the church and in Christ Jesus
throughout all generations, forever and ever. Amen.

WHAT AMAZES ANGELS

Through the church the manifold wisdom of God [is] made known to the rulers and authorities in the heavenly places. Ephesians 3:10

Things that impress us seldom impress angels. Angels are too dazzling to be impressed by fame or glamour. Angels are too strong to be impressed by athletic strength or military power. Angels are too smart to be impressed by scholarly brilliance.

Angels are not easily impressed, but there is something so marvelous that the angels still haven't fully figured it out, something so good that the angels never stop celebrating. What amazes even "the rulers and authorities in the heavenly places"? God's wisdom displayed through the church.

When you look at the church, you may see nothing amazing: just a building that could use a few repairs and a group of people with plenty of problems. But when angels look at the church, they see an astonishing display of God's wisdom. They see Jesus as the light of the world and the church as the rainbow of colors produced by his light. They see the beautiful variety of God's wisdom in Christ shining through the variety of cultures and personalities in the church worldwide. They see the church on earth sharing "the unsearchable riches of Christ." They see the church in heaven shining with a glory that surpasses even the splendor of angels. They see what God does through Christ in his church, saving sinners and bringing them to glory, and the angels marvel at wisdom so miraculous and mysterious.

PRAYER

Lord, may we see your church as the angels see it. Show us your amazing wisdom, love, and power. To you be glory in the church and in Christ Jesus for ever and ever. Amen.

Revelation 5:11-13, 7:9-17 ESV

[11] Then I looked, and I heard around the throne and the
living creatures and the elders the voice of many angels,
numbering myriads of myriads and thousands of thousands,
[12] saying with a loud voice, "Worthy is the Lamb who was
slain, to receive power and wealth and wisdom and might
and honor and glory and blessing!"

[13] And I heard every creature in heaven and on earth and
under the earth and in the sea, and all that is in them, saying,
"To him who sits on the throne and to the Lamb be blessing
and honor and glory and might forever and ever!"

[7:9] After this I looked, and behold, a great multitude that
no one could number, from every nation, from all tribes and
peoples and languages, standing before the throne and before
the Lamb, clothed in white robes, with palm branches in
their hands, [10] and crying out with a loud voice, "Salvation
belongs to our God who sits on the throne, and to the Lamb!"
[11] And all the angels were standing around the throne and
around the elders and the four living creatures, and they fell
on their faces before the throne and worshiped God,
[12] saying, "Amen! Blessing and glory and wisdom and
thanksgiving and honor and power and might be to our God
forever and ever! Amen."

[13] Then one of the elders addressed me, saying, "Who are
these, clothed in white robes, and from where have they
come?" [14] I said to him, "Sir, you know." And he said to me,
"These are the ones coming out of the great tribulation. They
have washed their robes and made them white in the blood of
the Lamb.[15] "Therefore they are before the throne of God,
and serve him day and night in his temple; and he who sits
on the throne will shelter them with his presence. [16] They
shall hunger no more, neither thirst anymore; the sun shall
not strike them, nor any scorching heat. [17] For the Lamb in
the midst of the throne will be their shepherd, and he will
guide them to springs of living water, and God will wipe
away every tear from their eyes."

ANGEL PRAISES

"Worthy is the Lamb who was slain, to receive power and wealth and wisdom and might and honor and glory and blessing!" Revelation 5:12

What Christ has done for humanity is so huge that the benefits overflow even to angels. Angels feed on the glory of God—it's their nourishment and pleasure—so every fresh display of God's glory expands their happiness even more. Angels always knew God is love, but when God the Son became human and died to rescue sinful people, God showed his love to be greater than even the angels could have guessed. That makes the angels praise Jesus the Lamb more gladly than ever.

Angels praise the Lamb who was slain for another reason as well: they prize their own heavenly happiness even more when they see what it cost the Lord to provide such happiness to humans. Eternal enjoyment of God is so precious that God paid the price of his own Son's blood to purchase it for sinful people. The holy angels don't need Christ to die for them in order to be fit for heaven; but when they see what Christ paid for humans to be there, the angels know better than ever what a huge treasure it is to belong to the Lord and enjoy him for eternity.

Angels rejoice that Christ became human. Shouldn't we rejoice that Christ is one of *us*? Angels rejoice that Christ died for other beings. Shouldn't *we* rejoice that Christ died for *us*? Angels are amazed at what God does for his church. Shouldn't every person in the church be amazed? And if you're outside the church, shouldn't you look for the way inside? It's through faith in Jesus.

PRAYER

"Unto God Almighty, sitting on the throne, and the Lamb, victorious, be the praise alone." King of angels, Lord of love, accept our songs of praise in Jesus' name. Amen.

Hebrews 2:5-18 NIV

5 It is not to angels that he has subjected the world to
come, about which we are speaking. 6 But there is a place
where someone has testified: "What is man that you are
mindful of him, the son of man that you care for him? 7 You
made him a little lower than the angels; you crowned him
with glory and honor 8 and put everything under his feet."

In putting everything under him, God left nothing that is
not subject to him. Yet at present we do not see everything
subject to him. 9 But we see Jesus, who was made a little
lower than the angels, now crowned with glory and honor
because he suffered death, so that by the grace of God he
might taste death for everyone.

10 In bringing many sons to glory, it was fitting that God,
for whom and through whom everything exists, should make
the author of their salvation perfect through suffering. 11 Both
the one who makes men holy and those who are made holy
are of the same family. So Jesus is not ashamed to call them
brothers. 12 He says, "I will declare your name to my brothers; in the presence of the congregation I will sing your
praises." 13 And again, "I will put my trust in him." And
again he says, "Here am I, and the children God has given
me."

14 Since the children have flesh and blood, he too shared
in their humanity so that by his death he might destroy him
who holds the power of death—that is, the devil— 15 and
free those who all their lives were held in slavery by their
fear of death. 16 For surely it is not angels he helps, but
Abraham's descendants. 17 For this reason he had to be made
like his brothers in every way, in order that he might become
a merciful and faithful high priest in service to God, and that
he might make atonement for the sins of the people. 18 Because he himself suffered when he was tempted, he is able to
help those who are being tempted.

HIGHER THAN ANGELS

Do you not know that we will judge angels? 1 Corinthians 6:3

The Bible hints that in God's new creation, humanity will hold a position higher than angels. This thought is almost too much to grasp. How can small, sinful humans rise above mighty, holy angels?

Hebrews 2 explains. God has not appointed angels as rulers over the world to come. God created *man* in his image to rule all things. At present we don't see man ruling all things, but we see in Jesus God's plan for humanity. The Son of God joined humanity in a position lower than the angels for awhile, but now Jesus is crowned with glory and honor. The Son of God did this to make many people sons of God. Indeed, Jesus calls them brothers. Christ came not to help angels but people of faith, "Abraham's descendants." Christ became like his brothers and sisters so that we might become like him: holy like him, loving like him, and reigning with the King of angels forever.

Are the angels upset or envious to know that people will be promoted above them? No, they are thrilled. Angels don't lose when humanity gains. Their supreme delight is Christ, so their delight grows with every human who is remade to be like Christ.

They rejoice at their King's wisdom and generosity in making small, sinful humanity so grand and glorious. In the circle of joy around God's throne, angels become happier and happier as each new member of the Lord's royal family receives a crown.

PRAYER

Lord Jesus, Son of God and Son of Man: "By your own eternal Spirit rule in all our hearts alone; by your all-sufficient merit raise us to your glorious throne." Amen.

2 Corinthians 3:17-4:7

[17] Now the Lord is the Spirit, and where the Spirit of the
Lord is, there is freedom. [18] And we all, with unveiled face,
beholding the glory of the Lord, are being transformed into
the same image from one degree of glory to another. For this
comes from the Lord who is the Spirit.

[4:1] Therefore, having this ministry by the mercy of God,
we do not lose heart. [2] But we have renounced disgraceful,
underhanded ways. We refuse to practice cunning or to tamper with God's word, but by the open statement of the truth
we would commend ourselves to everyone's conscience in
the sight of God. [3] And even if our gospel is veiled, it is
veiled to those who are perishing. [4] In their case the god of
this world has blinded the minds of the unbelievers, to keep
them from seeing the light of the gospel of the glory of
Christ, who is the image of God. [5] For what we proclaim is
not ourselves, but Jesus Christ as Lord, with ourselves as
your servants for Jesus' sake. [6] For God, who said, "Let light
shine out of darkness," has shone in our hearts to give the
light of the knowledge of the glory of God in the face of Jesus Christ.

[7] But we have this treasure in jars of clay, to show that
the surpassing power belongs to God and not to us.

EVER-INCREASING GLORY

We all, with unveiled face, beholding the glory of the Lord, are being transformed into the same image from one degree of glory to another. 2 Corinthians 3:18 ESV

Suppose you see a drooling baby in soiled diapers. Nearby you see some soldiers in splendid uniforms. If someone tells you that this stinky little infant will command those elite troops someday, it might sound ridiculous. But what if that little stinker's father is a king? For the time being, you and I are God's babies. But a day is coming when we will enter our full inheritance and be robed in dazzling white. We will even have authority over God's elite troops, the angels (1 Corinthians 6:2-3). It might sound ridiculous to say that puny, smelly sinners like us will someday take command of spotless, mighty angels. But it is going to happen, for our Father is King. We will reign with him forever (Revelation 22:5). Jesus says, "The one who conquers, I will grant him to sit with me on my throne, as I also conquered and sat down with my Father on his throne" (Revelation 3:21).

This glorious future should affect the present. Already now Christians are meant to shine with ever-increasing glory. Often, like babies crying for a bottle, we cry for God to feed us. Like babies fighting over worthless wrapping paper, we bicker and sue each other over things with no eternal value. Like babies who need their diapers changed, we sometimes think that cleaning up our sins is all Jesus came to do. Yes, clean diapers are necessary, but at some point shouldn't an heir to the throne realize that ahead lies something greater than clean diapers? To be a Christian is not just to be forgiven and cleaned up. It is to be destined for a glory that reflects the glory of God our Father and Jesus our elder Brother.

PRAYER

Father and King, by your Spirit transform us with ever-increasing glory. May we conduct ourselves, and treat others, as royalty, in light of our inheritance in Christ. Amen.

Ephesians 1:3-23 NIV

3 Praise be to the God and Father of our Lord Jesus
Christ, who has blessed us in the heavenly realms with every
spiritual blessing in Christ. 4 For he chose us in him before
the creation of the world to be holy and blameless in his
sight. In love 5 he predestined us for adoption to sonship
through Jesus Christ, in accordance with his pleasure and
will— 6 to the praise of his glorious grace, which he has
freely given us in the One he loves. 7 In him we have redemption through his blood, the forgiveness of sins, in accordance with the riches of God's grace 8 that he lavished on
us. With all wisdom and understanding, 9 he made known to
us the mystery of his will according to his good pleasure,
which he purposed in Christ, 10 to be put into effect when the
times reach their fulfillment—to bring unity to all things in
heaven and on earth under Christ…

13 And you also were included in Christ when you heard
the message of truth, the gospel of your salvation. When you
believed, you were marked in him with a seal, the promised
Holy Spirit, 14 who is a deposit guaranteeing our inheritance
until the redemption of those who are God's possession—to
the praise of his glory…

17 I keep asking that the God of our Lord Jesus Christ, the
glorious Father, may give you the Spirit of wisdom and revelation, so that you may know him better. 18 I pray that the
eyes of your heart may be enlightened in order that you may
know the hope to which he has called you, the riches of his
glorious inheritance in his holy people, 19 and his incompara-
bly great power for us who believe. That power is the same
as the mighty strength 20 he exerted when he raised Christ
from the dead and seated him at his right hand in the heavenly realms, 21 far above all rule and authority, power and dominion, and every name that is invoked, not only in the present age but also in the one to come. 22 And God placed all
things under his feet and appointed him to be head over everything for the church, 23 which is his body, the fullness of
him who fills everything in every way.

HEAD OVER EVERYTHING

God... appointed him to be head over everything. Ephesians 1:22-23

When God the Son became human, he gave us a status even higher than angels, and he blessed us even more than he blessed angels. Still, the blessing for angels is far greater than it would have been if the Lord had not become human.

Jesus is their head as well as ours. By becoming human, God the Son has come closer to angels than he was before. Angels are creatures, and the Creator is infinitely above them as he is infinitely above us. But by becoming human, the Son of God came closer to the angels, as closely connected to them as head and body. Their relationship to their Lord can be more intimate and joyful than ever.

With Christ as their head and ours, angels are blessed by their bond with the church. Angels celebrate the salvation of each new believer because they delight in every fresh display of God's glorious grace. Another reason they celebrate is that another splendid being is added to the eternal fellowship headed by Christ. Angels know that each repentant sinner is adopted by God as his child and becomes a prince or princess in his kingdom. The angels are thrilled to have another member of royalty join the eternal circle of joy around God's throne. You might not see yourself as royalty or see anything about yourself that would make angels excited to enjoy your company. But if you could see what God will someday make of you, you would know why angels feel honored and thrilled to associate with you. You will share in the splendor of Christ himself and reign with him in a way that even the angels will never cease to marvel at.

PRAYER

We praise you, Lord, for becoming one of us, for making us your royal children, and for including angels as well as us in the circle of blessing as we rejoice in you, our Head. Amen.

Hebrews 12:14-29

[14] Follow after peace with all men, and the sanctification without which no man will see the Lord, [15] looking carefully lest there be any man who falls short of the grace of God; lest any root of bitterness springing up trouble you, and many be defiled by it; [16] lest there be any sexually immoral person, or profane person, like Esau, who sold his birthright for one meal. [17] For you know that even when he afterward desired to inherit the blessing, he was rejected, for he found no place for a change of mind though he sought it diligently with tears. [18] For you have not come to a mountain that might be touched, and that burned with fire, and to blackness, darkness, storm, [19] the sound of a trumpet, and the voice of words; which those who heard it begged that not one more word should be spoken to them, [20] for they could not stand that which was commanded, "If even an animal touches the mountain, it shall be stoned" [21] and so fearful was the appearance that Moses said, "I am terrified and trembling."

[22] But you have come to Mount Zion, and to the city of the living God, the heavenly Jerusalem, and to innumerable multitudes of angels, [23] to the general assembly and assembly of the firstborn who are enrolled in heaven, to God the Judge of all, to the spirits of just men made perfect, [24] to Jesus, the mediator of a new covenant, and to the blood of sprinkling that speaks better than that of Abel.

[25] See that you don't refuse him who speaks. For if they didn't escape when they refused him who warned on the earth, how much more will we not escape who turn away from him who warns from heaven, [26] whose voice shook the earth then, but now he has promised, saying, "Yet once more I will shake not only the earth, but also the heavens." [27] This phrase, "Yet once more", signifies the removing of those things that are shaken, as of things that have been made, that those things which are not shaken may remain. [28] Therefore, receiving a Kingdom that can't be shaken, let us have grace, through which we serve God acceptably, with reverence and awe, [29] for our God is a consuming fire.

JOYFUL ASSEMBLY

You have come to thousands upon thousands of angels in joyful assembly. Hebrews 12:22

Healthy faith is more than believing some nice ideas or doing some good things. Healthy faith is a sense of belonging to a stunning reality: the city of the living God. By faith you join countless angels in joyful assembly. You join a church family whom God loves as his firstborn. You join God, the Judge who has become your Friend. You join godly people from previous ages who are now perfect in heaven. You join Jesus, whose blood speaks love and life for all who believe.

By faith you are not your own: you are caught up in God's plan "to bring all things in heaven and on earth together under one head, even Christ" (Ephesians 1:10). By faith you are not alone: you belong to a grand group that spans every century and reaches into eternity, a group that unites all races of humanity and all ranks of angels in the communion of the Holy Spirit.

You live each moment "in the sight of God and Christ Jesus and the elect angels" (1 Timothy 5:21). Let this awareness shape every action and attitude. Always be thankful. With reverent awe, worship the fatherly Fire who burns brightly without destroying you. Treat other people with care and respect, knowing they may rise above angels. Remember your own destiny as royalty called to serve and reign with the King of angels, and "live a life worthy of the calling you have received" (Ephesians 4:1).

PRAYER

"Teach me to love you as your angels love, one holy passion filling all my frame: the fullness of the heaven-descended Dove; my heart an altar, and your love the flame." Amen.

Hebrews 1 NIV

1 In the past God spoke to our ancestors through the prophets at many times and in various ways, 2 but in these last days he has spoken to us by his Son, whom he appointed heir of all things, and through whom also he made the universe. 3 The Son is the radiance of God's glory and the exact representation of his being, sustaining all things by his powerful word. After he had provided purification for sins, he sat down at the right hand of the Majesty in heaven. 4 So he became as much superior to the angels as the name he has inherited is superior to theirs.

5 For to which of the angels did God ever say, "You are my Son; today I have become your Father"? Or again, "I will be his Father, and he will be my Son"? 6 And again, when God brings his firstborn into the world, he says, "Let all God's angels worship him." 7 In speaking of the angels he says, "He makes his angels winds, his servants flames of fire." 8 But about the Son he says, "Your throne, O God, will last for ever and ever, and righteousness will be the scepter of your kingdom. 9 You have loved righteousness and hated wickedness; therefore God, your God, has set you above your companions by anointing you with the oil of joy." 10 He also says, "In the beginning, O Lord, you laid the foundations of the earth, and the heavens are the work of your hands. 11 They will perish, but you remain; they will all wear out like a garment. 12 You will roll them up like a robe; like a garment they will be changed. But you remain the same, and your years will never end." 13 To which of the angels did God ever say, "Sit at my right hand until I make your enemies a footstool for your feet"?

14 Are not all angels ministering spirits sent to serve those who will inherit salvation?

KING OF ANGELS

Jesus is superior to the angels ... Let all God's angels worship him. Hebrews 1:4,6

In the old comic strip *Hagar the Horrible*, the pudgy Viking Hagar is looking for a fight. He bangs on a castle door and shouts, "Is Og the Awful in there? Come out and face me!" The castle door opens and out steps a ferocious giant, bristling with weapons. His waist is higher than Hagar's head. Little Hagar shrinks back in terror and gasps, "Are *you* Og the Awful?" "No," replies the giant, "I'm just his butler."

Angels are mighty and overwhelming. But great as they are, cherubim and seraphim, angels and archangels, are still only God's butlers, his servants and throne attendants. The Lord himself is infinitely higher, greater, and more glorious than all of them combined. The angels are dazzling, but that tiny baby lying in Bethlehem's manger whom the angels announced and praised was infinitely greater. Within the form of that tiny baby was hidden all the splendor and greatness of God himself.

Angels, though splendid and strong, are still only God's servants. Jesus is God's one and only Son, equal in splendor with God the Father. If even the most magnificent angels cover their faces before the Lord Jesus and devote themselves to praising and serving him, you can only imagine how great Jesus himself must be. Jesus is "much superior to the angels. For to which of the angels did God ever say, 'You are my Son?'" God has many angels, but only one eternal Son. "Let all God's angels worship *him*."

Let all God's people also worship him.

PRAYER

Lord Jesus, king of angels, ruler of all things, we praise you for your power, splendor, and love. Help us to know you better, so that we may love and worship you more. Amen.

Acknowledgements

Most of the meditations in this book were first published by Back to God Ministries in various printings of *Today: The Family Altar*. I owe a great debt to Joel Nederhood, former director of Back to God and editor of *Today*. Joel invited me to join Back to God Ministries and mentored me during my early years there. He encouraged me in writing daily meditations to help people know Jesus firsthand through his inspired Word. Joel remains a lover of Jesus, a cherished friend, and a partner in God's mission.

My parents, Marvin and Nell Feddes, led our family in daily Bible reading, meditation, and prayer. Their love and their pattern of spending time with Jesus each day continues to bless my life. Thank you, Mom and Dad!

Family of Faith Church is a congregation of fellow believers who encourage one another in daily worship and home discipleship. My family and I are blessed and built up through belonging to such a body.

My wife, Wendy, is an unfailing support and encouragement through her love for Christ and her love for me. In addition, she helped to proofread this book, though any errors that remain are my responsibility. Our daughter Jaclyn read the book, corrected some things, and designed the cover. Our entire family brings me joy and energizes me for ministry.

My dear Savior and Lord, Jesus Christ, has done more for me than I can say. He is far more magnificent than anything I can put into words. I pray that he will use these Scriptures and my meditations, despite the inadequacy of my efforts, to help others know him and delight in him.

Christian Leaders Institute

Christian Leaders Press is the publishing arm of Christian Leaders Institute. CLI provides free online ministry training worldwide. All people called by God, regardless of income, can become well trained leaders at no cost to them. Local mentors and pastors in many countries partner with CLI faculty in equipping thousands of new leaders.

David Feddes serves as Provost at Christian Leaders Institute. He oversees the curriculum and works with other professors to make sure that every course provides high quality ministry training. Many classes feature video presentations and writings by Dr. Feddes. CLI's goal is to raise up revival leaders with hearts full of Holy Spirit fire and minds formed by biblical truth.

If you are seeking no-cost, high quality ministry training, or if you would like to support CLI financially so that more leaders can be equipped for God's mission, please visit the CLI website: **www.christianleadersinstitute.org**

Made in the USA
San Bernardino, CA
21 December 2015